The Social Context of Coping

The Plenum Series on Stress and Coping

Series Editor:
Donald Meichenbaum, *University of Waterloo, Waterloo, Ontario, Canada*

Current Volumes in the Series:

A CLINICAL GUIDE TO THE TREATMENT OF THE
HUMAN STRESS RESPONSE
George S. Everly, Jr.

COPING WITH NEGATIVE LIFE EVENTS
Clinical and Social Psychological Perspectives
Edited by C. R. Snyder and Carol E. Ford

DYNAMICS OF STRESS
Physiological, Psychological, and Social Perspectives
Edited by Mortimer H. Appley and Richard Trumbull

HUMAN ADAPTATION TO EXTREME STRESS
From the Holocaust to Vietnam
Edited by John P. Wilson, Zev Harel, and Boaz Kahana

INFERTILITY
Perspectives from Stress and Coping Research
Edited by Annette L. Stanton and Christine Dunkel-Schetter

INTERNATIONAL HANDBOOK OF TRAUMATIC STRESS SYNDROMES
Edited by John P. Wilson and Beverley Raphael

POST-TRAUMATIC STRESS DISORDER
A Clinician's Guide
Kirtland C. Peterson, Maurice F. Prout, and Robert A. Schwarz

THE SOCIAL CONTEXT OF COPING
Edited by John Eckenrode

STRESS BETWEEN WORK AND FAMILY
Edited by John Eckenrode and Susan Gore

WOMEN, WORK, AND HEALTH
Stress and Opportunities
Edited by Marianne Frankenhaeuser, Ulf Lundberg, and Margaret Chesney

---

A Continuation Order Plan is available for this series. A continuation order will bring delivery of each new volume immediately upon publication. Volumes are billed only upon actual shipment. For further information please contact the publisher.

The Social Context
of Coping

Edited by
JOHN ECKENRODE

Cornell University
Ithaca, New York

PLENUM PRESS • NEW YORK AND LONDON

Library of Congress Cataloging-in-Publication Data

The Social context of coping / edited by John Eckenrode.
     p.   cm. -- (The Plenum series on stress and coping)
  Includes bibliographical references and index.
  ISBN 0-306-43783-X
  1. Stress (Psychology) 2. Adjustment (Psychology) 3. Social
networks--Psychological aspects. I. Eckenrode, John. II. Series.
  [DNLM: 1. Adaptation, Psychological. 2. Psychology, Social.
3. Social Environment. 4. Social Support. WM 172 S6775]
BF575.S75S63 1991
155.9'042--dc20
DNLM/DLC
for Library of Congress   91-21238
                                        CIP

ISBN 0-306-43783-X

Printed in the United States of America

To my Father and Mother

Contributors

Carol S. Aneshensel, School of Public Health, University of California, Los Angeles, California 90024-1772

Evelyn J. Bromet, Department of Psychiatry and Behavioral Science, State University of New York at Stony Brook, Stony Brook, New York 11794-8790

Ralph Catalano, School of Public Health, University of California, Berkeley, California 94720

Margaret Chesney, Center for AIDS Prevention Studies, University of California, San Francisco, California 94143

Thomas J. Coates, Center for AIDS Prevention Studies, University of California, San Francisco, California 94143

Mary Ellen Colten, Center for Survey Research, University of Massachusetts–Boston, Boston, Massachusetts 02116

Mary Amanda Dew, Department of Psychiatry, University of Pittsburgh School of Medicine, Pittsburgh, Pennsylvania 15213

David Dooley, Program in Social Ecology, University of California, Irvine, California 92717

John Eckenrode, Department of Human Development and Family Studies, and the Family Life Development Center, Cornell University, Ithaca, New York 14853-4401

Susan Folkman, Center for AIDS Prevention Studies, University of California, San Francisco, California 94143

Susan Gore, Department of Sociology, University of Massachusetts–Boston, Boston, Massachusetts 02125

Benjamin H. Gottlieb, Department of Psychology, University of Guelph, Guelph, Ontario, Canada N1G 2W1

Gail Ironson, Department of Psychology, University of Miami, Coral Gables, Florida 33124

David S. Johnson, Pacific Graduate School of Psychology, Palo Alto, California 94117-1030

Ronald C. Kessler, Department of Sociology, University of Michigan, Ann Arbor, Michigan 48109

Nan Lin, Department of Sociology, Duke University, Durham, North Carolina 27706

Leon McKusick, Center for AIDS Prevention Studies, University of California, San Francisco, California 94143

Leonard I. Pearlin, Human Development and Aging Program, Center for Social and Behavioral Sciences, University of California, San Francisco, California 94143-0848

Karen Rook, Program in Social Ecology, University of California, Irvine, California 92717

Peggy A. Thoits, Department of Sociology, Vanderbilt University, Nashville, Tennessee 37235

Fred Wagner, Community Mental Health Clinic, Guelph, Ontario, Canada N1G 2W1

Donald Wertlieb, Eliot-Pearson Department of Child Study, Tufts University, Medford, Massachusetts 02155

Jeanne Westcott, Department of Sociology, State University of New York at Albany, Albany, New York 12222

Elaine Wethington, Department of Human Development and Family Studies, Cornell University, Ithaca, New York 14853-4401

Foreword

I am very pleased to have been asked to do a brief foreword to this second CRISP volume, *The Social Context of Coping.* I know most of the participants and their work, and respect them as first-rate and influential research scholars whose research is at the cusp of current concerns in the field of stress and coping.

Psychological stress is central to human adaptation. It is difficult to visualize the study of adaptation, health, illness, personal soundness, and psychopathology without recognizing their dependence on how well people cope with the stresses of living. Since the editor, John Eckenrode, has portrayed the themes of each of the chapters in his introduction, I can limit myself to a few general comments about stress and coping.

Stress research began, as unexplored fields often do, with very simple—should I say simplistic?—ideas about how to define the concept. Early approaches were unidimensional and input–output in outlook, modeled implicitly on Hooke's late-17th-century engineering analysis in which external load was an environmental stressor, stress was the area over which the load acted, and strain was the deformation of the structure such as a bridge or building.

The analogy between the capacity of a metal to resist strain—Hooke was interested in the elasticity of metals—and a person's capacity to resist psychophysiological damage under load has always been a tempting one for social scientists. Current research on resistance resources, social support, constructive thinking, hardiness, learned resourcefulness, dispositional optimism, self-efficacy, and sense of mastery—to name some of the fashionable personality and social mediators of stress effects—reflects the productive power of this analogy.

However, though the analogy might provide a good starting point for framing the question of what provokes resiliency, when this physical analogy is taken too literally as explanation, certain key psychological processes that are needed for a thorough comprehension of psychological stress and the emotions that flow from it—e.g., grasping the personal significance of the person–environment relationship; responding to feedback about the flow of events; and managing demands, constraints, and opportunities—are left out. The participants in this volume understand this very well.

In light of this, as interest in psychological stress increased, so did the complexity of its conceptualization, leading to a greater focus on individual differences in motivation and cognition as mediators of the person–environment relationship. Most researchers now take for granted that the appraisal of harm/loss, threat, and challenge—and coping too—has a powerful role in the response to stressful encounters, and that we need to know more about the social and personality factors that shape the appraisal process. These factors are now central variables and processes in stress theory, research, and measurement.

As a serious target for theory and research, the concept of coping itself began to emerge in the 1960s and 1970s and really blossomed in the 1980s. There were and still are challenges about how to think about coping—for example, whether it is best regarded as a stable trait, a contextual process, or both; the social and personal factors that influence it; how it affects adaptational outcomes; and the interventions one might use to change it for the better. These topics come up frequently in this book, and the research and ideas reported in *The Social Context of Coping* advance our thinking about them substantially.

A principle of coping that had previously been ignored—namely, that what a person wants to accomplish in a stressful transaction underlies the choice of coping strategy—has also begun to appear in some of the chapters, and I would like to take brief notice of it. In stressful transactions between a parent and child, spouses and lovers, co-workers, and so on, I am convinced that the coping process depends, to a substantial degree, on intentions toward the other person in the relationship and toward the relationship itself. In an anger encounter, for example, if a person wants to preserve the relationship, the coping strategy is more likely to involve suppression of the anger than if that person wants to repair a damaged self-esteem; in the latter case, the coping strategy is more likely to involve escalation of the anger and efforts to malign the other. So in addition to social and personality variables, situational goals or intentions also play a role in shaping coping.

This book deals with many of the most important issues on which an understanding of stress, coping, and adaptation is predicated, and it should become an important resource for a wide range of researchers, scholars, and professionals.

RICHARD S. LAZARUS
University of California, Berkeley
Berkeley, California

Preface

This book represents the second volume of contributions by members of the Consortium for Research Involving Stress Processes (CRISP) and their colleagues. The first volume, entitled *Stress between Work and Family* (1990), appeared as an earlier book in this series. The consortium was founded in 1983 with the support of the William T. Grant Foundation and has been meeting twice a year since that time. Interdisciplinary in nature, the consortium's mission is to increase communication and collaboration among researchers who represent various disciplines and to provide a forum for the articulation of unresolved issues in the field. Therefore, this volume represents not only the efforts of each of the authors of these chapters but also reflects discussions that have taken place in the consortium meetings. All the chapters deal with issues of stress and coping from a variety of perspectives, but two concepts link the chapters to each other: context and process. Attention to context serves to expand the topic of coping beyond an overly narrow concern with the individual's adaptational efforts. A focus on process reinforces the dynamic nature of the stress and coping process.

Many people made this volume possible in addition to the authors of the following chapters. I would especially like to acknowledge the support of Robert Haggerty, president of the William T. Grant Foundation, whose vision, guidance, and patience made our consortium possible. Linda Pickett and Frank Kessel, representing the Grant Foundation at our meetings, were a continuing source of encouragement. Finally, I would like to thank those consortium members who provided valuable feedback on the chapters presented here, but who do not themselves appear as authors in this volume. These include Blair Wheaton, Camille Wortman, Robert Weiss, Joan Liem, Ramsay Liem, and Patricia Cohen.

JOHN ECKENRODE

Ithaca, New York

Contents

Chapter 4. Development, Stress, and Role Restructuring: Social Transitions of Adolescence 55

Carol S. Aneshensel and Susan Gore

Chapter 5. Age Differences in Workers' Efforts to Cope with Economic Distress 79

Karen Rook, David Dooley, and Ralph Catalano

Chapter 11. Translating Coping Theory into an Intervention

Susan Folkman, Margaret Chesney, Leon McKusick, Gail Ironson, David S. Johnson, and Thomas J. Coates

Leonard I. Pearlin

1

Introduction and Overview

JOHN ECKENRODE

INTRODUCTION

It is clear that the concept of coping, like that of stress, is not a unified construct with readily agreed-upon meaning. Rather, it more accurately represents a general rubric or metaconstruct under which a number of phenomena are embedded. What distinguishes coping from other aspects of human behavior is its relevance to adaptation in the face of stressful life experiences or conditions. As such, a prerequisite for coping is the presence of an event or condition appraised as harmful or threatening to the individual (cf. Lazarus & Folkman, 1984). In this volume, we will be concerned with conscious, purposive behaviors or cognitions initiated in response to the experience of a chronically stressful situation or following the occurrence of a stressful life event. We will not be concerned here with automatic, biologically based responses to stressors, such as reflexive behaviors.

It is clear, however, that the term *coping* has been applied to more than the behaviors and cognitions associated with a person's attempts to respond to stressors. For example, coping *resources* have been discussed as representing characteristics of the person or his/her environment that are associated with low levels of distress or physical symptoms following the onset of stressors. Antonovsky (1979) has termed these *resistance*

JOHN ECKENRODE • Department of Human Development and Family Studies, and the Family Life Development Center, Cornell University, Ithaca, New York 14853-4401.

The Social Context of Coping, edited by John Eckenrode. Plenum Press, New York, 1991.

resources. These may be psychological characteristics of the person, such as self-esteem or a sense of mastery, social competence or skills, characteristics of the person's social environment, such as social network characteristics and levels of available social support, or achieved statuses such as education, financial resources, or occupational prestige.

Persons possessing what normatively are considered favorable resources (e.g., higher feelings of mastery, more material resources) have consistently been shown to fare better in the face of stressful circumstances than their not-so-advantaged peers. What has not been so clear is how such resources actually influence the cognitions and behaviors of persons who are confronted with situations appraised as harmful or threatening (Gore, 1985). It is intuitively reasonable to suggest that stable personality traits such as self-esteem, supportive social relationships, and higher levels of socioeconomic resources buffer stress because such characteristics are linked to more effective coping responses. Indeed, such evidence can be found in the research literature. For example, Pearlin and Schooler (1978), in a Chicago-based community study, showed education level and family income to be related to coping strategies found to be effective for certain types of chronic strains, such as maintaining optimistic outlooks in the face of financial or job-related strain. Billings and Moos (1981), in another community study, found that persons with few social resources also tended to use avoidance more than persons with higher levels of social resources. Strickland (1978) reviewed studies linking beliefs in self-efficacy to more active modes of coping with health-threatening events.

Such consistency is not always found in the literature, however. For example, in a community study of 85 married couples, Folkman, Lazarus, Gruen, and DeLongis (1986) found that the personality variables of interpersonal trust and mastery showed very few relationships to specific coping behaviors reported by these respondents in response to a recent stressful event. Pearlin and Schooler (1978) also present data showing that coping resources in the form of mastery beliefs and self-esteem were more effective in buffering the effects of role strains over which the respondent has little control, such as work-related strains, whereas active coping responses were more effective in diminishing the consequences of strains in role domains over which the respondent had some control, such as in the marital relationship.

Such findings argue against a simple notion of resources leading to coping responses. They also reinforce a view of coping as being sensitive to situational constraints, rather than as an invariant mode of responding irrespective of the stressor being confronted. Although there is some evidence for consistency of coping responses within a particular stressor domain, the literature finds little evidence for invariant coping styles or traits across different types of stressors (Kessler, Price, & Wortman, 1985; Lazarus & Folkman, 1980). The power of the situation to influence the choice of coping response is evident here. Indeed, the person's definition of the situation, in terms of cognitive appraisals of stressor characteristics such as its degree of controllability, are linked to the choice of coping responses (Lazarus & Folkman, 1984).

Like coping resources, coping responses have been conceived in the literature as a multidimensional set of cognitions and behaviors called upon to help the person manage or tolerate the demands imposed by chronic or acute stressors. The range of cognitions and behaviors that may serve as coping strategies is indeed enormous, with the categorization of coping strategies having posed a major challenge to researchers in this field. One popular assessment tool, the Ways of Coping Checklist (Folkman & Lazarus, 1984) contains 67 distinct responses, which fall into 8 discrete categories (Folkman, Lazarus, Dunkel-Schetter, DeLongis, & Gruen, 1986): confrontive coping, (e.g., expressing anger), distancing (e.g., making light of the situation), self-controlling (e.g., keeping feelings to oneself), seeking social support (e.g., talked to someone to find out more about the situation), accepting responsibility (e.g., criticized or lectured oneself), escape–avoidance (e.g., wished the situation would go away), planful problem solving (e.g., making a plan of action and following it), and positive reappraisal (e.g., changed or grew as a person in a good way). Pearlin and Schooler (1978) discuss the role of specific coping responses as falling into three general categories: altering the problem directly, changing one's way of viewing the the problem, and managing emotional distress aroused by the problem.

Moos and his colleagues (e.g., Moos & Schaefer, 1986) have presented a very useful framework for organizing the myriad of cognitions and behaviors that could hypothetically be included under the coping umbrella. First, they outline a set of adaptive tasks common to many transitions and crises. These include (1) establish the meaning and understand the personal significance of the situation; (2) confront reality and respond to the requirements of the external situation; (3) sustain relationships with family members and friends as well as with other individuals who may be helpful in resolving the crisis and its aftermath; (4) maintain a reasonable emotional balance by managing upsetting feelings aroused by the situation; and (5) preserve a satisfactory self-image and maintain a sense of competence and mastery. Specific coping strategies such as appraisal-focused coping, problem-focused coping, and emotion-focused coping can, in turn, be evaluated in terms of the degree to which they meet these general tasks.

THE SOCIAL CONTEXT OF COPING

There are numerous ways in which an individual's exposure to chronic or acute stressors and their attempts to manage the demands created by these experiences may be influenced by the social environment. Such influence may be either positive or negative, constraining or facilitating effective coping responses.

In many circumstances, coping efforts on the part of individuals are explicitly social in nature, whereby the person under stress actively seeks out the help and comfort of other people. Indeed, seeking social support is one of the factors that typically appears in assessments of coping responses (e.g., Folkman & Lazarus, 1980). It is as yet unclear under what circumstances help seeking is an effective coping strategy. There is general agreement that access to social supportive relationships and perceptions of feeling supported are important buffers to the negative psychological consequences of stressful experiences (Cohen & McKay, 1984; Kessler, Price, & Wortman, 1985). However, some studies have shown active help seeking to be ineffectual in reducing distress (Billings, Cronkite, & Moos, 1983; Coyne, Aldwin, & Lazarus, 1981; Pearlin & Schooler, 1978) or that there may be psychological costs associated with help seeking (Fischer, Goff, Nadler, & Chinsky, 1988). A distinction between social support that is actively solicited versus that which is spontaneously offered may help clarify this issue because there are several reasons why unsolicited support may be superior to assistance received as a result of help-seeking efforts (Eckenrode & Wethington, 1990).

Thoits (1986) has argued that social support may be conceptualized as *coping assistance*. She cites several examples of how a person's social relationships may influence an individual's coping responses. For example, others may help the person under stress appraise the situation differently, perhaps by providing a benign interpretation of events. They may also provide direct assistance or information concerning how to directly deal with the stressor. Having others nearby may also provide the opportunity for the ventilation of feelings, which may facilitate coping (Silver & Wortman, 1980). In addition, others may simply provide the person under stress with a safe haven from which to escape the immediate demands of the stressor and to replenish his or her energy level (Caplan, 1976). Perhaps most important, supporters may communicate emotional support in the form of expressions of caring and love that serve to help the person under stress maintain self-esteem and feelings of control and thus allow him or her to persist in coping efforts (Pearlin, Lieberman, Menaghan, & Mullan, 1981). Effective coping requires the avoidance of maladaptive responses as well as the adoption of adaptive responses. Significant others may serve a useful social control function for the distressed individual, reinforcing role obligations and normative modes of coping that may prevent the person from adopting more self-destructive forms of coping, such as excessive drinking or drug use (cf. Shiffman & Wills, 1985).

In addition to socially supportive relationships influencing the choice of coping behaviors, coping may also have an impact on the receipt of social support or the maintainance of social relationships. Dunkel-Schetter, Folkman, and Lazarus (1987) demonstrated that social support is more likely to be received when certain coping strategies are employed, such as problem solving and positive reappraisal. Given the cross-sectional nature of their study, it could not be determined whether coping led to the support or the support was instrumental in the person's initiation of coping strategies, but these authors cogently make the case that the way a person copes may well represent information to which his or her social world responds. Persons viewed by others as effectively managing the demands of the stressors they are encountering may elicit help for their efforts from their social networks, whereas persons who are seen as coping poorly may be viewed as unattractive and avoided (Coates, Wortman, & Abbey, 1979).

There is a more general sense in which interpersonal relationships may serve as the context for an individual's coping efforts. When exposed to stressful experiences, the person may use others as the basis for attaching meaning to those stressors and gauging how they are doing in their attempts to manage the demands of the situation. Wills (1987) and Taylor (1983) have discussed social-comparison processes as they relate to coping. For example, the person may compare him- or herself to others who are experiencing the same stressor but who are worse off, and in this way enhance their own self-image as an effective coper. Such downward social comparisons may be particularly likely the degree to which the stressor threatens the person's self-esteem.

In close relationships, we may also see a certain degree of synchrony or orchestration that takes place as each person seeks to cope with a common stressor or when one individual attempts to support the other in coping with stressors he or she is individually facing. For example, Weiss (1990) describes the sometimes explicit, but often subtle, processes by which husbands experiencing various types of work-related stress are supported by their wives. These support processes, which often begin with nonverbal cues, displays of emotion, or indirect disclosures may not involve direct help seeking but may well influence the ability of the distressed worker to manage the demands of the workplace.

The potential also exists for a lack of coordination in attempts at coping or in a lack of understanding with regard to the needs of the person currently under stress. For example, Wortman and her colleagues (e.g., Dunkel-Schetter & Wortman, 1982; Wortman, 1984) have described the mismatch that often occurs between the kinds of support a person suffering from cancer wants and the responses of intimates. Because of the discomfort these potential supporters may experience in coping with their own feelings about this stressor, they may encourage inappropriate or unhelpful coping on the part of the patient, such as remaining cheerful and optimistic. Persons facing a common stressor may also adopt coping strategies that may be incompatible and thus jeopardize each person's coping efforts, such as when a husband uses punitive discipline to cope with the stress of an aggressive teenager, whereas the mother seeks to adopt a noncoercive parenting style. Ineffectual methods of coping with stress may also entail social costs in the form of threatening the interpersonal relationships themselves. Elder and his associates (e.g., Liker & Elder, 1983) have shown that men who responded to losing a job during the Great Depression with increased levels of tension and irritability threatened the stability of their marriages.

Finally, we must consider the broader social structure as it may affect the development of coping resources and in the shaping of coping responses. Persons on higher social status, as reflected in educational and occupational attainment, have been consistently shown to have higher levels of coping resources, such as access to social support, and to engage in more effective coping responses (e.g., Pearlin & Schooler, 1978; Turner & Noh, 1983). Fatalistic beliefs about the world, often associated with persons living in poverty, may seriously compromise coping efforts in that the motivation for active, problem-focused coping responses is undermined (Wheaton, 1982). The poor, not having access to the range of social support from their informal networks that more privileged persons have, must often rely on institutional structures that too often are unresponsive and fail or bolster the individual's own ability to cope with stressors they are experiencing (Dill, Feld, Martin, Beukema, & Belle, 1980; Wilson, 1987).

It is clear, therefore, the social environment, whether defined broadly in terms of social structure or narrowly in terms of close social relationships, exerts powerful influences on the stress and coping process. The chapters in this volume seek to explicate some of these processes and by doing so they serve to add to our understanding of that complex phenomenon called coping.

ORGANIZATION OF THE VOLUME

This volume begins with a chapter by Elaine Wethington and Ronald Kessler in which they explore several underexplored issues related to the role of the situational context in influencing coping strategies and coping effectiveness. Most of the discussion centers around data these authors collected from a general population sample of 1,556 men and women. Two types of situational factors are considered, the objective characteristics of stressors, such as type and severity, and the social relational context in which coping occurs. For example, significant variations in the use of particular coping strategies were found, depending on the type of event encountered. Likewise, some coping strategies were found to be more efficacious than others in relieving distress.

The next three chapters of this book discuss developmental issues as relevant to stress and coping processes. In the first chapter, Donald Wertlieb uses the experience of divorce as the context within which to discuss the applicability of stress and coping models to our understanding of such stressors affecting children. What is clear from Wertlieb's discussion of the divorce literature is that divorce is not simply an "event" with which many children must cope, but, rather, it signifies a set of "complex processes over time which are only comprehensible in a phenomological context of the individual's and family's experiences of the 'events.'" He calls for conceptual differentiation among various chronic and acute aspects of the divorce experience as well as a differentiation of children's coping processes. His discussion of "developmental orchestration" also makes clear that the proper context for understanding a child's ability to cope successfully with divorce is the set of normative developmental tasks that are salient for that child when the divorce occurs and afterward. Wertlieb ends his chapter with a succinct but forward-looking discussion of intervention strategies, which makes clear that successful interventions with children experiencing divorce will need to take the developmental, familial, and environmental context of the divorce experience into account.

In the next chapter, Carol Aneshensel and Susan Gore provide further insight into the developmental issues affecting stress and coping processes with a discussion of stressful experiences among an ethnically and racially diverse group of adolescents growing up in Los Angeles. These authors argue against the tendency to export adult models of stress and coping to research with adolescents. They propose a model for undersanding the health consequences of stress among adolescents, which features the concept of "role restructuring." Their model explicitly recognizes that an understanding of stress or transitions within one role for an adolescent must include a consideration of the other social roles the adolescent occupies. From extensive interviews with 50 adolescents, two potentially stressful experiences constitute the focus of this chapter, the initiation of dating and school transitions. The detailed discussion of each transition serves to highlight the importance of the broader social context for gauging the stressfulness of these experiences.

Karen Rook, David Dooley, and Ralph Catalano focus their chapter on life course variations in coping with stressful life events, in this case economic distress resulting from work-related stressors. An important issue here is whether coping and coping effectiveness changes over the life course of adults. Their comprehensive review of the literature sheds light on the debate over whether coping skills tend to increase or decrease with age and points to needed methodological improvements in studies addressing this question. In the remainder of this chapter, these authors report on data collected as part of several large surveys conducted in Los Angeles County between 1978 and 1982. Several intriguing findings are reported with regard to age differences in the use of specific coping strategies. Not only did the use of coping strategies differ by age of the respondent, but the effectiveness of specific strategies appeared to change with age. These authors also discuss their results with regard to the implications for intervention.

The next two chapters focus on the role of gender in the stress and coping process. Peggy Thoits explores the hypothesis that men and women differ in their use of coping strategies and that these differences in coping strategies, if found, may be linked to gender differences in the appraisal of stressful events as to their controllability. Data on event perceptions, coping, and outcomes are reported for a sample of 200 college students who gave detailed descriptions of recent negative experiences. Contrary to common stereotypes about the different ways in which men and women cope with stress, the results did not reveal significant gender differences in perceptions of uncontrollability or use of problem-focused efforts. Women, however, were more expressive in describing the stressful event and their coping efforts and did use a greater number of coping strategies than men. This chapter, therefore, is consistent with other research that has failed to show pervasive gender differences in coping (e.g., Miller & Kirsch, 1988).

In their chapter, Susan Gore and Mary Ellen Colten discuss the role of self-esteem and interpersonal relationships in shaping the stress process for women and in helping to explain the higher rate of depressive symptoms commonly found women in community surveys. These authors conclude that interpersonal relationships form a somewhat different context for the development and maintenance of self-esteem for women than men. Their discussion highlights the need to link individual coping strategies and the emergence of stable coping resources to the social environment, which may have a different meaning for men and women. Both this chapter and the previous one by Thoits underscore the need to develop much more refined models of the stress and coping process in order to pinpoint gender differences in vulnerability to stress.

Although every chapter in this volume discusses in some way the role of social supports in the stress and coping process, three chapters have this as their central theme. Benjamin Gottlieb and Fred Wagner highlight the transactional nature of social support in close personal relationships as an antidote to many social support studies that treat this coping resource as a static feature of the social environment. Of particular concern are factors that constrain the expression of support or limit coping options in close relationships when a common stressor is encountered. Following a probing analysis of this issue that centers around a detailed review of three recent empirical studies, Gottlieb and Wagner discuss the results of a study of coping for parents of children who had been diagnosed with serious chronic illnesses. Intensive qualitative interviews with both parents revealed a complex web of positive and negative influences that spouses exerted on each other as they attempted to cope with their own needs and feelings, as well as the needs and feelings of their spouse and child. Sharp differences were found in how husbands and wives coped with the stressors associated with a child's illness, with wives often adopting a *public* form of coping in the presence of the husband different from their *private* forms of coping.

The chapter by Mary Amanda Dew and Evelyn Bromet serves to test the role of depression in having an impact on social support resources. The authors point out that such a concern is characteristic of clinical studies of depressed patients, whereas community surveys of normal populations generally view social support as an antecedent to depressive symptoms. They report data from a longitudinal study of over 700 women designed to study the health effects of the Three Mile Island accident. Their analyses suggest that an episode of depression is associated with a deterioration of marital support over time, both in terms of perceived levels of support and the actual relationship itself. Such a process has been hypothesized in the research literature, but this study represents one of the few empirical demonstrations of such an effect.

Nan Lin and Jeanne Westcott consider the events of marriage and marital disengagement from the perspective of social network theory and research. Their chapter outlines a process by which marriage leads to the integration of two social networks, whereas marital disruptions can be viewed as representing not only the dissolution of a given dyadic relationship but also a severing of the bridge linking these two social networks. This conceptualization is used by these authors to explore marital status differences in mental health and the impact of life events such as divorce or death of a spouse, as well as the role of gender in these processes. Their analysis adds some structural specificity to what are often passing and ill-defined references in the literature to the impact of "social network" on stress and coping. This conceptualization also helps define experiences such as marriage and divorce less as discrete events and more as dynamic social processes.

In their chapter, Susan Folkman, Margaret Chesney, Leon McKusick, Gail Ironson, David Johnson, and Thomas Coates present an explicit example of how coping theory and research may be utilized to design intervention strategies for individuals experiencing stress. The first part of their chapter provides a succinct theoretical overview of the role of cognitive appraisal and coping in the stress process. It is followed by a description and preliminary evaluation of Coping Effectiveness Training, an 8-week program developed and tested with persons affected by the AIDS epidemic in San Francisco. The value of this program is that it is directly derived from theory and research on stress and coping, and the preliminary evaluative data are encouraging.

The volume concludes with Leonard Pearlin's forward-looking review of the limitations to our current knowledge of coping processes and a guide to future directions for research in this field. He argues that a more complete understanding of coping will require more attention to the range of secondary stressors that are often associated with a primary stressful event like divorce. Second, he suggests that the personal significance of a stressful experience for the individual may well influence coping strategies and account for some of the wide variation we observe between persons in how they cope with the same objective stressor. Third, he seeks to add clarity to our understanding of the concept of coping itself, how it has been conceptualized, measured, and analyzed. Finally, he offers some provocative insights into issues of intervention and public policy. In all, this chapter revisits many of the themes other authors of this volume elaborated upon and provides the field with a challenging set of issues that will guide future research.

REFERENCES

Antonovsky, A. (1979). *Health, stress, and coping*. San Francisco: Jossey-Bass.
Billings, A., Cronkite, R. C., & Moos, R. (1983). Social-environmental factors in unipolar

depression: Comparisons of depressed patients and nondepressed controls. *Journal of Abnormal Psychology, 92,* 119–133.

Billings, A. G., & Moos, R. H. (1981). The role of coping responses and social resources in attenuating the stress of life events. *Journal of Behavioral Medicine, 4,* 139–157.

Caplan, G. (1976). The family as support system. In G. Caplan & M. Killelea (Eds.), *Support systems and mutual help: Multidisciplinary explorations* (pp. 19–36). New York: Grune & Stratton.

Coates, D., Wortman, C. B., & Abbey, A. (1979). Reactions to victims. In I. H. Frieze, D. Bar-Tal, & J. S. Carroll (Eds.), *New approaches to social problems* (pp. 21–52). San Francisco: Jossey-Bass.

Cohen, S., & McKay, G. (1984). Social support, stress, and the buffering hypothesis: A theoretical analysis. In A. Baum, J. E. Singer, & S. E. Taylor (Eds.), *Handbook of psychology and health* (Vol. 4; pp. 253–267). Hillsdale, NJ: Erlbaum.

Coyne, J. C., Aldwin, C., & Lazarus, R. S. (1981). Depression and coping in stressful episodes. *Journal of Abnormal Psychology, 90,* 439–447.

Dill, D., Feld, E., Martin, J., Beukema, S., & Belle, D. (1980). The impact of the environment on the coping efforts of low-income women. *Family relations, 29,* 503–509.

Dunkel-Schetter, C., & Wortman, C. (1982). The interpersonal dynamics of cancer: Problems in social relationships and their impact on the patient. In H. S. Friedman & M. R. DiMatteo (Eds.), *Interpersonal issues in health care* (pp. 69–100). New York: Academic Press.

Dunkel-Schetter, C., Folkman, S., & Lazarus, R. S. (1987). Correlates of social support receipt. *Journal of Personality and Social Psychology, 53,* 71–80.

Eckenrode, J., & Wethington, E. (1990). The process and outcome of mobilizing social support. In S. Duck (Ed.), *Personal relationships and social support* (pp. 83–103). Beverly Hills, CA: Sage.

Fischer, J. D., Goff, B., Nadler, A., & Chinsky, J. M. (1988). Social psychological influences on help-seeking and support from peers. In B. Gottlieb (Ed.), *Marshalling social support: Formats, processes, and effects* (pp. 267–304). Beverly Hills, CA: Sage.

Folkman, S., Lazarus, R. S., Dunkel-Schetter, C., DeLongis, A., & Gruen, R. J. (1986). Dynamics of a stressful encounter: Cognitive appraisal, coping, and encounter outcomes. *Journal of Personality and Social Psychology, 5,* 992–1103.

Folkman, S., Lazarus, R. S., Gruen, R. J., & DeLongis, A. (1986). Appraisal, coping, health status, and psychological symptoms. *Journal of Personality and Social Psychology, 50,* 571–579.

Gore, S. (1985). Social support and styles of coping with stress. In S. Cohen & S. L. Syme (Eds.), *Social support and health* (pp. 263–278). New York: Academic Press.

Kessler, R., C., Price, R. H., & Wortman, C. B. (1985). Social factors in psychopathology: Stress, social support, and coping processes. *Annual Review of Psychology, 36,* 531–72.

Lazarus, R. S., & Folkman, S. (1980). An analysis of coping in a middle-aged community. *Journal of Health and Social Behavior, 21,* 219–239.

Lazarus, R. S., & Folkman, S. (1984). *Stress, appraisal, and coping.* New York: Springer.

Liker, J. K., & Elder, G. H., Jr. (1983). Economic hardship and marital relations in the 1930's. *American Sociological Review, 48,* 343–359.

Miller, S. M., & Kirsch, N. (1988). Sex differences in cognitive coping with stress. In R. C. Barnett, L. Biener, & G. C. Baruch (Eds.), *Gender and stress* (pp. 278–307). New York: The Free Press.

Moos, R. H., & Schaeffer, J. A. (1986). Life transitions and crises: A conceptual overview. In R. H. Moos (Ed.), *Coping with life crises* (pp. 3–28). New York: Plenum Press.

Pearlin, L. I., & Schooler, C. (1978). The structure of coping. *Journal of Health and Social Behavior, 19,* 2–21.

Pearlin, L. I., Lieberman, M. A., Menaghan, E., & Mullan, J. T. (1981). The stress process. *Journal of Health and Social Behavior, 22,* 337–356.

Shiffman, S., & Wills, T. A. (Eds.). (1985). *Coping and substance use.* New York: Academic Press.

Silver, R. L., & Wortman, C. B. (1980). Coping with undesirable life events. In J. Garber & M. Seligman (Eds.), *Human helplessness: Theory and application* (pp. 279–375). New York: Academic Press.

Strickland, B. R. (1978). Internal-external expectancies and health-related behaviors. *Journal of Consulting and Clinical Psychology, 46,* 1192–1211.

Taylor, S. E. (1983). Adjustment to threatening events: A theory of cognitive adaptation. *American Psychologist, 38,* 1161–1173.

Thoits, P. A. (1986). Social support as coping assistance. *Journal of Consulting and Clinical Psychology, 54,* 416–423.

Turner, R. J., & Noh, S. (1983). Class and psychological vulnerability among women: The significance of social support and personal control. *Journal of Health and Social Behavior, 24,* 2–15.

Weiss, R. S. (1990). When work stress comes home. In J. Eckenrode & S. Gore (Eds.), *Stress between work and family* (pp. 17–37). New York: Plenum Press.

Wheaton, B. (1982). The sociogenesis of psychological disorder: An attributional theory. *Journal of Health and Social Behavior, 24,* 2–15.

Wills, T. A. (1987). Downward social comparison as a coping mechanism. In R. C. Snyder & C. Ford (Eds.), *Coping with negative life events: Clinical and social psychological perspectives* (pp. 243–268). New York: Plenum Press.

Wilson, W. J. (1987). *The truly disadvantaged.* Chicago: University of Chicago Press.

Wortman, C. B. (1984). Social support and cancer: Conceptual and methodologic issues. *Cancer, 53,* 2339–2360.

2

Situations and Processes of Coping

ELAINE WETHINGTON and RONALD C. KESSLER

Despite many admirable and theoretically provocative attempts to understand the role of "coping" in the stress process and a myriad of studies to understand the relationship of particular sorts of coping strategies to outcomes in the stress process, several issues about coping and the coping process remain relatively unexplored. This chapter examines several such issues. For some issues, we provide new data. For others, we provide additional ideas about how data may be gathered.

The first of these issues regards situational determinants of coping strategies and coping effectiveness (see Figure 1). We divide situational determinants into two types: the situational context surrounding the victim and the type of event that occurs. Do context and type of situation affect an individual's choice of coping strategies? If so, what sorts of strategies do different contexts and stressor types evoke? Assuming that a choice of coping strategy takes place, does the choice of one coping strategy over another affect the outcome of the stressful situation? The effects of situations on choice of coping strategy are rationally plausible and anecdotally and empirically supported. The degree to which the choice of coping strategy ultimately affects psychological adjustment to the situation has received less research attention.

ELAINE WETHINGTON • Department of Human Development and Family Studies, Cornell University, Ithaca, New York 14853-4401.　**RONALD C. KESSLER** • Department of Sociology, University of Michigan, Ann Arbor, Michigan 48109.

The Social Context of Coping, edited by John Eckenrode. Plenum Press, New York, 1991.

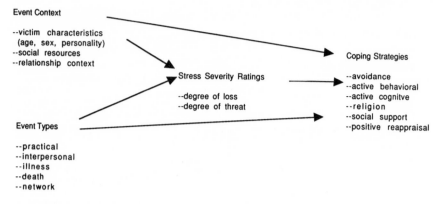

Figure 1. Conceptual linkages between event context, event types, stress severity ratings, and coping strategies.

Two general sorts of situational characteristics are known to be relevant to choice of coping strategy: (1) type of situation, for example, financial problem or marital difficulty, which specifies the *tasks* presented for coping; and (2) severity of the situation, defined in terms of the degree to which the situation involves the loss of valued persons or objects or threat of future harm, which influences the cognitive and affective responses of the victims, such as emotion management, constructive problem solving and vigilance for the future. Similarly, objective situational characteristics and severity are relevant when evaluating the efficacy of different coping strategies. To promote good emotional adjustment, coping should not only fit the demands of the situation but also alleviate the emotional and practical difficulties facing the individual.

The second of the issues to be addressed is the applicability of coping research based on outcomes of psychological adjustment and well-being to research where the outcome is the onset of a clinically significant depressive or affective disorder. Researchers have tended to assume that research on coping in community samples will generalize to research on clinical populations. However, onset of depressive episode is qualitatively distinct from depressed mood. In the second part of this chapter, we put this assumption to the test.

The third issue regards additional contexts of events that are relevant to coping. Event type and stress severity have been the focus of much previous research (see Figure 1). Yet other components of situations could be equally decisive. The coping challenges of situations do not necessarily reduce to objective tasks and demands brought about by discrete events. The degree of challenge evoked by situations also involves other aspects of event context, such as characteristics of the victim, social resources available to the victim, and relationship context. In particular, we wish to explore how the actions and reactions of others caught up in the same situation affect how an individual copes with a stressful situation. Significant others can play a role in the etiology, maintenance, and resolution of stress. Nevertheless, the role of close relationships in affecting individual coping is only beginning to be explored (Antonovsky & Sourani, 1988; Bolger, DeLongis, Kessler, & Wethington, 1989b; Gottlieb & Wagner, this volume).

This chapter explores each of these questions in turn. For the first two questions, we provide new data. It concludes with the call for new studies of coping, focused on these issues.

SITUATIONAL DETERMINANTS OF COPING AND COPING EFFECTIVENESS

In the past decade, a series of excellent studies have documented the development of a general theory of coping (e.g., Billings & Moos, 1981; Folkman, Lazarus, Gruen, & DeLongis, 1986a; Folkman, Lazarus, Dunkel-Schetter, DeLongis, & Gruen, 1986b; Miller, Surtees, Kreitman, Ingham, & Sashidharan, 1985). Those studies have overcome many of the limitations of previous research by using representative samples, standardized measures of stress, coping, and emotional adjustment, and by building systematic comparisons across stressful situations into the research designs. These studies have also documented that different situations call forth different coping strategies.

In spite of these efforts, the literature does not examine the situational determinants of coping effectiveness. Only Pearlin and Schooler (1978) explicitly considered the possibility that coping effectiveness varies as a function of the characteristics of stressful situations, and their analysis was confined to a consideration of chronic role-related stress (for which they documented considerable differences in coping effectiveness).

Mattlin, Wethington, and Kessler (1990) contributed to the growing body of research on situational determinants of coping. This study went beyond previous efforts in two ways. First, it presented the first large-scale analysis of situational determinants of coping effectiveness in response to a wide variety of stressful life events and chronic difficulties. Most previous studies on coping utilize nonrepresentative samples and idiosyncratic measures. Second, this study documented that, over and above the effects of individual strategies, combinations of particular strategies promote good emotional adjustment to stress.

We based our analyses of situational determinants of coping on a general population sample of 1,556 men and women. The target population for the study was nonblack, intact married couples in the Detroit metropolitan area. Interviewing took place in the spring and summer of 1985; the interviews were face-to-face and averaged 78 minutes in length. The household interview response rate was 73%. Because this was a study of married couples, we attempted to interview both members of the couple. When an interview was successfully completed with one spouse, persistent attempts were made to interview the second. The response rate was 80% for the second spouse. The couple response rate, the product of the two spouse response rates, was .73 × .80 = 58%. Although considerably lower than the response rates typical in studies of *individuals*, this is comparable to the response rates found in other surveys of married couples (Hiller & Philliber, 1985).

The 1,556 respondents (out of a total sample of 1,755) included in the analysis are those who reported the occurrence of at least one experience judged to be stressful in the 12 months before the interview and who provided complete information about coping and emotional adjustment. The most common reason respondents were eliminated was because they experienced no event that the investigators judged to be objectively stressful; however, some were eliminated because they reported events that the investigators judged to be a consequence of the respondent's mental health (e.g., a hospitalization for depression). These exclusions limit the generalizability of the findings, on which we will comment extensively later.

In previous general population studies of coping, respondents have either been asked to describe their "typical" ways of coping with stress or to describe the ways they cope with one particular stressful situation. We took the second approach, based on evidence that assessments of "typical" coping are only weakly related to the ways people actually cope in particular situations (Folkman & Lazarus, 1980). Respondents selected their "most stressful situation" after a review with the interviewer of all the stressful situations that they had reported in response to interview questions about specific life events (defined as discrete occurrences, e.g., death of a loved one) and difficulties (defined as ongoing, chronic, stressful situations, e.g., serious problems getting along with spouse).

Study interviewers administered a series of informational probes whenever a respondent reported an event during the interview (e.g., "What happened?" "Can you tell me a little about that situation?"). The aim of these probes was not to measure the respondent's perception of how stressful the situation was but to gather information about the objective circumstances of the event that would likely be associated with the amount of stress it would cause. This information was recorded and was used later to code the event into any one of 500 event categories, distinguished by dimensions previous research had found to be associated with the stress experienced by the average person undergoing the event (e.g., layoff vs. voluntarily quitting a job, death of confidant vs. death of acquaintance, finding out one has cancer vs. treatment for a broken bone). In turn, these event categories were classified by their severity—major, moderate, or minor—on the dimensions of *loss* and *threat*. Loss was rated on the basis of evidence that some valued person, object, or idea was harmed (Brown & Harris, 1978). Threat was rated on the basis of evidence that future harm might result from the situation (Lazarus & Folkman, 1984; see also the concept of "danger," developed by Brown & Harris, 1978). All combinations of degree of loss and danger are possible for a situation.

These two coding distinctions—event versus difficulty and degree of loss and threat—are significant advances in studies of coping. The distinction between events and difficulties is important because the kinds of strategies used to manage long-term stressful situations almost certainly differ from those used to manage acute stressors. Theoretical models that emphasize how subjective appraisal of situations affect coping (e.g., Folkman & Lazarus, 1980; McCrae, 1984; Parkes, 1984, 1986; Stone & Neale, 1984) have documented the effects of perceived threat and controllability on coping choice.

In addition to our classifications of event versus difficulty and degree of loss and threat, we also divided events into the six categories of Respondent Illness, Respondent Practical (financial, legal, job-related), Interpersonal (arguments and difficulties between the respondent and others), Death of a Loved One, Network Illness, and Network Other (events other than illness and death occurring to someone other than the respondent). Billings and Moos (1981) classified events into a somewhat similar set of categories and found significant associations between event type and reports of coping.

This study evaluated six different types of coping strategies: avoidance ("How much did you do things to take your mind off the situation?"), positive reappraisal ("How much did you try thinking about the situation in a different way so that it didn't upset you so much?"), religion ("How much did you rely on your religious beliefs to help you cope?"), active cognitive ("How much did you try to think of possible ways to improve the situation?"), active behavioral ("How much did you do things to improve the situation?"), and social support ("Did you talk to anyone about this situation?").[1] The extent to which a strategy was employed was assessed in a single question for each of the coping strategies.[2] The use of single items is a limitation because it reduced the ability of our analyses to detect subtle variations in coping; nevertheless, as reported later, the distribution of coping responses did vary across situational type, as predicted.

Using the six coping dimensions assessed in this study, exploratory cluster analyses were carried out to determine whether individuals evidenced clear *multivariate* patterns, or profiles, of coping. Menaghan (1983) has suggested that coping profiles of this sort exist, but empirical examinations of this possibility are rare (Pearlin & Schooler, 1978). In our analyses, two substantive profiles were detected: *versatility* and *passivity*. Versatile copers, who comprised 49% of the sample, reported using virtually all coping strategies. Passive copers, less than 4% of the sample, reported using each strategy either "not at all" or "only a little." Two dichotomous variables were constructed to indicate being in the versatile or passive groups, and these were then used as predictors in multiple regression analyses of coping effectiveness, controlling simultaneously for the main effects of the separate coping strategies.

Multivariate regression analyses were used to evaluate the efficacy of various coping strategies. Efficacy was evaluated as the significant coefficient for a given coping strategy in a regression predicting levels of psychological adjustment, controlling for event type, for example, illness, degree of loss and danger in the situation, and the confounding demographic factors of age, gender, and socioeconomic status. Subgroup analyses were also conducted among groups defined by event type, event severity, and acuteness versus chronicity of the stress. Psychological adjustment, following the literature on coping, was measured by self-reported symptoms of anxiety and depression. These outcomes were measured with items from the anxiety and depression subscales of the revised Hopkins Symptom Checklist (Derogatis, 1977).

Our analyses, in sum, parallel those used in previous general popu-

---

[1]Although this series was based on a typology developed by Stone and Neale (1984), the categories were revised, based on pretest interviewing. Active cognitive coping was added to the scheme on the basis of its frequent mention in response to open-ended questions about "other" coping strategies. We also eliminated several Stone and Neale coping categories, based on their low response frequencies in the pretest. Catharsis, acceptance, and relaxation were dropped.

[2]Respondents were asked, "How much did you do things like this after (most stressful situation)": Response options were "a lot," "some," "a little," "not at all." The question about social support was asked in a different format; information was obtained about whether or not the respondent sought support, rather than the frequency with which it was sought.

lation surveys of coping effectiveness (Billings & Moos, 1981; Folkman *et al.*, 1986a, 1986b; Miller *et al.*, 1985; Pearlin & Schooler, 1978). We interpret the associations between coping and adjustment as evidence that coping affects adjustment, although, as in the previous studies, we use cross-sectional data on exposure to stress and adjustment. This is a serious problem and can only be justified by the fact that a more reliable nonexperimental design has not yet been developed for studies of coping in the general population (Kessler, Price, & Wortman, 1985).

Our analysis documented that situational influences can be found not only on the use of particular coping strategies but also on their effectiveness as strategies. Many of our results are consistent with previous research. Active behavioral and versatile coping occur most frequently in response to practical problems (Billings & Moos, 1981; Folkman *et al.*, 1986b; Pearlin & Schooler, 1978). Passive coping is rare. Religion is most commonly reported by those coping with the long-term illness or death of a loved one (McCrae, 1984). Active behavioral coping is least likely in response to a death, and religion is less likely to be used in response to practical problems. Our overall findings regarding the efficacy of different sorts of coping strategies can be summarized simply: Religion, active behavioral, and versatile coping are generally efficacious strategies, whereas avoidance, cognitive reappraisal, and active cognitive coping are not. Passive coping, although rare, is sometimes efficacious. Although previous research has not demonstrated precisely the same pattern, the divergence in efficacy between types of strategies has internal consistency.

Some of our findings, however, are significant departures from previous research and suggest that it will be necessary to modify the findings of earlier investigations in several ways. We explored these departures more thoroughly in analyses of subgroups: events versus difficulties, high versus low severity, event type. As a result of the smaller sample sizes, we appropriately consider these findings less robust.

Perhaps the most striking finding of this sort is that *positive reappraisal*, generally thought to be associated with good emotional adjustment to stress, appears in our analyses to be maladaptive. Analyses of specific types and classifications of life events, however, paint a more complex picture. Positive reappraisal helps reduce distress associated with the death of a loved one but interferes with adjustment in situations of low degree of threat or situations that pose practical problems. These negative effects are most likely to occur when reappraisal is used without related action (that is, not actually doing something about the problem), suggesting that reappraisal is harmful if it interferes with action to resolve a problem.

Another divergence from prior research findings involves the relationship between active cognitive and active behavioral coping. Most investigations (including Stone & Neale, 1984) have merged these strategies into one ("Did you think or do something in order to cope?"). Consistent with the findings of Billings and Moos (1981), though, we find that active cognitive coping is generally associated with poor emotional adjustment and active behavioral coping with good adjustment. These opposing associations emerged in a multivariate analysis of the coping profiles. Thinking about ways to make a situation better, in other words, is harmful when it is not accompanied by action. The fact that action is generally adaptive underscores the benefits of problem-focused coping. The fact that cognitive coping is generally a harmful strategy suggests that it is likely to be used in situations that cannot be changed, a state that would almost certainly increase their stressfulness. It is also possible that it is dangerous to ruminate over a problem (Nolen-Hoeksema, 1987), especially if its magnitude grows in the meantime.

In our analyses, religion emerged as an efficacious strategy, when coping with the death of a loved one and with similar events that pose a high degree of loss. Several previous investigations (Folkman et al., 1986b; Veroff, Douvan, & Kulka, 1981) report findings that are consistent with this. When confronted with illness and death, feelings of helplessness and depression may be moderated by the belief that one's fate is in the hands of God. (To reduce this to the language of coping, religion can facilitate positive reappraisal of the situation.) Our data show that religion is efficacious in the same situations as positive reappraisal, although religion is more efficiacious than reappraisal and more consistently beneficial.

We also document the importance of using multiple coping strategies. Having a "versatile" coping profile is associated with good emotional adjustment to stressful events, particularly practical and interpersonal events. Yet, these effects were not large. As a matter of fact, we find less evidence in favor of versatility than Pearlin and Schooler (1978). This discrepancy with their research may be due to the fact that our analyses controlled for the additive effects of individual strategies, whereas the Pearlin and Schooler analysis did not.

"Passive" coping, moreover, can be associated with good emotional adjustment, such as in chronically stressful situations that pose high loss or threat. Indeed, the efficacy of passivity in these situations suggests that passivity should be considered seriously in future research.

We also found that engaging in the behaviors we define as coping are generally less effective among people exposed to a chronic difficulty than those exposed to an acute stressor. There are many possible interpretations of this difference. For instance, the power of coping strategies to promote adjustment may become weaker as the stress continues. Yet given what is known about coping with chronic situations, this is unlikely. Longitudinal studies of people coping with intractable problems show that resilience to stress increases rather than decreases over time (Zarit, Todd, & Zarit, 1986). Pearlin and Schooler (1978) also suggested another explanation: That some situations are so intractable and so beyond the control of individuals who experience them, that endurance is more efficacious than action that would be useless, perhaps even harmful, if it sapped energy or increased frustration. This latter interpretation is quite consistent with our finding, noted before, that passivity is associated with good adjustment. But just as plausibly, our finding that coping is not generally associated with good emotional adjustment to chronic difficulties is a function of the research design, in which respondents were asked to nominate the one problem that was the most stressful of the preceding year. The nomination of a chronic situation could be indicative of inability to resolve that problem successfully, or "failed coping" (Kessler *et al.*, 1985). If this is the case, then it is not at all surprising that coping does not facilitate good adjustment among respondents who nominate chronic difficulties. A more representative sampling of chronic difficulties, one that did not ask respondents to nominate their most stressful problems, supports the methodological interpretation by documenting that coping promotes good emotional adjustment in the face of chronic strains (Pearlin & Schooler, 1978).

Obviously, situational factors are not fully determinant of coping efficacy or choice. The very complexity of situations may reduce the correspondence that can be observed between situation and coping choice. For example, a financial problem may require strict budgeting on the part of all family members, but complete honesty with the children could cause emotional problems. In a situation that mixes danger and loss, for example, the imminent closing of a business, the danger may evoke a need for continued vigilance, whereas the loss may evoke a need for emotional management; management of emotion might encourage a relaxation of vigilance, or the maintenance of vigilance might interfere with the control of emotions.

DISTRESS, DISORDER, AND COPING

There has been a great deal of interest in the role of stress and coping processes in "depression." Nevertheless, in the literature, depression has been conceptualized both as a continuum of self-reported symptoms (as reported in the foregoing section of this chapter) and as a discrete diagnosis of depressive disorder, based on clinical observation and judgment or structured diagnostic interview (Parker & Brown, 1982).

Discussions of findings, however, have tended to minimize the consequences that different ways of measuring the outcome may have for understanding processes of coping and their role in adjustment to stress. For example, Billings and Moos (1982), although conceding that little research has addressed this issue, have argued that the same processes and variables are related to provoking depressed mood as well as clinically significant onsets of depression episodes.

There are several reasons to expect important differences between the stress processes that are related to depressed mood and the stress processes related to onset of depressive episode. Type of stressor may be important. For example, minor events are related to depressed mood, whereas only major events seem to be related to onset of major depressive disorder (Brown & Harris, 1978, 1989).

Researchers should anticipate differences, moreover, because depressed mood and clinical episodes are qualitatively distinct phenomena. Interview or clinical diagnosis of depression requires a large number of symptoms and a long period of presence (nearly every day for 2 weeks for the DSM-III-R Research Diagnostic Criteria [RDC; Spitzer, Endicott, & Robins, 1975]). In contrast, a "high score" on a symptoms list can come about through short-lived moods. Differences in the properties of the statistical distribution of distress and diagnosable depressive disorder may also be salient. Clinical depression is a rarer event than depressed mood and generally scored in a dichotomous fashion, rather than as a continuous variable. The extent to which two variables are dissimilarly distributed limits how similarly any third variable can be correlated with them. In particular, any third variable will be less strongly correlated with a case/noncase categorical variable than it will be correlated with a continuous symptom score.

The design of our community study made it possible to study the differing association between coping and the stress process in groups distinguished by the probability of suffering from depressive disorder. Following the preferred practice in psychiatric epidemiology (e.g., Cooper & Morgan, 1973), a two-stage procedure was used to ascertain the prevalence of depressive disorder in this sample. The first interview (from which all data reported in the foregoing section of this chapter originated) included a revised version of the depression stem question from version III-A of the Diagnostic Interview Schedule (DIS; Robins,

Helzer, Croughan, & Ratliff, 1981).[3] The beginning, end, and duration of the most recent episode was ascertained. (The sample was also screened for probable anxiety disorder during the past 6 months.)

Based on the series of depression episode questions, the respondents were divided into two categories: predicted depression cases and predicted noncases. Predicted cases were those who answered "yes" to the stem question and who reported episodes lasting 2 weeks or longer, a length of time generally regarded to denote a clinically significant episode of depression. All predicted cases were targeted for a second interview, as were their spouses. Seventy-three percent of the predicted cases and their spouses were successfully reinterviewed.

The second interview included a somewhat modified version of the depression section from the lifetime Schedule for Affective Disorders and Schizophrenia (SADS) (Bromet, Dunn, Connell, Dew, & Schulberg, 1986). The episodes investigated, however, were confined to those occurring in the 6 months prior to the interview. Psychiatric social workers were trained to conduct the second interview. Questions were devoted to classifying the episodes as major, episodic minor, or chronic intermittent in nature. Interviewers also recorded detailed clinical observations along with symptom ratings. The interviews, symptoms ratings, and observations were reviewed independently by two clinical study supervisors who assigned diagnoses based on Research Diagnostic Criteria (RDC; Spitzer *et al.,* 1975).

The focus of the analyses was on how coping differs between depressive cases and noncases. Comparative analyses were conducted using the confirmed "diagnosed" depressives and a subsample of "supernormals" drawn from the community sample. Simply stated, "supernormals" were those who answered "no" to both the depression and anxiety stem questions in the Time 1 interview. The sample for the analyses consisted of 133 "cases" and 764 "supernormals." Demographic characteristics of this analysis group closely approximate those of the sample target population.

Multiple regression analyses were used to examine the relationship of how respondents coped with life events and difficulties to distress and interview-based diagnosis, controlling for age, income, and severity of stress. These analyses thus provided an estimate of the independent relationship between a particular coping strategy and the criterion vari-

---

[3]The exact wording of this question was: "In the past 6 months was there a time lasting 1 continuous week or more when you felt sad, blue, or depressed most of the time, or when you lost all interest and pleasure in things you usually care about or enjoy?"

able (diagnosis or distress), taking into account all other coping strategies plus control variables.

Coping strategies had distinctly different relationships to distress and diagnosis, and these in turn varied in terms of whether it was life events or chronic difficulties that were being examined: The latter pattern is consistent with the findings reported earlier in this chapter. In general, strategies of coping with life events were more strongly related to distress than to diagnosis of depression. What is important, is that the hypothesis that strategies for coping with stress have different relationships with distress versus diagnosable depression was confirmed: The relationship between coping strategies and the outcomes varied by whether the outcome was measured as distress or as diagnosis. Most striking, the use of almost all coping strategies is associated with diagnosis, in the subgroup coping with a chronic life difficulty, but is not with higher distress. Testing the second hypothesis—that such differences in the relationships with coping were due to differences in the distribution of the distress scores versus diagnosis of depression—we conducted regression analysis using a dichotomously rescaled distress score as the outcome. The rescaled distress score largely replicated the findings obtained using the continuous scaling of the score. Thus we could reject the hypothesis that differences in the relationship to coping are merely a function of differences in the distributions of distress scores versus diagnosis.

Our results indicate the need to consider more carefully the differences in the relationship of coping strategies to distress versus depression. The two need to be distinguished when discussing research findings and constructing theoretical models. Overall, our results, though tentative, caution against oversimplification in discussions of stress, coping, distress, and depression. Further research is needed.

SOCIAL INTERACTION AND "INDIVIDUAL" COPING

Others in the environment can *cause* stress. This statement borders on trivial truism, but this truism underlies the argument presented here. Conflicts and tensions with network members, close significant others as well as more distantly related individuals, are a potent source of stress (Bolger, DeLongis, Kessler, & Schilling, 1989a). Overt conflict, however, is just one of the possibilities that concern us here. Significant others can be the victims of circumstances that provide coping challenges, such as the problems arising when a child falls victim to serious illness or a spouse to unemployment. Others can engage in behavior, such as trouble with the law or having an affair, that expose their loved ones to unexpected and serious stress.

The burdens on network members are many. Those undergoing stress require special treatment that facilitates their emotional control, such as listening, comfort, and reassurance as well as practical help, such as help with chores, special health care, and feeding. These emotional and practical tasks presented to helpers are often perceived as distressing in their own right. Indeed, in the community sample of adults analyzed in this report, problems occurring to someone other than the focal respondent are the most common sort of problem nominated as "the most stressful situation of the year" (42.8%).

Yet other individuals' exposure to stress is only part of the way the personal context of relationships relates to the stress process. Another process to consider is how important others may also affect the individual's response to a problem (see chapter by Gottlieb and Wagner in this volume). Research on coping assumes that victims mobilize social support from their significant others. Yet relatively little is known about the processes of mobilization or the costs and benefits of certain sorts of mobilization strategies to both victim and helper (Eckenrode & Wethington, 1990). Do others, in an attempt to shield themselves from more stress, ignore signals for help? What impact does relationship context have on help seeking and emotion management? About these processes, relatively little is known. The literature on coping that has sampled the general population, moreover, has not often considered the possibility that coping can be "mutual." Nor do individually based survey research designs generally collect data from more than one individual in a household, thus making inference of "mutual" coping more difficult to predict.

In our own study, we sampled married couples. Theoretically, an analysis of "mutual coping" with stressful situations could be conducted. Unfortunately, the research design, which asked individuals to nominate the most stressful situation of the year, resulted in only a minority of couples mentioning the same stressful situation. Descriptions of aspects of the events presented for coping in the situations, moreover, were more often than not discrepant between members of a couple: For example, one spouse might say that the most stressful aspect of a child's serious crisis had been fear of the outcome for the child, whereas the other spouse found it most difficult to cope with the anger and emotion toward the child generated by the event. Discrepancies such as these make it difficult to conduct a conventional analysis of mutual coping. Patterns of interaction in families and their history of stress might make each couple somewhat unique in its response to a given stressor. Still, we wish to speculate on how "mutual processes" may be relevant to the study of situational determinants of coping. Observations of the couples' coping with the same situation are used as a qualitative data base for speculation.

For example, one spouse's choice of coping strategies could affect how the other spouse copes. First, the affected individual might simply take on the problem to solve him- or herself, without involving—or even informing—the spouse. Second, the affected individual might decide on a strategy that limits the strategies of the other spouse, such as deciding that no action will be taken and asking the other spouse to follow this strategy as well. Third, the affected spouse might be incapable of action and refer all of the coping to the other. It is interesting to note that each of these three "unilateral" coping strategies could pose some emotional costs to the spouse, whose actions are constrained and contingent on choices decreed by the other.

Our data pose many examples of these unilateral coping strategies and dramatize the negative effects on spouses. In our data, one respondent coping with impending death reported that the other spouse's refusal to admit that death was near was the "most stressful aspect" of the situation, because he could not express his own feelings to her. In another case, one spouse's refusal to cope led to overburden for the other: One spouse was burdened with all of the practical difficulties arising from a court case involving a child, whereas the other refused to get involved in the day-to-day hassles and blamed the child for the situation.

More commonly, though, the burden of coping is shared more consenually, especially when the stressor affects both members of the couple. Sharing patterns that arise by consensus may be compensatory or parallel. To present a sex-typed example of the compensatory pattern, a husband might be engrossed in handling the financial problems brought on by an event, whereas a wife might be engaged in smoothing feelings and emotions in the family. Such compensatory patterns are widely reported in our study by both dual-earner and one-earner families. Sharing the burden could also proceed in a more parallel manner, with the husband and wife taking turns coping with the problem. In our own data, we have examples of how health care for a sick child shifts from wife to husband, depending on the time of day, and how "looking in" on aged parents is divided day by day between the members of a dual-career couple. There are also couples who collaborate in providing emotional comfort for stricken friends.

The examples presented emphasize the positive aspects of mutual coping, particularly those in which there has been open communication and discussion between the spouses. Research in the related area of social support, however, suggests that not all outcomes of even open discussion processes are uniformly positive. One spouse may agree to take on a strategy that has negative effects in the long term. To return to examples from our own data, a husband whose spouse developed a fatal disease reported that he would better "adjust" to the situation if he spent more time preparing for her death. Yet he felt that his dying wife experienced this behavior as threatening, implying that he had given up on her. The husband, in deference to her emotional state, minimized the severity of her symptoms and adopted a more optimistic demeanour in her presence. It is not clear whether this second set of strategies, although poignantly sensitive to the feelings of the wife, would be as efficacious in minimizing the husband's own problems or in moderating his future grief.

We do not mean to focus merely on extreme examples here or to minimize the positive effects of coordinated coping between spouses. We do mean to imply, though, that the study of mutual coping will require carefully designed, intense research. We believe that the use of daily diary methodology we have undertaken recently (Bolger *et al.*, 1989b), and direct investigator observation of married couples, will be necessary in order to provide new insights into the processes of mutual coping.

SUMMARY AND CONCLUSION

The purpose of this chapter has been to describe our own attempts to carry forward research on coping with stress and to provide some new information about how future research can both improve our understanding of individual coping processes and develop new theory in this area. The statistical associations between individual coping efforts, stress, and psychological adjustment are very modest in our research and in the research of others. Such modest associations should not be taken to show that the real-world relationships between coping, stress, and psychological adjustment are unimportant. Rather, they point out that the scientific understanding and measurement of these processes is imprecise.

We believe that the three issues with which we considered all warrant further attention because they will yield new understanding and precision to stress research. First, the situational determinants of coping and coping effectiveness warrant more serious attention. The most critical need in this area is to develop more reliable and valid measures of those qualities of situations that pose both restraints and challenges to individual coping. Second, future research must discriminate between different sorts of psychological adjustments, in particular, between reports of bad mood and onsets of serious psychological disorder in response to stress. Third, future research must consider the processes of "mutual coping." To reduce the study of coping to considering the efforts of only one individual may lead researchers away from one of the most potent predictors of psychological adjustment after stress: the perception of social support in the environment. ("But if the while I think on thee, dear friend,/ All losses are restored and sorrows end." [Shakespeare, Sonnet XXX, c. 1593])

ACKNOWLEDGMENTS

The research was supported by MERIT Award 1-R01-MH42714, Research Scientist Development Award 1-K01-MH00507, and by Grants 2-R01-MH41135 and 1-R01-MH42714, all from the National Institutes of Mental Health. The authors wish to thank Jean Converse, Jane McLeod, Stanley Presser, and the students of the 1985 Detroit Area Study for their assistance in collecting these data. Niall Bolger, James Coyne, Anita DeLongis, Jay Mattlin, Elizabeth Schilling, and Camille Wortman contributed significantly to the research program described in this chapter.

REFERENCES

Antonovsky, A., & Sourani, T. (1988). Family sense of coherence and family adaptation. *Journal of Marriage and the Family, 50,* 79–92.

Billings, A. G., & Moos, R. H. (1981). The role of coping responses and social resources in attentuating the stress of life events. *Journal of Behavioral Medicine, 4,* 139–157.

Billings, A. G. & Moos, R. H. (1982). Stressful life events and symptoms: A longitudinal model. *Health Psychology, 1,* 99–117.

Bolger, N., DeLongis, A., Kessler, R. C., & Schilling, E. (1989a). The effects of daily stress on negative mood. *Journal of Personality and Social Psychology, 57,* 808–818.

Bolger, N.,, DeLongis, A., Kessler, R. C., & Wethington, E. (1989b). The contagion of stress across multiple roles. *Journal of Marriage and the Family, 51,* 175–183.

Bromet, E. J., Dunn, L. O., Connell, M. M., Dew, M. A., & Schulberg, H. C. (1986). Long-term reliability of diagnosing lifetime major depression in a community sample. *Archives of General Psychiatry, 43,* 435–440.

Brown, G. W., & Harris, T. O. (1978). *Social origins of depression: A study of psychiatric disorder in women.* New York: Free Press.

Brown, G. W., & Harris, T. O. (1989). *Life events and illness.* New York: Guilford Press.

Cooper, B., & Morgan, H. G. (1973). *Epidemiological Psychiatry.* Springfield, IL: Charles C Thomas.

Derogatis, L. R. (1977). *SCL-90: Administration, scoring, and procedures manual for the revised version.* Baltimore, MD: Johns Hopkins University.

Eckenrode, J., & Wethington, E. (1990). The process and outcome of mobilizing social support. In S. Duck (Ed.), *Personal Relationships and Social Support* (pp. 83–103). Beverly Hills: Sage.

Folkman, S., & Lazarus, R. S. (1980). An analysis of coping in a middle-aged community sample. *Journal of Health and Social Behavior, 21,* 219–239.

Folkman, S., Lazarus, R. S., Gruen, R. J., & DeLongis, A. (1986a). Appraisal, coping, health status, and psychological symptoms. *Journal of Personality and Social Psychology, 50,* 571–579.

Folkman, S., Lazarus, R. S., Dunkel-Schetter, C., DeLongis, A., & Gruen, R. J. (1986b). The dynamics of a stressful encounter: Cognitive appraisal, coping and encounter outcomes. *Journal of Personality and Social Psychology, 50,* 992–1003.

Hiller, D. V., & Philliber, W. W. (1985). Maximizing confidence in married couple samples. *Journal of Marriage and the Family, 35,* 729–732.

Kessler, R. C., Price, R. H., & Wortman, C. B. (1985). Social factors in psychopathology: Stress, social support, and coping processes. *Annual Review of Psychology, 36,* 531–572.

Lazarus, R. S., & Folkman, S. (1984). *Stress, appraisal, and coping.* New York: Springer.

McCrae, R. R. (1984). Situational determinants of coping responses: Loss, threat, and challenge. *Journal of Personality and Social Psychology, 46,* 919–928.

Mattlin, J., Wethington, E., & Kessler, R. C. (1990). Situational determinants of coping and coping effectiveness. *Journal of Health and Social Behavior, 31,* 103–122.

Menaghan, E. G. (1983). Individual coping efforts: Moderators of the relationship between life stress and mental health outcomes. In H. B. Kaplan (Ed.), *Psychosocial stress: Trends in theory and research* (pp. 157–191). New York: Academic Press.

Miller, P., Surtees, P. G., Kreitman, N. B., Ingham, J. G., & Sashidharan, S. P. (1985). Maladaptive coping in reactions to stress: A study of illness inception. *Journal of Nervous and Mental Disease, 173,* 707–716.

Nolen-Hoeksema, S. (1987). Sex differences in unipolar depression. *Psychological Bulletin, 101,* 259–282.

Parker, G., & Brown, L. (1982). Coping behaviors that mediate between life events and depression. *Archives of General Psychiatry, 39,* 1386–1391.

Parkes, K. R. (1984). Locus of control, cognitive appraisal, and coping in stressful episodes. *Journal of Personality and Social Psychology, 46,* 655–668.

Parkes, K. R. (1986). Coping in stressful episodes: The role of individual differences, environmental factors, and situational characteristics. *Journal of Personality and Social Psychology, 51,* 1277–1292.

Pearlin, L. I., & Schooler, C. (1978). The structure of coping. *Journal of Health and Social Behavior, 22,* 2–21.

Robins, L. N., Helzer, J. E., Croughan, J. & Ratcliff, K. L. (1981). National Institute of Mental Health Diagnostic Interview Schedule: Its history, characteristics, and validity. *Archives of General Psychiatry, 38,* 381–389.

Silver, R. L., & Wortman, C. B. (1980). Coping with undesirable life events. In J. Garber & M. E. P. Seligman (Eds.), *Human helplessness* (pp. 279–375). New York: Academic Press.

Spitzer, R. L., Endicott, J., & Robins, E. (1975). *Research diagnostic criteria (RDC) for a selected group of functional disorders,* Instrument No. 58 (ed. 2). New York: Biometrics Research, New York State Psychiatric Institute.

Stone, A. A., & Neale, J. M. (1984). New measures of daily coping: Development and preliminary results. *Journal of Personality and Social Psychology, 46,* 892–906.

Veroff, J., Douvan, E., & Kulka, R. A. (1981). *The inner American: A self-portrait.* New York: Basic Books.

Zarit, S. H., Todd, P. A., & Zarit, J. M. (1986). Subjective burden of husbands and wives as caregivers: A Longitudinal Study. *The Gerontologist, 26,* 260–266.

3

Children and Divorce

Stress and Coping in Developmental Perspective

DONALD WERTLIEB

INTRODUCTION

For several decades now, divorce has been a topic of intensive concern to researchers from various disciplines, to mental health clinicians, to child development specialists, and to those involved with the construction of social policy. As our knowledge base has expanded and evolved, so has our appreciation of the complexity of the tasks of studying and comprehending the divorce experience. Demographers indicate that despite the recent leveling-off of the divorce rate, a decline in the rate is not expected, and large numbers of children will continue to be effected. Current statistics highlight this in terms of predicting that 60% of children will spend at least some portion of their developing childhood or adolescent years in a single-parent situation (Norton & Glick, 1986). Among black children, some predictions are as high as 94% who will experience a single-parent situation (Hofferth, 1985). "Growing up divorced has become an alternative developmental path for a substantial number of children in the country" (Kalter, 1987, p. 587). Among the theses of this chapter is that our focus needs to be upon various alternative developmental paths along which divorce might be an event. Further, divorce is better conceptualized as one element in a complex series

DONALD WERTLIEB • Eliot-Pearson Department of Child Study, Tufts University, Medford, Massachusetts 02155.

The Social Context of Coping, edited by John Eckenrode. Plenum Press, New York, 1991.

of events or experiences that may influence the course of these alternative developmental paths.

Considerations for the exploration of the nature of these "alternative developmental paths" are the substance of this chapter. Through selective review of the literature with an emphasis upon a particular integrative focus provided by the "stress and coping" paradigm, an agenda relevant to both researchers and clinicians is offered. The agenda calls for increasingly differentiated and developmentally sensitive concepts and measures of stress and coping processes. Such a conceptual framework accounts for and emerges from recent empirical data and marks crucial considerations for future research and intervention. A related and urgent task involves the cross-fertilization of divorce literatures in child development, family sociology, and related disciplines (Falicov, 1988; Furstenberg, 1985).

Divorce researchers benefit greatly from the comprehensive literature reviews made available in recent years (see Blechman, 1982; Bloom, Asher, & White, 1978; Demo & Acock, 1988; Emery, 1988; Emery, Hetherington, & Dilalla, 1984; Hetherington & Camara, 1984; Kalter, 1987; Kitson & Raschke, 1981; Teachman, 1982). Bloom *et al.*'s scholarly review was forceful in documenting the "highest cost" of divorce and the pervasiveness of its effects on individuals and society. The conceptual advance provided by Hetherington and Camara (1984) broadened the attention of researchers toward the complex processes of dissolution and reconstitution in family life and suggested the heuristic value of adopting a "stress and coping" model. These reviewers provided strong and broad shoulders from which we can now perch for a reconsideration of the divorce experience with the benefit of more recent data now exploding in the various concerned fields.

A brief historical foray highlights some of the caveats of which the producer or consumer of divorce research needs constant wariness. A particular reframing or reconceptualizing of the divorce experience is then offered. Then articulation of stress and coping processes and their developmental orchestration generates a base from which to consider specific issues in intervention and continued research.

SIRENS OF HISTORY

Lest history repeat itself, it is useful to examine certain "errors" or weaknesses that pervade much of the field's research to date and that hamper our efforts to draw conclusions, integrate findings, and make applications. These include numerous "conceptual blinders" and limitations of design and methodology, many of which are highlighted in the existing reviews just noted. Aside from errors, weaknesses, or deficits are the wrinkles or obstacles that emerge more from just "differences" in approach or perspective. For instance, Santrock and Madison (1985) offer a framework for evaluating divorce research that takes into account the advantages and disadvantages of three "traditions" of research—the clinical tradition, the family sociological tradition, and the quasi-experimental/developmental tradition. In considering both the deficits and the differences characterizing divorce research, four issues are of particular concern: (1) the psychopathological bias; (2) the context bias; (3) the transactional challenge; and (4) the heterogeneity challenge.

The Psychopathological Bias

With mental health clinicians being perhaps first and most on the front lines in terms of dealing with the "effects" of marital disruption and divorce on children, it is not surprising that a substantial portion of theory and clinical research emphasizes associations between divorce and mental health or behavior problems. A vast literature, often using retrospective and cross-sectional designs and "clinical" samples (e.g., patients or clients in the mental health care delivery system) etches in the minds of many a notion that the strong correlation between divorce and psychopathology is somehow automatic, causal, necessary, or sufficient. Early epidemiological research contributed to this psychopathological bias as it documented the relationships between marital status and a range of physical and psychological disorders. The analysis offered by Bloom *et al.* (1978) is especially helpful in differentiating alternative explanatory hypotheses for these correlations. However, as was the case nearly 15 years ago, "there is far less certainty about the *reasons* for the statistical relationships . . . than there is about the fact of such relationships" (Bachrach, 1975, p. 5). In designing and interpreting studies that address divorce variables, it is important to use more than just a "deficit comparison lens" (Ganong & Coleman, 1986).

Perhaps most influential in countering the influence of the "psychopathological bias" and in opening the way to a richer appreciation of how the divorce experience affects children's development is the attention to resiliency and invulnerability in a child's life course. This enlightenment is evident in many areas of psychiatric and clinical research (Anthony & Cohler, 1987; Garmezy, 1987; Rutter, 1987) as well as in more specific divorce research (Wallerstein, 1983). In a compelling and integrative analysis of the divorce process, Ahrons and Rogers (1987) "normalize" the separation–divorce–remarriage transition. They describe its institutional and functional dimensions and balance these with its psycho-pathological dimensions. Much recent research aimed at identifying cor-relates of behavior symptomatology in children of divorce has been more explicit in noting that levels of symptomatology are often "within the 'normal' range" (e.g., Copeland, 1985; Wertlieb, Springer, Weigel, & Feldstein, 1987; Wertlieb, Weigel, & Feldstein, 1987a), thus calling into question the assumption of divorce as an automatic cause or effect of behavior pathology. Our old preoccupation with risk, vulnerability, and illness is now complemented with an appreciation of competence, re-silience, and health. As will be discussed further later, these adaptations to the psychopathological bias are among the factors that enhance the heuristic value of a stress and coping perspective.

The Context Bias

To grow up as a child of divorce in the 1950s was surely a different experience than growing up as a child of divorce in the 1980s. A few recent studies provide some guidance as to what similarities and dif-ferences might be relevant, but rarely are the influences of such cohort differences directly addressed in generalizing our understandings of the divorce experience. For instance, one might speculate on how the analy-ses by Elder, Nguyen, and Caspi (1985) of data on family adaptation and parenting behavior during the Great Depression might compare to a similar model generated with contemporary families who might exhibit a broader range of family composition and marital histories.

Though not specific to concerns about divorce among children, Orton's (1982) comparison of children's worries reported in 1939 (Pinter & Lev, 1940) to worries of children in 1977 revealed some remarkable constancy (e.g., "failing a test" ranked number 1 both in 1939 and in 1977) as well as intriguing changes. For example, in 1977 children ranked as fourth "someone dying in my family"; in the 1939 sample, this item ranked 39th for boys and 31st for girls. Neither Orton (1982) nor Pinter and Lev (1940) included divorce or marital separation as a specif-ic item on their Worries Inventory. An item, "My father going away" ranked 49th and 52nd of 53 items for boys and girls, respectively in the 1939 study. In the 1977 survey, the item ranked 37th of 62 items. Among the 9 items added for the 1977 survey, 2 were more directly relevant to children's worries about divorce, "One of my parents not living with me" and "Having to choose which parent to live with," and these ranked 49th and 57th, respectively.

Three other features of divorce research bear scrutiny as manifesta-tions of contextual constraints to which a life-span developmental approach sensitizes us. The age or developmental stage of the child at the time of separation, divorce, or remarriage, as well as the time elapsed between the "event" and the data collection remain crucial variables to be included in any model of the divorce adjustment process. Along with gender differences associated with direct and/or interactive effects and when analyzed longitudinally, the salience of these contextual or developmental variables comes into bold relief (see, for example, Brady, Bray, & Zeeb, 1986; Hetherington, Cox, & Cox, 1985). We will return to these issues in our subsequent discussion of developmental orchestration.

The final observation suggesting caution in generalizing over or across recent studies of the effects of divorce on children comes from an investigator who has done two landmark studies, one in California (Hess & Camara, 1979) and another in New England (Camara & Resnick, 1988). Important qualitative and quantitative differences in "response rate" and recruitment processes may reflect regional differences in salient attitudes and behaviors that must be considered in constructing an understanding of the divorce experience (Camara, 1986, personal communication). For instance, a New England "reserve" that seemed associated with a lower response rate to similar recruitment procedures might also extend to influence the family's experience of divorce as well as their openness in describing the experience to the researcher.

In an important critique of certain statistical methodologies that have become de rigueur in the field, Glenn and Shelton (1983) and Glen and Kramer (1987) document the influence of a geographical "divorce belt" comprised of some midwestern mountain and Pacific regions of the country. White men and women who resided in the "divorce belt" at age 16 had a later divorce rate about 45% higher than people from other regions of the country. Much of the divorce research available to date has paid little attention, if any, to these probably crucial cohort factors or regional differences. These and other sampling issues require increased consideration in order to address both methodological and substantive concerns of the field (e.g., Kitson, Sussman, Williams, Zeehandelaar, Shickmanter, & Steinberger, 1982).

The Transactional Challenge

Contemporary research in divorce and in child and family development has been duly criticized as of questionable ecological validity or relevance (e.g., Bronfenbrenner & Crouter, 1983; Kurdek, 1981). Kagan (1979) decried research aimed at "absolute principles which declare that a particular set of external conditions is inevitably associated with a fixed set of consequences for all children" (p. 886). Sameroff and Seifer

(1983) and Elder *et al.* (1985) caution against the "conceptual blinders" that for so long have led to an understatement of the child as a producer of socialization. A commitment to developmental perspectives, family systems perspectives, and a stress and coping model ensures at least a conceptual appreciation of the complex transactional processes involved in the divorce experience. Operationalization of these constructs and application of appropriately sophisticated data-analytic methods remains a challenge. Nonetheless, dynamic and reciprocal interactions among children, parents, and institutions (e.g., families, courts) must be described and interpreted.

The Heterogeneity Challenge

When contemporary divorce research began to flourish in the early 1970s, one of its first accomplishments was to throw off the shackles and blinders indigenous to the rich and respectable bodies of research on "father absence" and "broken families." This enlightenment acknowledged that there may indeed be profound differences among the impacts of family change occasioned by death, desertion, or divorce. More recently, conceptualizations call into play notions of "alternative developmental path" (Kalter, 1987), "emerging family forms" (Brody, Neubaum, & Forehand, 1988) "diverse postdivorce and family forms" (Zaslow, 1988), or family diversity as "multidimensional developmental pathways" (Bernardes, 1986). In appreciating the extant data on divorce effects, a likely necessary step is to recognize these as data on "mother-custody" families, given the predominance of this structure in most studies to date. Indeed, it is the intriguing, controversial, and still relatively primitive research on comparison of children across a range of custody arrangements or postdivorce family forms that heightens the salience of this particular historical siren, the heterogeneity challenge (see Clingempeel & Reppucci, 1982; Furstenberg & Nord, 1985; Koel, Clark, Phear, & Hauser, 1988; Maccoby, Depner, & Mnookin, 1988). As suggested by Hetherington and Camara (1984):

> A modified version of the models of family stress and systems theory may be useful in trying to explain the diversity of outcomes following divorce. The adaptation to divorce is based on an interaction between past and present life hardships, and stressful life experiences, the perception of the situation, and the personal, familial and extrafamilial resources available to deal with the stressful concomitants of divorces. These will vary with the social and cultural ecology in which the family is embedded, with the life stage of the family members, and with the historical cohort to which the family belongs. The interplay among these facts and their impact changes over time and vary for different family members. (pp. 405–406)

RECONCEPTUALIZING DIVORCE

Consistent with the historically derived caveats just enumerated is the broadening of our concept of divorce along two related dimensions:

1. Rather than using the traditional static notion of "divorce" as an "event" in the life course of an individual or family, consider divorce as a marker for a range of constellations or patterns that include numerous "events" or linked contingencies.
2. Rather than concretize or reify divorce in terms that connote some consensually validated "event" or circumstance that "happens," consider divorce in terms of complex processes over time that are only comprehensible in a phenomenological context of the individual's and family's experiences of the "events."

The necessity for adoption of these reconceptualizations derives from efforts to integrate recent theory and research in the field and has strong basis conceptually, phenomenologically, and empirically. What emerges then is an appreciation of divorce as an accumulation, concatenation, and imbrication of stressful experiences and coping processes woven into a range of fabrics referred to before as alternate developmental pathways.

Event versus Events

At the dawn of research on the effects of divorce on children, we followed the lead of adult research and quickly confirmed the event of divorce to be a factor in children's adjustment problems. Divorce appeared as the second most stressful life event on the checklist designed to identify and quantify the deleterious influences of stress on children's well-being (death of a parent ranked first) (Coddington, 1972). Further, it seemed that this divorce event could be reliably isolated as a common element in the backgrounds of substantial proportions of children in need of mental health services (Felner, Stolberg, & Cowen, 1975; Kalter, 1977; McDermott, 1970). However, it was not long before the necessity of including related events became apparent. Even in the simplest terms of using the legal domain to chart the series of relatively discrete "events" potentially captured by ticking-off "divorce" on a Life Events checklist reveals this necessity. A physical departure of a parent, a legal separation, a divorce decree from the court, a custody "battle," a remarriage, and another divorce are among the likely or possible events of the constellation even this narrowly conceived. Even minor broadening introduces increased likelihood of "stressful life events" such as a move to a new home or school, a downward shift in family income or standard of living, arrival of new siblings (step- or otherwise). The conceptualization and findings offered by Felner, Farber, and Primavera (1983), Hetherington and Camara (1984), Stolberg, Kiluk, and Garrison (1986), and Sandler, Wolchik, Braver, and Fogas (1986) all emphasize a view of multiple and cumulative "events" underlying the divorce adjustment process.

Another aspect of this dimension of our reconceptualization is reflected in the early conclusion by Bloom *et al.* (1978) that the operationalization or measurement of a "marital history" variable is likely to yield better data than our more traditional "marital status" variable. The challenge is immense, given that Kellam, Ensminger, and Turner (1977) identify 86 levels of the variable "family structure," with it still tied to a rather limited range of recent past events that define a current structure. As they then go on to demonstrate, even an elaborate, cumbersome, perhaps obsessive taxonomy such as theirs can generate useful theoretical and empirical guidelines for researching the correlates of divorce. For instance, their analyses highlighted that the presence of an additional adult in the home—parent, boyfriend, grandmother, or other—may be a crucial positive factor in a child's adjustment.

Events versus Experiences

The study of divorce is not immune to the clash or dialectic between nomothetic and idiographic perspectives that pervades much of behavioral science. Nomothetic orientations aspire toward the identification of commonalities or universals in the divorce experience and often culminate in stage theories or typologies that capture extremely important dimensions of divorce processes that shape alternative developmental pathways. For instance, the longitudinal clinical research by Wallerstein (1983) generates a very useful notion of six ordered psychological tasks facing the child of divorce:

1. Acknowledging the reality of the marital rupture
2. Disengaging from parental conflict and distress and resuming customary pursuits
3. Resolving the loss
4. Resolving anger and self-blame
5. Accepting the permanence of the divorce
6. Achieving realistic hope regarding relationships.

Though these six "interrelated, hierarchical coping tasks" do indeed capture significant aspects of the divorce experience for many children, they are neither exhaustive nor comprehensive. Extant data do not confirm that they are universal in their sequencing. And, as will be further addressed later, it is probably important to weave this particular line or temporal pattern of tasks with numerous others that ultimately converge to form any individual child's developmental course. Even within a single family, there can be a range of experiences, adaptations, or outcomes evident for siblings. Wallerstein (1983) emphasizes the particular role in the strife-torn family constellation and their individual developmental position and psychological strengths and resourcefulness (p. 232) as factors in this variability. Similarly, Brody and Forehand (1988) call upon Rowe and Plomin's (1981) notion of "nonshared environmental influences" to help capture the variation and heterogeneity of children's divorce experiences, even in a single family.

Idiographic orientations aspire to capturing the depths and complexities of an individual's singular experience of the divorce process, emphasizing the unique phenomenology generative of each of those pathways. In striving for the synthesis of these sometimes clashing emphases on "subjective" and "objective" methods, data, and conclusions, divorce researchers can identify salient dimensions of individual differences, acknowledge the complex multivariate web of relationships, and offer frameworks reflecting a range of typical processes and unique features. The following vignette illustrates some of this complexity:

Ms. M. sought consultation to insure that her recent decision to divorce her husband of 15 years was the "right" one for her and her two children, ages 7 and 10. A sophisticated and educated woman, she was distraught in her understanding from the popular literature that even under the best circumstances, divorce would likely exert an untoward influence on the lives of her children. Another goal of the consultation was "damage control," how could she best minimize the risks and maximize the children's short-term and long-term adjustment.

The initial interview highlighted the uniqueness of each individual's divorce experience. The 10-year-old boy focused his concerns on missing his best friend whom he had to leave behind when the family relocated to more affordable housing several towns away from where he grew up. His anger at both parents was explicit, with part of it manifest in his refusal to get involved in his new school, as evident in his declining grades. In contrast, the younger sister spoke longingly of the lost and idealized father, often blaming the mother as the main provocateur in the continuing parental marital conflict.

Mother's sense of being abandoned and overwhelmed by these family dynamics was only accentuated by the day-to-day dread she experienced as she reentered a professional career ladder, discovering how deep and far-reaching changes in her field had been while she was off raising her family.

Intimately intertwined, yet significantly distinctive and demanding of quite disparate entrees for therapeutic engagement—the diverse dimensions of this one family's divorce experiences illustrate the necessity of more highly differentiated analysis of divorce impacts.

ADVANCING WITH STRESS AND COPING MODELS

In calling upon stress and coping models as heuristic and interpretive models for divorce experiences as reconceptualized here, it is important to consider recent general developments in stress and coping theory as well as specific linkages to divorce-related research. A parallel and most challenging task is to integrate stress and coping theory and data with the concepts, methods, and findings of child development research. In general terms of the state-of-the-art, the following contributions are especially informative and influential: Eckenrode and Gore (1990); Lazarus and Folkman (1984); Pearlin, Lieberman, Menaghan, and Mullen (1981); McCubbin, Sussman, and Patterson (1983); and Walker (1985). Among the landmarks and guiding lights for integration of stress and coping models with child development are the contributions by Compas (1987a,b), Rutter (1981, 1985, 1987), Garmezy (1987), Garmezy and Rutter (1983), Johnson (1986), and Felner, Rowlison, and Terre (1986). Rather than attempt a comprehensive review of these crucial general and child development contributions, the emphasis here will be to illustrate a few of the promises or successes associated with the integration and linkage to divorce-specific research. In particular, two themes of these literatures highlight promise and problems in understanding the impact of divorce on children's lives. One theme reflects the need for increasing differentiation of what we term *stress and coping processes*. A second theme reflects the need for examining *developmental orchestration* of these processes.

Differentiating Stress and Coping

Contemporary stress and coping models increasingly emphasize the distinctions among what are variously termed *chronic life strains, major life events,* and *daily hassles* as elements of the stress process. When divorce is reconceptualized in the manner proposed here, some of these distinctions come quickly into play. Rather than keep a narrow focus on divorce as an "event" in the life of the child, one must consider the chronic life strain of living in a single-parent home as well as the day-to-day "hassle" inherent in such experiences as including parents in a school event or "transitioning" into and out of a visitation with the noncustodial parent. In constructing models of the "effect of divorce," one must include consideration of predivorce variables such as the chronic life strain of parental conflict or the impact of marital dissatisfaction on parenting competence (e.g., Brody & Forehand, 1988; Emery, 1988; Forehand, Long, & Brody, 1988).

The research program constructing The Divorce Events Schedule for Children (DES-C) (Sandler *et al.*, 1986) illustrates a promising methodology for the description and quantification of the multiple stressors associated with the divorce experience. Further, their checklist of 62 items provides for both "objective" and "subjective" ratings of stressfulness. The authors are duly optimistic about how their instrument will contribute to our understanding of the effects of divorce on children and facilitate the development of interventions aimed at high-risk subpopulations. Data on the relationship between children's scores on the DES-C and adjustment outcomes such as behavior symptoms have yet to be published, but one would expect the relationship to be at least as strong as the statistically significant $r = .30$ that is consistent across numerous studies (e.g., Johnson, 1986; Wertlieb, Weigel, & Feldstein, 1987a).

In anticipation of such data, there are already indications from recent stress and coping research that an immediate process of refinement may be called for in order to interpret or apply such findings. For instance, Compas (1987a,b) concludes that chronic strains and daily stressors may be more salient than major life events as predictors of children's psychological and behavioral difficulties. The DES-C items include examples of strains, events, and hassles without scoring algorithms to take into account what might be a crucial differentiation. Not only does the "daily hassles" dimension require explicit consideration, but a possibly complementary dimension termed *daily uplifts* may be required (Kanner, Feldman, Weinberger, & Ford, 1988). Uplifts are "the positive experience such as the joy derived from manifestations of love, relief at hearing good news, the pleasure of a good nights rest, and so on" (Kanner, Coyne, Schaefer, & Lazarus, 1981, p. 6). In their extension of work by Kanner, Harrison, and Wertlieb (1985), Kanner *et al.* (1988) document unique contributions by both hassles and uplifts to various indexes of children's psychosocial adjustment. Future research will need to examine the utility of such differentiations for our stress assessment technology and its relevance to divorce specific experiences.

An additional example of the task of differentiating "stress" is inherent in the now well-documented finding that levels of family conflict or interparental hostility, both predivorce and postdivorce, may be more salient predictor of children's adjustment difficulties than just the simple structural distinction between intact versus separated or divorced families (Camara & Resnik, 1988; Emery, 1982, 1988; O'Leary & Emery, 1984). Introduction of a high versus low conflict variable into designs that test relationships between a child's exposure to divorce and his or her psychosocial status begins to refine our appreciation of factors associated how children and families cope with divorce (Camara & Resnick, 1988).

Not only do we need increased differentiation in our stress constructs and measures, but also, we need differentiations and coherent frameworks for assessing children's coping processes. Some promising initial work in this area has been reported by Curry and Russ (1985) and Wertlieb, Weigel, and Feldstein (1987b). In terms of a specific role for individual differences in coping associated with children's divorce adjustment, the data provided by Krantz, Clark, Pruyn, and Usher (1985) are of particular interest. Appraisals of divorce and appraisals of coping options were significantly related to indexes of psychosocial adjustment by boys from families who had experienced separation or divorce. Boys using fewer "adaptive statements" or more "maladaptive statements" about divorce situations exhibited more problems in postdivorce adjustment in the home. "Adaptive statements" included positive or mixed positive/negative evaluations of the situation as well as an optimistic or accepting focus. "Maladaptive statements" were those that indicated a sense of responsibility or blame for parental behavior or well-being or those that took a negative or pessimistic focus. Boys able to recognize many options or alternatives for managing stressful divorce situations presented in a semiprojective format exhibited better psychosocial adjustment. The patterns for girls were less clear or consistent, and as the authors note, numerous methodological considerations impose a cautious stance in interpreting these preliminary data.

Among the coping cognition observed in children postdivorce, clinical lore and practice have emphasized the child's "self-blame" as a frequent element. Wallerstein and Kelly (1980) highlight this stance as a feature of coping most evident in the younger children their sample, ages 2½ to 5 years; other accounts include this dynamic in older children and even adults whose parents divorced (Hodges, 1986). In contrast, several researchers have remarked upon the absence of self-blaming cognition in their samples (e.g., Kurdek & Siesky, 1980; Krantz et al., 1985). In ferreting out the nature of these inconsistencies, some explanations may be found in methodological differences or problems, for instance, the contrast of clinical and normal samples. For example, if self-blame is associated with the experience and appraisal processes of younger individuals, is its presence in the older children a manifestation of a psychopathological process and/or developmental lag? On another tack, it is likely that the use of a stress and coping paradigm might eventually clarify such inconsistent findings. For instance, it remains unclear whether the "self-blaming" stance toward his or her parents' divorce is best understood as a manifestation of a young child's ego-centrism or immature capacity to comprehend the complexity of family relationships and contexts, or rather, an effort on the part of the child to conceive or inject a degree of control into a set of stressful situations that are distressing in large part due to the "uncontrollability" they reflect. Two features of stress and coping models lend optimism to the quest for understanding. From one, in emphasizing the processual nature of coping and its unfolding phenomenology, it may be possible to describe and predict differential correlates or paths for the "self-blame" dynamic. Two, in emphasizing the role of moderators, mediators, and buffers in the coping process, in particular those involving perceptions of control, hypotheses can be generated and tested systematically (e.g., Weigel, Wertlieb, & Feldstein, 1989). For instance, the function and meaning of "self-blame" and the cognitive and affective associations to control are likely to be quite different for the 4-year-old child in the midst of a heated divorce and the 18-year-old adolescent who experiences the dissolving of his parent's marriage from the distance of his freshman year away at college. Among the most compelling reasons for attending to this level of complexity is that the design of interventions is likely to be better informed through such a framework, as will be discussed later.

One last example of recent data documenting the promise of stress and coping models is drawn from Kurdek and Sinclair's (1988) pioneering comparisons of nuclear, stepfather, and mother-custody families. In their study, both specific family processes and particular coping strategies reported by junior-high-school students were related to psychosocial adjustment, whereas differences in adjustment across the three family structures were nonsignificant. Consistent with the earlier discussion of conflict as a salient stress dimension, better adjustment was reported by children who also reported less family conflict. In addition, what might be termed *social support,* both within the family and within the peer group, as well as a tendency not to use "negative externalizing strategies" such as ventilation or passive problem solving were associated with better adjustment. Controversy abounds in how to conceptualize and measure social support as part of the coping process (e.g., Thoits, 1986; Heitzmann & Kaplan, 1988); nonetheless, these preliminary data warrant elaboration.

Developmental Orchestration

The previous examples have been offered to suggest the present or future promise of stress and coping models for the study of children and divorce. The next examples underscore that to realize this utility, an explicit and overriding consideration of "developmental orchestration" is deemed crucial and necessary.

Developmental orchestration refers to the complex continuities and changes over time in an individual's behavior or "personality." In particular, the mutually influencing and reciprocating processes within the individual and between the individual and his or her surroundings determine a developmental course such that an experience at one point may have restricted or pervasive influence at any variety of points, some sooner and some later. In the seemingly simple case of divorce, one might be tempted to focus upon a young child's behavioral maladjustment in the 2-year period following the event and then focus on his or her adjustment evident as behavior symptoms subside, and he or she "gets over it." With the aid of conceptualizations such as Wallerstein's (1983) "psychological tasks for the child of divorce," briefly outlined here, one can trace developmental progress at least in some relatively narrow trajectory.

In broadening one's perspective and placing the divorce events and experiences in proper developmental context, a more comprehensive view emerges, consistent with current stress and coping theory. In proposing his "Developmental Vulnerability Model" of long-term effects of divorce on children, Kalter (1987) makes a major contribution in focusing on developmental orchestration processes. He identifies three key developmental areas—domains of behavior or "personality" referred to before—and suggests how a divorce experience might be a factor in a child's coping with any of these tasks. The three areas are managing anger and aggression, separation–individuation, and gender identity. He illustrates "their role as central factors in the emergence of specific emotional, social and behavioral problems associated with children of divorce. . . . Though more easily discerned in a post-divorce family [these are] applicable to many families in which a divorce has never occurred" (p. 598). Kalter (1987) goes on to pose that

> The long-term negative effects of divorce . . . can be understood as due in large measure to developmental vulnerabilities sustained or created by these post-separation issues. Problems that are first seen in the crisis period of the divorce . . . may draw their staying power from the ongoing contributions of particular family interaction as well as the effects of these systemic stresses on the individual child. Similarly, . . . difficulties which arise *de novo* years after divorce may have their roots in the post-divorce interaction of family dynamics and child development. (p. 598)

Thus coping with divorce, along with all the other stresses and challenges posed in growing up, becomes a strand, albeit a significant strand, in a complex web of developmental processes.

Implicit in the discussion thus far are simple and basic precepts that a child's age or developmental state is an important consideration. Slightly more complex are the references to interactions of such variables with gender (e.g., Hetherington *et al.*, 1985; Krantz *et al.*, 1985). As stated by Elder *et al.* (1985):

> The developmental implications of social change can only be studied within a theoretical framework that relates individual and family change. Individuals are changed by their changing families and families are changed by changing the developmental course of members. Both of these processes are likely to emerge when the life course dynamics of families and individuals are studied over time. (pp. 372–373)

Even with the relatively simple and basic assumption that the child's age or developmental stage will influence, even determine the divorce adjustment process, one faces a complex, confounded body of evidence. Wallerstein (1983) argued that "despite significant individual differences, the child's age and developmental stage appear to be the most important factors governing the initial responses to parental divorce. Stage of development profoundly influences the child's need for, and expectation of, the parent, and the perception of the stress, as well as the child's available armamentarium of coping and defensive strategies" (p. 279). Reflecting on the same study at its 5 year follow-up, Wallerstein concludes that "neither age nor sex proved to be significant in separating troubled children from the children who were well adjusted" (p. 281). In focused, systematic assessments of children's perceptions of and beliefs about the divorce experience, some investigators find few age-related differences (e.g., Kalter & Plunkett, 1984; Kurdek & Berg, 1987; Wolchick, Sandler, Braver, & Fogas, 1985).

To some extent, these apparent discrepancies can be attributed to differences in methods and the age ranges of the study samples. Nonetheless, it is imperative that future research clarify these issues, given its centrality to the heuristic framework being proposed here. A number of specific variables may provide clues, even keys to building upon the appreciation of developmental process and orchestration. Among these are, for instance, a child's age at time of parental separation and time elapsed between the separation, the divorce, and the study data collection. Rarely are these variables the focus of data analyses. On the few occasions that such effects are examined, interesting findings emerge, as will be noted later.

The difficulty of integrating research findings is increased when there is a lack of clarity over probably crucial distinctions between time since parental separation and time since divorce. Given that anywhere from a few months to several years might ensue between the time of a parent leaving the home and the actual legal divorce decree, any effort to understand the adaptation process must incorporate and measure these variables. In addition, findings mentioned regarding the impact of family conflict independent of separated or intact structures further broaden the design and measurement demands. Still further, one can assume that the findings from recent adult research regarding timing patterns in the process of deciding to separate, separating, reconciling, and/or divorcing will be echoed in defining the alternative developmental pathways of children. In their exploratory analyses of women's divorce adjustment, Melichar and Chiriboga (1985) operationalized process by focusing on the timing of steps or events such as deciding to separate and filing for divorce. Significant relationships with adjustment were found for age at marriage, years married, and taking relatively longer times in separating and divorcing. In a subsequent study, a longer interval between the decision to separate and the point of actual separation was associated with better adjustment for women (Melichar & Chiriboga, 1988). As such temporal markers are introduced into the study of children's divorce adjustment, important hypotheses can be reexamined. For instance, is longer exposure to parental conflict a salient determinant of maladjustment? Is the recovery or improved adjustment of the custodial mother and associated enhancement of her parenting competence a salient determinant of improved child adjustment?

Emery (1988) cites Furstenberg and Allison (1985) for their pioneering effort at disentangling confounds of child's age and time since separation. They described relationships that were inconsistent with expectations—longer periods of separation were associated with more adjustment problems. However, as they point out, any number of third variables might be involved. For instance, marriages ending earlier might have been more conflictual. Other researchers report nonsignificant correlations between adjustment outcomes and such temporal variables.

It is heartening to see more recent proposals such as Stolberg, Kiluk, and Garrison's (1986) Temporal Model of Divorce Adjustment attending to some of these matters. Emery's (1988) most recent review of the divorce literature also emphasizes the need for attention to temporal influences, and he offers some restrained optimism regarding the empirical construction of "growth curves" as an avenue toward addressing the age–cohort–period problem. With the advent of these more developmentally sensitive conceptual frameworks to guide research, more accurate and useful findings should become available. A particularly powerful example of how a stress and coping model can be applied is presented by Pearlin *et al.* (1981) in their conceptual and empirical exposition of the processes associating the economic strains of unemployment with depression. Similar studies of the stress and coping processes of divorce are needed, with particular attention to the pathways of children's adjustment.

Longitudinal studies to date (e.g., Wallerstein & Kelly, 1980; Hetherington *et al.*, 1985) have documented the necessity of conceptualizing short-term and long-term "effects" in the divorce adjustment process. In addition to incorporating the age/stage variables just mentioned, findings such as those reported by Hetherington *et al.* (1985) demonstrate the developmental orchestration manifesting as gender differences and age/gender interaction effects. In the 6-year follow-up of their 124 families originally studied at preschool age, they conclude that boys were more adversely effected by divorce, as noted in early childhood, whereas girls exhibited problems in association with parental remarriage, as noted in middle childhood. Further, the stability of the middle childhood behavior symptomatology differed for boys and girls such that internalizing symptoms characterized girls' problems and externalizing symptoms characterized boys' problems.

Caution must be exercised in accepting the assumption that data such as these are actually data on the "effects" of divorce. Indeed, Block, Block, and Gjerde (1986) presented data from their prospective longitudinal study that demonstrate that, at least for boys, some externalizing or undercontrol symptoms predate a parental separation or divorce, sometimes by several years. So, as Zaslow (1988) points out, it remains "unclear to what extent differences in children *following* divorce reflect predivorce family stress, the actual separation, postdivorce disequilibrium, or even long-standing differences in child behavior that may have contributed to family stress and parental separation" (p. 356).

Issues in Mental Health Intervention

A plethora of programs and approaches characterizes the formal services available in the mental health care system to address the needs of children of divorce. These range from traditional general services such as counseling and psychotherapy, to court-based guidance and mediation, to highly structured "psychoeducational" group programs for children and families (Hodges, 1986). A useful cataloging of some of these approaches was offered by Baker, Druckman, Flagle, Camara, Dayton, Egan, and Cohen (1980). However, as noted in this, as well as other reviews of the literature, there continues to be a lamentable paucity of valid systematic data on the effectiveness of such services.

To some extent, one might take a position that in order to intervene effectively, we must await a better understanding of what we are intervening in. Thus truly effective services will not be available until the basic developmental research agenda generates an understanding of the "effects" of divorce. This position is fallacious and ignores two important facts. One, traditionally and more generally, truly knowing or understanding the full nature and implication of a phenomena—be it a psychopathological state or a family process—has rarely been considered a prerequisite for intervening. Two, it is likely that the avenue of clinical research in which knowledge and understanding are generated in the process of intervening and evaluating interventions will be among the richest resources for mapping the numerous developmental pathways taken by children of divorce. Etiology need not be confirmed in order to structure effective interventions. Nor does an effective intervention necessarily imply etiology. Again, with these assumptions or elements, the stress and coping framework can generate some examples of problems and potentials for intervention.

Within the frameworks of their temporal model of divorce adjustment and preventive mental health, Stolberg and his colleagues (Stolberg et al., 1986) have compared interventions aimed at preventing the deterioration of parents' adjustment and providing children and parents with social support and training in social skills. By including pre- and postintervention measurement as well as follow-up, they were able to detect substantial increases in children's self-esteem and social skills as well as enhanced adaptation by parents. As they note, "The intervention strategy was firmly based on a model of divorce adjustment and individual developmental, familial, and environmental processes normally facilitating and interfering with post-divorce adjustment. Program effectiveness may be attributed to the goodness-of-fit between these real needs and the procedures utilized" (p. 118).

Not only does the Stolberg et al. work reflect a major advance in clinical research strategy, but its hypotheses and findings have been bolstered by partial replication. Pedro-Carrol and Cowan (1985) implemented a modified version of the child segment group component of the Stolberg et al. (1986) intervention. They documented significant improvement by children after the intervention in terms of teacher ratings of problem behavior and competence, parent ratings of adjustment, and self-reported anxiety. The use of multiple ratings by multiple observers in multiple settings is an especially positive feature of their research design, a feature that must characterize our continuing efforts to evaluate our interventions. Additional replication data were reported by Pedro-Carroll, Cowen, Hightower, and Guare (1986).

As relatively advanced as these contributions are in contrast to the utter dearth of evaluation research in the prior decades (Bloom *et al.*, 1978; Wertlieb, Budman, Demby, & Randall, 1984) the degree of sophistication yet to be required and achieved is significant. Again, stress and coping models provide some guidance for meeting this challenge.

It is by now de rigeur for divorce research reports to conclude with a paragraph or two of implications for intervention derived from the conceptual or empirical thrust of the study reported. The explicit or implicit compatibility with stress and coping paradigms can be considered as advice for interveners, intervention evaluators, as well as basic developmental or clinical researchers. For instance, Plummer and Koch-Hattem (1986) identified important differences between men and women in how they navigated the postdivorce experience. Their findings suggested that women might benefit from intervention aimed at altering their appraisal processes, given that the meanings and perceived severity of the divorce was highly correlated with adjustment by women in their sample. In contrast, for men, it was the pile-up of stressors and social network size that accounted for significant portions of the variance in divorce adjustment. The researchers suggest that interventions for men might be better advised to tap these realms with programs of stress reduction and social network enhancement. The individual difference dimensions, including gender, may be among the keys emphasized by stress and coping models that will allow for better focused intervention.

Kalter (1987) echoes this call for better differentiated conceptualization, implementation, and evaluation of intervention, noting that "the family dynamic-child developmental processes described here can be expected to overwhelm any brief, single effort at preventive intervention. Potentially fruitful strategies would recognize the contribution of ongoing family interactions to the persistence or emergence of postdivorce problems in child adjustment" (pp. 598–599). The developmental orchestration evident in the alternative developmental paths traveled by children of divorce and being increasingly described and mapped with markers of stress and coping processes may be open to our intervention. As refinements such as those noted in this chapter are integrated with the next generation of program evaluation designs spawned by efforts such as Stolberg *et al.* (1986) and Pedro-Carrol and Cowan (1985), we can anticipate significant progress in understanding the myriad ways in which children and families cope with divorce and how we might enhance those processes.

ACKNOWLEDGMENTS

   This chapter benefited from ongoing discussion with colleagues in the Consortium for Research in Stress Processes (CRISP) funded by the W. T. Grant Foundation, New York. My thanks to Joan Liem and Patricia Cohen for comments on a preliminary version of this chapter and to Rose Chioccariello for preparation of the manuscript.

REFERENCES

Ahrons, L., & Rogers, R. (1987). *Divorced families: A multi-disciplinary developmental view.* New York: Norton.

Anthony, E. J., & Cohler, B. (Eds.). (1987). *The invulnerable child.* New York: Guilford.

Bachrach, L. (1975). *Marital status and mental disorder* (DHHS Publication ADM 75-217). Washington, DC: USGPO.

Baker, O. V., Druckman, J., Flagle, J., Camara, K., Dayton, C., Egan, J., & Cohen, A. (1980, February). *The identification and development of community-based approaches for meeting the social and emotional needs of youth and families in variant family configurations.* Final Report. Palo Alto, CA: American Institutes for Research.

Bernardes, J. (1986). Multidimensional developmental pathways: A proposal to facilitate the conceptualization of "family diversity." *The Sociological Review, 34,* 590–610.

Blechman, E. A. (1982). Are children with one parent at psychological risk? A methodological review. *Journal of Marriage and the Family, 11,* 179–195.

Block, J. J., Block, J., & Gjerde, P. F. (1986). The personality of children prior to divorce: A prospective study. *Child Development, 57,* 827–840.

Bloom, B. L., Asher, S. J., & White, S. W. (1978). Marital disruption as a stressor: A review and analysis. *Psychological Bulletin, 85,* 867–894.

Brady, C. P., Bray, H. J., & Zeeb, L. (1986). Behavior problems of clinic children: Relation to parental marital status, age and sex of child. *American Journal of Orthopsychiatry, 56*(3), 399–412.

Brody, G., & Forehand, R. (1988). Multiple determinants of parenting: Research findings and implications for the divorce process., In E. M. Hetherington & J. D. Arasteh (Eds.), *Impact of divorce, single parenting, and step-parenting on children* (pp. 117–133). Hillsdale, NJ: Lawrence Erlbaum.

Brody, G., Neubaum, E., & Forehand, R. (1988). Serial marriage: A heuristic analysis of an emerging family form. *Psychological Bulletin, 103,* 211–222.

Bronfenbrenner, U., & Crouter, A. (1983). The evolution of environmental models in developmental research. In W. Kessch (Ed.), P. H. Mussen (Series Ed.), *Handbook of child psychology, Vol. 1, History, theory and methods* (pp. 357–414). New York: Wiley.

Camara, K. A., & Resnick, G. (1988). Interparental conflict and cooperation: Factors moderating children's postdivorce adjustment. In E. M. Hetherington & J. Arasteh (Eds.), *Impact of divorce, single-parent, and stepparenting on children* (pp. 169–195). Hillsdale, NJ: Lawrence Erlbaum.

Clingempeel, W. G., & Reppucci, N. D. (1982). Joint custody after divorce: Major issues and goals for research. *Psychological Bulletin, 91,* 102–127.

Coddington, R. D. (1972). The significance of life events as etiological factors in the disease of children: A survey of professional workers. *Journal of Psychosomatic Research, 16,* 7–18.

Compas, B. E. (1987a). Coping with stress during childhood and adolescence. *Psychological Bulletin, 101*(3), 393–403.

Compas, B. E. (1987b). Stress and life events during childhood and adolescence. *Clinical Psychological Review, 7*, 275–302.

Copeland, A. P. (1985). Individual differences in children's reaction to divorce. *Journal of Clinical Child Psychology, 14*(1), 11–19.

Curry, S. L., & Russ, S. W. (1985)., Identifying coping strategies in children. *Journal of Clinical Child Psychology, 14*, 61–69.

Demo, D., & Acock, A. (1988). The impact of divorce on children. *Journal of Marriage and the Family, 50*, 619–648.

Eckenrode, J., & Gore, S. (Eds.), (1990). *Stress between work and family.* New York: Plenum Press.

Elder, G. H., Jr., Nguyen, T. V., & Caspi, A. (1985). Linking family hardship to children's lives. *Child Development, 56*, 361–375.

Emery, R. E. (1982). Interparental conflict and the children of discord and divorce. *Psychological Bulletin, 92*, 310–330.

Emery, R. E. (1988). *Marriage, divorce and children's adjustment.* Newbury Park, CA: Sage Publications.

Emery, R. E., Hetherington, E. M., & Dilalla, L. F. (1984). Divorce, children and social policy. In H. W. Stevenson & A. Siegel (Eds.), *Child development research and social policy* (pp. 189–266). Chicago: University of Chicago Press.

Falicov, C. J. (1988). Family sociology and family therapy development framework: A comparative analysis and thoughts on future trends. In C. Falicov (Ed.), *Family transitions: A comparative analysis and thoughts on future trends* (pp. 3–51). New York: Guildford Press.

Felner, R. D., Farber, S. S., & Primavera, T. (1983). Transitions and stressful life events: A model for primary prevention. In R. D. Felner, L. A. Tason, T. N. Mortisugu, & S. S. Farber (Eds.), *Preventive psychology: Theory, research and practice* (pp. 199–215). New York: Pergamon.

Felner, R. D., Rowlison, R. T., & Terre, L. (1986). Unraveling the Gordian Knot in life change inquiry: A critical examination of crisis, stress, and transitional frameworks for prevention. In S. M. Auerbach & A. L. Stolberg (Eds.), *Crisis intervention with children and families* (pp. 39–63). Washington, DC: Hemisphere Publishing.

Felner, R. D., Stolberg, A., & Cowen, E. L. (1975). Crisis events and school mental health referral patterns of young children. *Journal of Consulting and Clinical Psychology, 43*, 305–310.

Forehand, R., Long, N., & Brody, G. (1988). Divorce and marital conflict: Relationship to adolescent competence and adjustment in early adolescence. In E. M. Hetherington & J. D. Arasteh (Eds.), *Impact of divorce, single parenting, and stepparenting on children* (pp. 155–167). Hillsdale, NJ: Lawrence Erlbaum.

Furstenberg, F. F. (1985). Sociological ventures in child development. *Child Development, 56*, 281–288.

Furstenberg, F. F., & Allison, P. D. (1985). *How marital dissolution affects children: Variations by age and sex.* University of Pennsylvania; Unpublished manuscript.

Furstenberg, F. F., & Nord, C. W. (1985). Parenting apart: Patterns of child-rearing after marital disruption. *Journal of Marriage and the Family, 47*, 893–904.

Ganong, L. S., & Coleman, M. (1986, May). A comparison of clinical and empirical literature on children in stepfamilies. *Journal of Marriage and the Family, 48*, 309–318.

Garmezy, N. (1987). Stress, competence, and development: Continuities in the study of schizophrenic adults, children vulnerable to psychopathology, and the search for stress-resistant children. *American Orthopsychiatric Association, 57*, 159–174.

Garmezy, N., & Rutter, M. (Eds.). (1983). *Stress, coping and development*. New York: McGraw-Hill.

Glenn, N. D., & Kramer, K. B. (1987). The marriages and divorces of the children of divorce. *Journal of Marriage and the Family, 49*, 811–825.

Glenn, N. C., & Shelton, B. A. (1983). Pre-adult background variables and divorce: A note of caution about overreliance on explained variance. *Journal of Marriage and the Family, 45*(2), 405–410.

Heitzmann, C., & Kaplan, P. (1988). Assessment of methods for measuring social support. *Health Psychology, 7*, 75–109.

Hess, R. D., & Camara, K. A. (1979). Postdivorce relationships as mediating factors in the consequences of divorce for children. *Journal of Social Issues, 35*, 79–96.

Hetherington, E. M., & Arasteh, J. D. (Eds.). (1980). *Impact of divorce, single parenting, and step-parenting on children*. Hillsdale, NJ: Lawrence Erlbaum.

Hetherington, E. M., & Camara, K. A. (1984). Families in transition: The processes of dissolution and reconstitution. In R. Parke (Ed.), *Review of child development research* (Vol. 7, pp. 398–439). Chicago: University of Chicago Press.

Hetherington, E. M., Cox, M., & Cox, R. (1985). Long term effects of divorce and remarriage on the adjustment of children. *Journal of the American Academy of Child Psychiatry, 24*(5), 518–530.

Hodges, W. F. (Ed.). (1986). *Interventions for children of divorce: Custody Access and psychotherapy*. New York: Wiley & Sons.

Hofferth, S. (1985). Updating children's life course. *Journal of Marriage and the Family, 47*, 93–115.

Johnson, J. (1986). *Life events as stressors in childhood and adolescence*. Newbury Park, CA: Sage Publications.

Kagan, J. (1979). Family experience and the child's development. *American Psychologist, 34*, 886–891.

Kalter, N. (1977). Children of divorce in an outpatient psychiatric population. *American Journal of Orthopsychiatry, 47*, 40–51.

Kalter, N. (1987). Long-term effects of divorce on children: A developmental vulnerability model. *American Journal of Orthopsychiatry, 57*(4), 587–600.

Kalter, N., & Plunkett, J. W. (1984). Children's perceptions of the causes and consequences of divorce. *Journal of the American Academy of Child Psychiatry, 23*(3), 326–334.

Kanner, A. D., Coyne, J. C., Schaefer, C., & Lazarus, R. S. (1981). Comparison of two modes of stress management: Daily hassles vs. major life events. *Journal of Behavioral Medicine, 4*, 1–39.

Kanner, A. D., Harrison, A., & Wertlieb, D. (1985, August). *Development of the Children's Hassles and Uplifts Scales*. Poster session on stress, coping, and chronic illness. Division 38, Annual Meeting of the American Psychological Association, Los Angeles, CA.

Kanner, A. D., Feldman, S. S., Weinberger, D. A., & Ford, M. E. (1988). Uplifts, hassles, and adaptational outcomes in early adolescents. *Journal of Early Adolescence, 7*, 371–394.

Kellem, S., Ensminger, M., & Turner, R. (1977). Family structure and the mental health of children. *Archives of General Psychiatry, 34*, 1012–1022.

Kitson, G. C. (1985). Marital discord and marital separation: A county survey. *Journal of Marriage and the Family, 47*(3), 693–700.

Kitson, G. C., & Raschke, H. J. (1981). Divorce research: What we know; what we need to know. *Journal of Divorce, 4*, 1037.

Kitson, G. C., Sussman, M. B., Williams, G. K., Zeehandelaar, R. B. Schickmanter, B. K., & Steinberger, J. L. (1982). Sampling issues in family research. *Journal of Marriage and the Family, 11*, 965–981.

Koel, A., Clark, S., Phear, W., & Hauser, B. (1988). A comparison of joint and sole legal custody agreements. In E. M. Hetherington & J. D. Arasteh (Eds.), *Impact of divorce, single parenting and stepparenting on children.* Hillsdale, NJ: Lawrence Erlbaum.

Krantz, S. E., Clark, J., Pruyn, J. P., & Usher, M. (1985). Cognition and adjustment among children of separated of divorced parents. *Cognitive Therapy and Research, 9*(1), 61–67.

Kurdek, L. A. (1981). An integrative perspective on children's divorce adjustment. *American Psychologist, 3,* 856–866.

Kurdek, L. A., & Berg, B. (1987). Children's beliefs about parental divorce scale: Psychometric characteristics and concurrent validity. *Journal of Consulting and Clinical Psychology, 55*(5), 712–718.

Kurdek, L. A., & Siesky, A. E. (1980). Children's perception of their parents' divorce. *Journal of Divorce, 3,* 339–378.

Kurdek, L. A., & Sinclair, R. J. (1988). Adjustment of young adolescents in two-parent nuclear, stepfather, and mother-custody families. *Journal of Consulting and Clinical Psychology, 56*(1), 91–96.

Lazarus, R. S., & Folkman, S. (1984). *Stress, appraisal and coping.* New York: Springer.

Maccoby, E., Depner, C., & Mnookin, R. H. (1988). Custody of children following divorce. In E. M. Hetherington & J. D. Arasteh (Eds.), *Impact of divorce, single parenting, and stepparenting on children* (pp. 91–114). Hillsdale, NJ: Lawrence Erlbaum.

McCubbin, H., Sussman, M., & Patterson, J. (Eds.). (1983). *Social stress and the family: Marriage and family review* (Vol. 6, 1, & 2). New York: Haworth.

McDermott, J. F. (1970). Divorce and its psychiatric sequence in children. *Archives of General Psychiatry, 23,* 421–427.

Melamed, B. G., and Bush, J. (1987). Parent-child influences during medical procedures. In S. M. Auerbach & A. L. Stolberg (Eds.), *Crisis intervention with children and families* (pp. 123–148). Washington, DC: Hemisphere Publishing.

Melichar, J., & Chiriboga, D. A. (1985). Timetables in the divorce process. *Journal of Marriage and the Family, 47*(3), 701–708.

Melichar, J. F., & Chiriboga, D. A. (1988). Significance of time in adjustment to marital separation. *American Journal of Orthopsychiatry, 58*(2), 221–227.

Norton, A., & Glick, P. (1986). One parent families: A social and economic profile. *Family Relations, 35,* 9–17.

O'Leary, K. D., & Emery, R. E. (1984). Marital discord and child behavior problems. In M. D. Levine & P. Satz (Eds.), *Middle childhood: Development and dysfunction* (pp. 345–364). Baltimore: University Park Press.

Orton, G. (1982). A comparative study of children's worries. *Journal of Psychology, 110,* 153–162.

Pintner, R., & Lev, J. (1940). Worries of school children. *Journal of Genetic Psychology, 56,* 67–96.

Pearlin, L. I., Lieberman, M. A., Menaghan, E. G., & Mullan, J. T. (1981, December). The stress process. *Journal of Health and Social Behavior, 22,* 337–356.

Pedro-Carroll, J., Cowen, E., Hightower, D., & Guare, J. (1986). Preventable intervention with latency-age children of divorce: A replication study. *American Journal of Community Psychology, 14,* 277–290.

Pedrol-Carroll, J. L., & Cowen, E. L. (1985). The children of divorce intervention program: An investigation of the efficacy of a school-based prevention program. *Journal of Consulting and Clinical Psychology, 53*(5), 603–611.

Plummer, L. P., & Koch-Hattem, A. (1986). Family stress and adjustment to divorce. *Family Relations, 35,* 523–529.

Rowe, D. C., & Plomin, R. (1981). The importance of nonshared environmental influences in behavior development. *Developmental Psychology, 17,* 315–324.

Rutter, M. (1981). Stress, coping, and development: Some issues and some questions. *Journal of Child Psychology and Psychiatry 22*, 323–356.

Rutter, M. (1985). Resilience in the face of adversity: Protective factors and resistance to psychiatric disorder. *British Journal of Psychiatry, 147*, 598–611.

Rutter, M. (1987). Psychosocial resilience and protective mechanisms. *American Journal of Orthopsychiatry, 57*, 316–322.

Sameroff, A., & Seifer, F. (1983). Familial risk and child competence. *Child Development, 54*, 1254–1268.

Sander, I. N., Wolchik, S. A., Braver, S. L., & Fogas, B. S. (1986). Significant events of children of divorce: Toward the assessment of risky situations. In S. M. Auerbach & A. L. Stolberg (Eds.), *Crisis intervention with children and families* (pp. 65–83). Washington, DC: Hemisphere Publishing.

Santrock, J. W., & Madison, T. D. (1985). Three research traditions in the study of adolescents in divorced families: Quasi-experimental, developmental, clinical, and family sociological. *Journal of Early Adolescence, 5*(1), 115–128.

Stolberg, A. L., Kiluk, D. J., & Garrison, K. M. (1986). A temporal model of divorce adjustment with implications for primary prevention. In S. M. Auerbach & Arnold L. Stolberg (Eds.), *Crisis intervention with children and families* (pp. 105–121). Washington, DC: Hempishere Publishing.

Teachman, J. D. (1982). Methodological issues in the analysis of family formation and dissolution. *Journal of Marriage and the Family, 11*, 1037–1053.

Thoits, P. (1986). Social support as coping assistance. *Journal of Consulting and Clinical Psychology 54*, 416–423.

Walker, A. J. (1985). Reconceptualizing family stress. *Journal of Marriage and the Family, 47*, 827–837.

Wallerstein, J. S. (1983). Children of divorce: Stress and developmental tasks. In N. Garmezy & M. Rutter (Eds.), *Stress coping and development in children* (pp. 265–302). New York: McGraw-Hill.

Wallerstein, J. S., Corbin, S. B., & Lewis, J. M. (1988). Children of divorce: A 10-year study. In E. M. Hetherington & J. D. Arasteh (Eds.), *Impact of divorce, single parenting, and stepparenting on children* (pp. 197–214). Hillsdale, NJ: Lawrence Erlbaum.

Wallerstein, J. S., & Kelly, J. B. (1980). *Surviving the breakup: How children actually cope with divorce*. New York: Basic Books.

Weigel, C., Wertlieb, D., & Feldstein, M. (1989). Perceptions of control, competence and contingency as influences on the stress-behavior symptom relation in school-age children. *Journal of Personality and Social Psychology, 56*(3), 456–464.

Wertlieb, D., Budman, S., Demby, A., & Randall, M. (1984). Marital separation: Stress and intervention. *Journal of Human Stress, 10*, 18–27.

Wertlieb, D., Springer, T., Weigel, C., & Feldstein, M. (1987). Temperament as a moderator of children's stressful experiences. *American Journal of Orthopsychiatry, 57*, 234–245.

Wertlieb, D., Weigel, C., & Feldstein, M. (1987a). Stress, social support and behavior symptoms in middle childhood. *Journal of Clinical Child Psychology, 16*, 204–211.

Wertlieb, D., Weigel, C., & Feldstein, M. (1987b). Measuring children's coping. *American Journal of Orthopsychiatry, 57*, 548–560.

Wolchik, S., Sandler, I. N., Braver, S. L., & Fogas, B. S. (1985). Events of parental divorce: Stressfulness ratings by children, parents, and clinicians. *American Journal of Community Psychology, 14*(1), 59–74.

Zaslow, M. J. (1988). Sex differences in children's response to parental divorce: Research methodology and postdivorce family forms. *American Journal of Orthopsychiatry, 58*(3), 355–378.

4

Development, Stress, and Role Restructuring

Social Transitions of Adolescence

CAROL S. ANESHENSEL and SUSAN GORE

Much of the impetus for the accelerating emergence of adolescent stress research flows from a growing recognition that the outcomes associated with exposure to stress are highly prevalent among adolescents. These unfortunate consequences are illustrated most poignantly by the high rate of suicide among young people. Suicide is currently the third leading cause of death among adolescents and young adults (USDHHS, 1986), and these rates are increasing (Murphy & Wetzel, 1980). Reports also document high (Albert & Beck, 1975; Kandel & Davies, 1982; Kaplan, Hong, & Weinhold, 1984; Schoenbach, Kaplan, Wagner, Grimson, & Miller, 1983; Teri, 1982) and increasing prevalence rates (Klerman & Weissman, 1989) of depression in adolescent and young-adult populations, and this disorder, significant in and of itself, also figures prominently as a risk factor for suicide (Neinstein, 1984; Sommer, 1984; Wells, Deykin, & Klerman, 1985). In addition, high rates of substance use and abuse among adolescents may reflect attempts of youth to cope with stressful life experiences or with emotional distress (Huba, Wingard, & Bentler, 1980) and thus are another element in an overall picture of

CAROL S. ANESHENSEL • School of Public Health, University of California, Los Angeles, California 90024-1772.　**SUSAN GORE** • Department of Sociology, University of Massachusetts–Boston, Boston, Massachusetts 02125.

The Social Context of Coping, edited by John Eckenrode. Plenum Press, New York, 1991.

heightened risk at this stage of life. Although these stress-related mental health conditions are important objects of inquiry in their own right, it is equally important to identify the mechanisms through which stress arises in the lives of adolescents, the subject of this chapter.

DEVELOPMENTAL ISSUES

Research concerning stress and psychological disorder among adolescents has become increasingly influenced by the paradigms employed in similar research among adults. This parallelism flows from the recognition that stress is associated with psychological disorder among adolescents as well as among adults (Burke & Weir, 1978; Compas *et al.*, 1986a,b; Gad & Johnson, 1980; Greenberger, Steinberg, & Vaux, 1982; Langner, Gersten, & Eisenberg, 1974; Siegel & Brown, 1988; Vaux, 1981; and see Thoits, 1983, for a review of the adult literature) and from substantive concerns with developmental trajectories, that is, how stress and disorder in adolescence persist over time into adulthood (Robins, 1983). Much of the adult literature has focused upon the issue of differential vulnerability by way of identifying factors that regulate the adverse impact of stress, including social characteristics such as class, gender, and race; social support; coping resources and behaviors; and self-concept (see Kessler, Price, & Wortman, 1985, for a review). A related theme addresses issues of exposure to stress and the differentials across groups defined by age, class, gender, and race–ethnicity (Aneshensel & Pearlin, 1987; Kessler, 1979). These twin themes of differential exposure and vulnerability to stress have begun to emerge in the adolescent literature but pose as yet unanswered questions concerning commonalities in stress processes across life stages and unique features of adolescence.

Although similarities in the stress process across the life course may exist, some features may not generalize from adult to adolescent experience. Achenbach (1974) and Rutter (1986), in explicating developmental approaches to psychopathology, argue cogently against the wholesale extrapolation of adult models of disorder to children and adolescents. They caution that child and adolescent models must take into account the vast differences in psychosocial functioning between young persons and adults. Other research pitfalls stem from the nonstatic nature of adolescence itself. For example, regarding the cognitive appraisal of threat—a key component of stress models—the perception and interpretation of environmental threats appear to change from early to late adolescence (Magnusson, 1982). Coleman (1978) similarly reports that the concerns of adolescents change over time, with early adolescents being most concerned with anxiety over heterosexual relationships, late adolescents having most conflict with parents, and fears of rejection from peer groups being most pronounced among middle adolescents.

There are issues as well about determining when adolescent risk-taking should be viewed as adaptive experimentation (Erickson, 1968) versus when it indicates an abnormal behavioral response to stress (see Baumrind, 1987, for a review of this issue) with damaging life-course implications. This, too, may be partially dependent upon age and the other temporal processes such as age of initiation of the behavior, regularity, and persistence of the behavior. Thus, in research on adolescence, age presents more of a problem than simply one of statistical control; the models need to reflect developmental stage, taking into account the great differences in maturity and social situation that exist during the adolescent years.

These developmental concerns arise in considering the basic model for exploring the health effects of life stress. There are three major classes of variables that are usually considered in models of the stress–illness relationship: the stressors and other features of stress exposure, the mediating and moderating factors that condition and translate responses to stress, and the "outcomes" or health effects of these processes. First, exposure to many stressors is contingent upon social role occupancy. Because adolescents and adults tend to occupy different social roles, these groups encounter different types of problematic life circumstances. Second, adults and adolescents are likely to differ in the resources they require and can bring to bear on these stressful circumstances. Social support, coping, self-concept, and other potential moderators of stress utilize social, cognitive, and emotional capabilities that are undergoing rapid developmental change during the adolescent years. Also, adolescents usually have had less experience than adults in coping with life's vicissitudes and therefore may be less skilled at avoiding or containing potential stressors or at managing the meaning or impact of these events and circumstances—the primary functions of coping activities (Pearlin & Schooler, 1978). Thus, adults and adolescents may respond differently to the same types of stressors and consequently manifest varying levels of psychological distress. Finally, the specific manifestations of psychological distress or disorder may differ between adolescents and adults (Achenbach, 1982; Rutter, 1986), and the health relevance of similar behaviors (e.g., having one alcoholic beverage daily) may be interpreted differently when occurring in the adolescent versus adult context.

In sum, exposure to life stress may evoke psychological distress in both adults and adolescents, but the precise nature of the interconnections among facets of the stress process may be qualitatively very different. This model, however, becomes even more complex with further specification of the stressor concept. In the next section, we propose a model of adolescent stress that takes the stressfulness of developmental transitions as the point of departure.

NORMATIVE AND NONNORMATIVE STRESSORS

That adolescents ordinarily experience rapid and extensive developmental change—physical, sexual, cognitive, emotional, and social maturation—contributes importantly to the image of adolescence as a period of life fraught with stress. This perspective originated in the early writings of G. Stanley Hall (1904) and A. Freud (1958), which portray adolescence as a period of "storm and stress." The very nature of adolescence as a period of transition between childhood and adulthood means that most teens encounter numerous life-change events with the potential to evoke stress (Hamburg, 1974; Petersen & Spiga, 1982). These changes include scheduled progressions of the life course, such as school transitions and puberty, and other changes that commonly happen at this time, such as the initiation of dating or sexual activity (Brooks-Gunn & Petersen, 1983; Simmons & Blyth, 1987). Moreover, the successful accomplishment of the psychosocial developmental tasks of adolescence virtually demands change in numerous established social relationships, as when adolescent and parent negotiate changing responsibilities and privileges as part of the adolescent's evolving autonomy (Smetana, 1991). These transitions are labeled *normative life events* because they are expected to occur during this stage of the life course.

This perspective is useful in distinguishing adolescence from other stages of the life course, but by itself it does not account for differences among adolescents in the experience of life stress. Also, investigations of pubertal and school changes in general show that these transitions *per se* tend not to have long-term or profound effects (Simmons & Blyth, 1987). Given that all or most adolescents encounter these transitions, how then are we to understand the normal functioning of most adolescents, as well as the experience of those who fail to manage these experiences?

This issue has been approached from several distinct perspectives in the general stress literature, perspectives that are present in the adolescent stress literature as well. In Figure 1, we present a model of adolescent stress and its health effects that draws upon both of these research traditions.

In Figure 1, we see normative life changes as setting in motion a

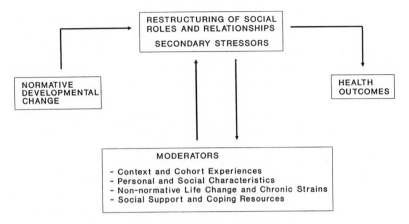

Figure 1. Health effects of developmental transitions: Mediating and moderating processes.

series of social dislocations that are consequential to health. Such normative transitions may be stressful in and of themselves or may engender stress because they produce other events or circumstances that are stressful.[1] Pearlin (1983) suggests that life events become distressing largely to the extent that these events create or exacerbate difficulties in the enactment of ongoing social roles, which he refers to as *role strains*. Of the types of role strains Pearlin identifies, one is particularly pertinent to the adolescent period—the concept of role restructuring. In Figure 1, we show developmental transitions leading to the restructuring of social roles, which mediates the relationship between these transitions and negative changes in health status. During adolescence, the adoption of new roles, such as dating or working, often creates pressure to redefine other existing roles, such as friendships or relations with parents. This type of role restructuring can pose difficulties more severe than those of ordinary role transitions because it is necessary to adapt to shifts in expectations, obligations, and norms among members of a stable role set whose prior relationships were guided by different rules (Pearlin, 1983). Also, preexisting roles may continue over this period, but the

---

[1]Transitions may also occur when there is some kind of breach or resolution of long-term stressful circumstances. This case, where the transition follows from a prior period of stress, is not usually seen as relevant to the problem of developmental transitions, except where individuals may be experiencing chronic anticipation stress of some change occurring, such as in preparing to enter the labor force. Most researchers see developmental transitions as setting in motion subsequent stressors rather than resulting from prior stressful conditions. However, our case materials show that both these processes are at work.

expectations and obligations of these roles may change qualitatively, posing adaptational challenges. As an example, many adolescents continue to occupy the student role throughout this period, but expectations for adultlike behavior in increasingly structured arrangements increase with progression through the school system. Developmental transitions, therefore, may be differentially stressful to adolescents depending upon the extent to which these transitions disrupt existing social relationships, creating secondary sources of stress.

We also see in Figure 1 that severe and less severe responses to stressful experiences are shaped by certain other conditions. These conditions that more precisely specify the stress experience are called *moderators* and are represented by the vertical lines that intersect the pathway between developmental transitions and the health status variables. Moderating variables include the individual's perceptions, needs, values, goals and aspirations, social support, and other coping resources. In Figure 1, we use a bidirectional arrow to link the social support and coping concepts to the pathway of stress responses in order to denote that effective coping can attenuate or "buffer" stress effects but also be jeopardized by these developmental changes. The chapter by Gore and Colten in this volume discusses this problem with reference to self-esteem, whereas our discussion here of social support is also illustrative of this more pervasive dynamic. Some moderator variables may be understood to exacerbate rather than alleviate the stress of developmental change. For example, Brooks-Gunn and Warren (1985) report that pubertal maturation (a biological transition) is more distressing for adolescent females training for a career in dance, which values a prepubertal appearance, than for other adolescent females whose activities and the adult roles to which they aspire are not threatened by these physical changes.

Also among these moderating conditions, we include other characteristics that determine the meaning and therefore stressfulness of the developmental transitions. Thus, the meaning of the event and hence its potential to evoke stress are shaped not only by individual characteristics and social resources but also by the context in which the event occurs. Wheaton (1990) has demonstrated, for example, that presumed negative events such as divorce or involuntary job loss may not be stressful or distressing to adults if these events represent exits from unsatisfactory situations. For adolescents, the timing of pubertal events appears to be a critical contextual factor: Pubertal maturation that occurs "on time," that is, when the largest numbers of youth experience it, is less distressing than maturation that occurs early or late relative to the maturation of peers. Also, the simultaneous clustering of several developmental changes is thought to be more distressing than the sequential occurrence of these life changes (Coleman, 1978; Simmons, 1987). The context in which normative life events occur, then, may influence the impact of the specific event. These contextual characteristics, many of which are defined in terms of the experience of the larger cohort in which the adolescent is a member, may moderate the degree of role restructuring that takes place, and, as will be discussed later, may reduce the level of disturbance within the social network.

In addition, normative events may become distressing because they occur in conjunction with nonnormative events or in the context of more chronically stressful life conditions. Although normative events occur to adolescents precisely because they are adolescents, nonnormative events are not scheduled transitions of the life course. Here we are referring to the kinds of eruptive events usually assessed in life-event inventories. Because these events frequently are also socially structured sources of stress, the term *nonnormative* is perhaps misleading (Aneshensel & Pearlin, 1987). However, it is important to differentiate events that happen to only some adolescents from those that occur to virtually all adolescents. The adult-centered stress literature has not focused on normative stressors, with the exception of some studies of retirement, birth of a child, and death of a spouse, and has progressed on the assumption that nonnormative stressors are more threatening because such events are likely to be unexpected, uncontrollable, and undesirable (Thoits, 1983). In contrast, adolescent researchers have emphasized the stress inherent in normative life-course transitions.

The relative importance of these two types of stressors and how they come to evoke stress among some adolescents but not others have yet to be explored thoroughly. Yet, the simultaneous presence of nonnormative stressors may provide an important context for understanding the variable impact of developmental transitions. For example, coping with normative events may not result in high levels of distress because such events can be anticipated and therefore more easily negotiated. However, in the context of other pressing life problems, and when parents, other significant adults, and peers are unable or unavailable to help youth anticipate and deal with such challenges, the adolescent's ability to master developmental transitions will be much more problematic. In Figure 1 we include other life stresses within the category of moderating variables to depict this idea that coping with nonnormative life stress may be contingent upon the other stressors experienced because other problems and disruptions alter the resources available for responding to developmental change. This representation emphasizes the impact of developmental processes on health status and casts other, perhaps more serious, life stresses as moderating factors. And, we know that non-developmental stresses also set in motion similar processes of role re-structuring and secondary stressors. This understanding of nonnor-mative life stresses as the independent variable most often guides stress research on adult populations, whereas Figure 1 provides a distinctive perspective on the processes specific to adolescent development.

Although Figure 1 depicts adolescents as sharing normative stressful experiences by virtue of their common life-course stage, they remain males and females of diverse racial–ethnic and social-class back-grounds. As with adults, the particular stressful life circumstances to which adolescents are exposed appear to be regulated by these and similar markers of their location in the social system. For example, Gad and Johnson (1980) report that young black adolescents experienced more negative life change events than white adolescents but not more positive change events; similar patterns were found for lower- versus middle- and high-socioeconomic-status adolescents. Burke and Weir (1978) find that female adolescents reported more stress than male ado-lescents in certain role domains, reflecting social relational issues of peer acceptance, isolation, difficulties with parents, and relationships with the opposite sex. Such findings are consistent with those of Bush and Sim-mons (1987) who argue that girls are more exposed to the sexual and interpersonal stresses of early to middle adolescence, and that with self-esteem more dependent upon the positive feedback of others, they are also less well equipped to deal with these stresses. Moreover, social char-acteristics shape the needs, values, resources, and past experiences that influence the individual's perception and evaluation of events and cir-cumstances as stressful or not. Consequently, teens of diverse social back-grounds are not only likely to encounter dissimilar conditions, but they are equally likely to respond in different ways to similar conditions. These group differences, like age, are often seen as outside or "ex-ogenous" to the stress process, but a current thrust in stress research is to be more attentive to the dynamics of these variables as significant com-ponents of the stress model (Barnett, Biener, & Baruch, 1987; Pearlin, 1989).

A final matter that should be introduced briefly here and that antic-ipates our discussion of stress in social relationships is the nature of the association between stress and social support. The dominant framework for investigating stress, social support, and mental health is some variant of the stress-buffering model, in which supportive relationships provide resources for dealing with stress and are modeled as existing prior to the occurrence of stress, and/or as being mobilized in response to stressful events. However, support also may change for the worse in response to stress and in turn impact upon mental health. In discussing this possibility, Thoits (1982) has shown how patterns of findings suggesting stress-buffering processes may in fact be concealing this type of process: That is, individuals who are characterized by high stress and low social support may be distressed because it was in the nature of their stressor events to bring about decrements in social support. As will become evident from the discussion of the data that follows, many of the stressors that adolescents face are, or derive from, transformations of relationships that in turn bring about decrements of parental and friendship support resources. This possibility is represented by the bidirectional arrow linking the social support moderator to the role restructuring and secondary stress mediators in Figure 1. Thus, as we shall see, study of the nature of stress in adolescence may inform some of the fundamental problems in the way we usually model the mental health effects of life stress.

This chapter focuses on one aspect of the intersection of development and the stress process—stress that emerges in the conduct of everyday life for adolescents as a consequence of development-related role changes. The emphasis of this analysis is on developmental role transitions, such as the adoption of dating roles, and how such changes initiate a series of dislocations within established social relationships, such as relationships with friends, that in turn generate stressful social experiences for both the adolescent encountering the transition and his or her role partners. We now describe our data set and turn to a consideration of how these types of role-bound stress arise within the specific roles typically occupied by adolescents, with a particular emphasis on the developmental restructuring of adolescent friendships.

THE QUALITATIVE INTERVIEWS

The sources of information for describing these types of stress-provoking experiences are qualitative interviews with 50 adolescents residing in greater Los Angeles, California. Interviews were conducted between August 1986 and February 1987. This is a convenience sample chosen to maximize diversity in the adolescents interviewed; it is not a probability sample representative of the general adolescent population. Instead, teens were selected to fill cells in an *a priori* stratification table of age, sex, and race–ethnicity. Specifically, an attempt was made to interview males and females representing early, middle, and late adolescence in each of the three major racial–ethnic groups residing in this geographical region: blacks, Hispanics, and non-Hispanic whites. Ethnic–

racial diversity was obtained by targeting neighborhoods containing a high density of one of these three groups according to census data. In addition, teens were selected from middle-, lower-middle, and low-socioeconomic-status groups. This selection was accomplished by targeting neighborhoods known to vary in terms of income and housing costs according to census data.

In general, recruitment efforts were successful in obtaining a sample reflecting the diversity of life conditions encountered by adolescents. The racial–ethnic breakdown is 19 whites, 11 blacks, and 20 Hispanics. There are 26 males and 24 females. Eleven of the youth are 12 to 13 years old, 21 are 14 to 15 years old, and 18 are 16 to 17 years old. The socioeconomic circumstances of these teens range from affluent to below poverty levels.

Interviewers located potential respondents by going to sites frequented by teens, such as schoolyards, parks and recreation areas, and shopping malls, and by canvassing households in selected neighborhoods. Interviewers randomly approached a teen in these locations, described the study, and asked whether he or she was interested in being interviewed. The interviewer then contacted the adolescent's parent or guardian at home to describe the study and to obtain informed consent from the parent or guardian. After consent was obtained, the adolescent's assent was formally obtained. Interviews took place at the adolescent's home or in a nearby location (e.g., porch, car) if a private location within the home was not available. The interviews varied in length from a half hour to 2 hours, averaging approximately 1 hour.

The semistructured interviews focused on identifying particularly difficult and problematic aspects of the adolescent's life. Most of the interview schedule or guide posed open-ended questions concerning both general problems and problems in specific areas of life, such as family life, peer relations, and school and/or work. Respondents were asked about aspects of their life that were particularly bothersome or upsetting, whether any major crises had occurred during the past year, whether they had any day-to-day problems or hassles, and whether anything was different from the way it was a year earlier. Irrespective of responses to these general questions, the adolescents were also asked about problems at home or with their family, at school or with other students or teachers, at work or with coworkers or supervisors, and so forth. In order to elicit information about coping activities, respondents were asked about how they dealt with any problems identified during the course of the interview. In addition, the interview contained several questions concerning positive aspects of the adolescent's life.

Finally, the interviewer asked whether there were aspects of the respondent's life or self that he or she would change if possible and whether there was anything that had not happened during the past year that he or she expected to happen. The intent of the latter questions was to identify sources of stress that arose not from the presence of a noxious condition but from the absence of a positive or desired-after condition or event.

The interviews were conducted by professional interviewers from the Institute for Social Science Research, Survey Research Center, University of California, Los Angeles. Two females and one male interviewer conducted the survey. The male interviewer and one female interviewer were white; the other female interviewer was black. All three were middle-aged.

All interviews were audiorecorded and transcribed. The data were then analyzed qualitatively with a content analysis. Each transcript was reviewed by one of the investigators to identify major themes appearing in the responses given to the open-ended questions. These responses were categorized according to the domain of functioning involved (e.g., family, friends) and the nature of the event or circumstance (e.g., conflict over rules, exclusion from group activities). Once these categories were established, the transcripts were reevaluated and verbatim responses assigned to appropriate categories. Two graduate research assistants then reviewed the tabulations and transcripts to identify misclassifications and omissions. Discrepancies were resolved through consensus.

We have selected from the volume of material generated in these interviews the data pertaining to two developmental transitions—initiation of dating and school transitions—that have figured prominently in the literature on adolescent stress. In the following sections we expand the conceptualization of these transitions as normative life events to describe the conditions under which these events are experienced as stressful or not.

DATING TRANSITIONS AND ROLE RESTRUCTURING

The initiation of love relationships is often considered a normative life-change event because adolescence is the stage of the life course when these relationships are typically experienced for the first time and prepare the youth for intimate relationships in adulthood. Therefore, it is not surprising that several of the teens in this study mentioned having their first boyfriend or girlfriend as a significant event that had occurred during the past year. Theoretically, the assumption of a new role is stress-provoking precisely because the role is new: The lack of prior experience in enacting the role creates uncertainty over appropriate behavior. Adolescents initiating dating activities may have only a vague idea of how they are supposed to act toward their role partners, or of what they can expect of their partners. Alternatively, they may have a clear image, if only from the media, but lack confidence about their ability to enact this new role. Yet, those who had recently started dating uniformly described this event as positive, as if a major hurdle had been cleared. None of these teens described this change as negative or stressful. However, several teens expressed dissatisfaction with not dating. For example, one expressed an unfulfilled need to have someone with whom he could express affection. These teens cited several obstacles to dating, including not being old enough, parents not allowing it, and not being able to afford dating. For many teens, then, difficulties surrounding the acquisition of the dating role appear to be more disruptive before dating starts, when there is a sense that entry into the role is delayed, than at the actual point of transition into this role.

Because the transition was sought after, however, does not mean that the relationship, once established, was free of problems. The difficulties experienced in these relationships resulted in part from the ambiguity surrounding dating roles. Thus, conflict frequently centered on standards of appropriate behavior concerning issues such as fidelity and reciprocity. Some teens felt that their partners violated the very rules to which they themselves were expected to conform. One teen, for example, complains that her boyfriend gets angry when she talks to other boys but that he feels free to talk to other girls: "I go, it has to be an equal relationship. I go, either I talk to guys and you talk to girls, or I don't talk to guys and you don't talk to girls." The single most troublesome aspect of these relationships, however, was the unwanted breakup of specific dating relationships, which often left the adolescent emotionally devastated. Reestablishing these relationships was one of the most commonly mentioned events that were hoped for but which had not happened. In contrast, some teens felt trapped in relationships that they had been unable to end. Overall, exits from dating relationships appeared to be more stressful than the initial entrance into the dating role.

Thus, although the initiation of dating *per se* did not appear to be particularly troublesome, teens were frustrated by being unable to have a relationship in general or with a particular person and often experienced difficulties with their partners once a relationship had been established. Dating role transitions, then, are more accurately portrayed as a series of related occurrences that extend over time than as a discrete event. Furthermore, these transitions do not stand alone as isolated events. We turn now to a consideration of how these dating role transitions generate secondary sources of stress in other social roles.

Most teens make these transitions during these years, but they do so at their own pace. Consequently, there is considerable diversity among adolescents in their level of involvement in love relationships, even among age-mates. Friendship networks, therefore, tend to be developmentally heterogeneous. Moreover, the social development of some network members proceeds more rapidly than that of others. Over time, then, the friendship group is likely to become increasingly diverse, with some members having serious love relationships and others having only limited if any such involvements.

This developmental diversity needs to be underscored, for it has important consequences for the structure and functioning of the friendship network. As some members of the group begin to date, or to develop serious love relationships, there is pressure to change the established friendship group. Those with extensive heterosexual involvements typically curtail activities with friends to accommodate increasing activities with dating partners. These changes may produce mismatches among friends in expected, desired, and actual levels of shared activities. Preferences for types of activities also diverge as some friends seek new activities that include opportunities for interactions with members of the opposite sex. Alternately, as some friends become committed to one partner, they may become disinterested or uncomfortable in group activities that provide contact with other potential dating partners. In this manner, the increasing involvement of some friends in relationships with members of the opposite sex generates pressure to redefine established same-sex friendship groups.

The developmental change of some adolescents translates into problematic social circumstances for other adolescents. Dating-initiated changes in the amount or type of friendship activity of some adolescents alter the friendship experiences of their friends, especially those who have not yet made these changes. The maturational variation among role set members leaves some adolescents feeling abandoned by their friends and others feeling trapped by established friendships. In this manner, teens are influenced not only by their own dating role transitions but by the transitions that occur to their friends as well. The restructuring of adolescent friendships to accommodate dating activities, therefore, affects both those who are taking up these activities and those who are not yet involved in dating activities.

The accounts of the adolescents interviewed in this study illustrate how these transitions alter the composition of the friendship groups and the transactions that occur within it. A 14-year-old girl who is dating, for example, recounts how she cannot discuss some of her problems with her closest friend who is not interested in boys but must rely instead on another friend:

> I could talk to Joanie better because she understands more. . . . Marie she doesn't like guys. So it's better to talk to Joanie because she knows. . . . It's hard, but I could still tell Marie most of the stuff I tell Joanie.

A 15-year-old expresses the opposite sentiment:

> Their boy problems. . . . They just always like to talk about their boy problems and it's upsetting, you know it's depressing to not get along with their boyfriends a lot. . . . But that's what friends talk about.

We see illustrated here both sides of the transactional dilemma involved in the restructuring of adolescent friendships. The previously established friendship inadequately meets the emergent needs, interests, and commitments of the dating adolescent. On the other hand, the person who is not dating finds these new topics of conversation less than compelling. What once was presumably satisfactory to both friends is now satisfactory to neither. In extreme mismatches, such disjunctures can terminate the friendship.

Another manifestation of these restructuring strains centers on shared activities, on the amount of time spent together, and on the types of activities that take place. The adolescent who takes up the dating role faces potentially conflicting demands from friends and from dating partners. One 17-year-old girl provides a vivid account of her difficulties in balancing her relationships with her friends and her boyfriend:

> Sometimes my boyfriend and my friends don't get along. . . . My friends expect me to be with them all the time and my boyfriend expects me to be with him all the time. One of my friends just recently broke up with her boyfriend, so neither of them have boyfriends right now. So, we're like the Three Musketeers, until my boyfriend gets in the picture, and just forget about them and be all with him. . . . Before it was, I just pretty much went out with my friends all the time and then I would go out to a party with my boyfriend, but now it's like Friday night I go out with my friends and Saturday night I go out with my boyfriend. My friends expect things to be the same, but they're not.

Such conflicts may attack the very foundation of the original friendship, generating uncertainty over whether the person is still valued and cared for by his or her now-dating friend. Simply put, friends may feel displaced by the dating partner and that they can no longer rely on their former friend to "be there for me."

These types of strains emerge even when most members of the role set are involved in dating activities because friends may differ in the intensity and depth of their dating or love relationships, and the timing of such episodes may be such that some youth are dating regularly, whereas their friends are between boy- or girlfriends. Consequently, friends may also differ in the extent to which they are invested in the friendship group—in what they seek from group members and in what they are willing to give to other members. Alternately, the preferred activities of some friends may no longer appeal to others because these activities conflict with commitments to dating partners. For example, one 17-year-old girl with a steady boyfriend describes her frustration with friends who also date:

> It always seems like we always have to do what they want to do. . . . Like when we go out, sometimes we go visit the guys that they like, but that's no fun for me. . . . A lot of times we do things we all want to do. Like we'll all plan to go to the movies or something. . . . Lately, we've been doing things that I want to do, I guess.

The transition involving one social role—dating—may therefore evoke stressful circumstances in another role—friendships. The impact of such transitions is not confined to the individual making the transition. His or her role partners—both friends and girlfriends or boyfriends—may believe that insufficient time is spent with them and feel neglected, jealous, or possessive. In this manner, the development-related transitions of one adolescent become potential stressors for other adolescents. Interestingly, this tension at the boundary of the two types of roles is likely to have profound implications for the adolescent's peer support system, and it is the disruption of the friendship support system that might explain why early maturing youth—if dating is also initiated sooner—experience more psychological distress.

SCHOOL TRANSITIONS AND ROLE RESTRUCTURING

The restructuring of friendship groups that occurs during adolescence stems not only from dating role transitions but from other role transitions that occur as some members of the role set take on new interests and activities. School-related transitions, in particular, appear to produce substantial dislocation and readjustment in friendships, perhaps because school is a central physical, social, and psychological location of friendship activities. Indeed, when asked what they liked about school, the teens in this study commonly cited the opportunity to see friends.

Changing schools is an inevitable occurrence during adolescence and, like initiating dating, is typically considered a normative change event. The structure of school systems usually necessitates several school changes during these years: elementary to junior high or middle school, to senior high school, to vocational school, college, or the end of formal education. Almost without exception, the teens in this study who had recently experienced one of these transitions described the change as a difficult, troublesome, or stressful experience. A frequently mentioned difficulty encountered in changing schools was having to adapt to new teachers, frequently multiple new teachers. This change meant adapting to new expectations, usually for a greater amount of schoolwork that was evaluated more stringently than in lower grades. Students also reported being expected to do more of this work independently, on their own, with little direct instruction from teachers. Often the demands from different teachers piled up to create an overload of assignments. Thus, the normal progression through the school system proved to be demanding for many of the teens making these transitions.

Other adolescents expressed concern about anticipated school transitions that had not yet occurred. For example, one girl was afraid of entering junior high school because she had heard that students there were mean and used drugs. Older adolescents were concerned about finishing high school. Some feared they were not performing well enough to get into college, whereas others found the prospect of going to college intimidating and frightening. One 17-year-old girl says, for example:

> I wish I could put myself back a couple of years, so I didn't have to go to college. . . . I think I'm too scared about failing out my first year of college, or just being away from home. I guess I'm just scared that I'll hate college. . . . I guess college scares me.

At times, this uncertainty was expressed as a generalized anxiety about the sense of change. For example, a 15-year-old boy says, "I don't want to get old. I want to stay young forever, but you can't." A 16-year-old boy expresses a related sentiment: "Time is going too fast for me. Everything is starting to happen. When I was younger it was going slowly." Still other teens find school unfulfilling or irrelevant and eagerly anticipate leaving school, feeling trapped in a role they cannot give up at present.

Thus, anticipated transitions and discomfort in existing roles both serve to create stress for some adolescents. As we saw for dating role transitions, the periods leading up to and following these transitions may be as trying for the adolescent as the actual event itself, suggesting that the ability to anticipate normative changes brings with it stress as well as the ability to prepare for change. These transitions are best conceptualized, then, as a process of related occurrences extending over time.

As with dating transitions, school-related transitions also generate sets of secondary stressors, by setting in motion a series of dislocations in other social roles.

The most potent of these secondary stressors is the dissolution of existing friendship groups. In some instances, friends are left behind in the lower-grade school. In other instances, most of the friendship group moves intact to a new school, but the group does not survive intact in the new environment. Parenthetically, similar difficulties were mentioned by teens who changed schools either because they had moved or for other reasons, that is, when this transition was nonnormative. A 16-year-old boy describes the transition into high school:

> Yes, going into high school. It's totally different. When I went to junior high and elementary, I loved school. A lot of friends. But once you got to high school, everybody's doing their own thing. It's different, you know, that's the biggest hassle I can think, changing schools. It's a hassle, you know. All your friends split up. You don't see them. . . . I went to Jackson because I heard it was a better school so I had to sneak into Jackson just to get in there. So I snuck into Jackson and I knew some kids that I went to elementary school with, but they had changed. They weren't like they used to be and I used to have a lot of close friends in elementary, but when I got back there, they were changed. . . . They got into stuff that I didn't get into.

Changing schools, then, becomes stress-provoking when it alters existing friendships and necessitates establishing new friendships, and, as in the case with dating, the transition impacts the individual making the change, and those who are left behind, as it were, when these events occur to others in their friendship group. One 16-year-old boy expresses his sentiments about being left behind: "All of them graduated, they left. . . . I wanted to leave with them. . . . I still miss them." Adolescents who had changed schools almost invariably mentioned having to make new friends as a substantial readjustment that they had to make. Thus, we can see that the ease of making new friendships is an important dispositional characteristic that can moderate the stressfulness of these changes in the social environment. And, regarding social supports, the quality of relationships with parents and siblings may be highly significant to weathering these transitions that disrupt the peer network.

Although new friendships usually had been started, most of those whose social networks had undergone these types of changes continued to express a sense of loss. For example, one 17-year-old male makes the following statement months after his friends have left:

> In a way I did hang out with a group of friends, but they all went their own way. I have a good friend who went into the army. . . . My best friend. . . . I hardly see them now. I'm the only one. All my friends are gone from my school now. Jack up the street he goes to North High now and another friend dropped out. One gradu-

ated and moved away. . . . [School is] boring. . . . My friends are all gone. I have lots of friends but no one I really see out of school except for the girls. I spend most of my time talking to the girls. . . . I tried to make new friends or talk to people that I never really talked to that much. I kind of got the feeling that "Oh, now that your friends aren't around you're going to talk to me."

This adolescent finds his social life at school radically changed because the developmental role transitions of his friends have left him bereft of male friends. In the case of this youth, it appears that his best friends were older by at least a grade. Again, we see that his major sources of support are not in the same age cohort, and this lack of network homogeneity in making important transitions is a significant source of stress. This restructuring of friendships, however, also results from less dramatic shifts than changing schools. As members of the role-set advance in the school system or mature, their concerns may diverge from those of their friends, particularly friends in lower grades. A 17-year-old girl describes her sense of abandonment:

My friends . . . last year they were juniors and I was a sophomore and now that I'm a junior and they're seniors . . . they don't care anything about me anymore. Then I start turning to other people that I know and then they get mad at me because I'm not turning to them. . . . Well, I try to talk to them but they don't listen, so who needs them anymore, you know? Forget them. . . . When I have problems and turn to them they don't care. . . . I have one more year left of school and all my friends are like lower than me now, and I'm thinking of like how am I going to react to them when I'm in the senior year and they're younger than me. My senior friends influenced me not to be like that and stuff, so I hope I don't.

A 15-year-old expresses similar frustrations about the involvement of his friends with older teens:

Sometimes they can be flaky. Say it was like going somewhere after school. Then they meet with a group of their bigger friends, say 18 years old or something, and then they just forget about me.

In sum, some strains pertaining to friendships emanate directly from changes in the composition of the friend network. In some instances, these changes occur because a network member has moved or changed schools, events that impact on the person who leaves the network and those who remain behind. In other instances, the composition of the network changes because the interests and affections of its members change.

DISCUSSION

This chapter has examined some of the ways in which developmental change produces social stress, and in some cases, loss of peer support for adolescents. Although we have presented data on the implications of role transitions and lack of synchrony in these changes within friendship networks, we have also emphasized the importance of studying the linkages between development-related change events, other stressful features of the social environment, social supports, and intrapsychic coping resources. In particular, we have attempted to elucidate the linkages between development-related change events and the ongoing needs and difficulties in established social relationships.

One key dynamic of adolescent development is that social maturation generates social role transitions—entrances into and exits from social roles—that are experienced as stressful. In some instances, these transitions involve taking up an entirely new role, one that has not been occupied previously, such as dating or beginning to work. Role transitions, however, do not necessarily involve new roles and may instead involve movement into and out of specific role relationships, such as changing schools. In these instances, the adolescent continues to occupy a given role, but the role set changes, and he or she must adapt to the expectations, values, and behaviors of different role partners. As we saw for the case of progression through the school system, this process of readjustment can be stressful because previous ways of behaving may be no longer appropriate, acceptable, or adequate. Although these transitions are usually considered normative life-change events, the events themselves are but markers of a particular stage in a process, road signs signifying a specific juncture in a series of related occurrences. Interesting also is that although transitions can be understood as normative—experienced by all youth within a particular time frame—the variable timing and intensity of such changes in the original cohort can make a particular youth's experience nonnormative.

Development-related role transitions may be stress-provoking in and of themselves, but what is more important is that they may set in motion a chain-reaction of secondary stressors in areas of social functioning not directly involved with the primary stressor. Thus, transitions involving one role may alter the social transactions that occur within a different role or relationship. This was illustrated quite clearly for the impact of dating role transitions on established friendships. In this instance, the adoption of a new role frequently changed the adolescent's enactment of another role, typically curtailing the amount of time and energy invested in the friendship role and creating or exacerbating conflict with friends. Similar restructuring strains also emerged in adolescents' relationships with their parents. As Pearlin (1983) has argued, enduring discordant elements of social interaction within social roles are critical to the creation of stress because these roles are central to the organization and meaning of the individual's life and to the structure and functioning of the social system. These secondary stressors, therefore, may be more potent than the primary change event.

The patterns described here also illustrate a process of social contagion of stress, the transmission of stress from one individual to others, and from one domain of functioning to another (Bolger, DeLongis, Kessler, & Wethington, 1990). Teens making developmental changes in their social relationships become potential sources of stress to others in their social environment. In this manner, the developmental changes of some adolescents create problematic social conditions for other adolescents, particularly those who have not yet made these developmental changes themselves. Although we have limited our discussion to a consideration of same- and opposite-sex peers, these transitions also generate a set of changes in family roles as well. Processes of this nature help us to understand why it is that reports of one's own life-change events provide only a partial understanding of experienced stress, and why so-called "nonevents" can be as meaningful and stressful as the occurrence of undesirable events.

The development-related changes described here generate problematic social circumstances for adolescents in large part because the role set is no longer as homogeneous in values and behaviors; thus, expectations are easily violated. The character of the friendship itself is called into question, as reflected in the frequency with which themes of loyalty and betrayal were evidenced in the transcripts. As such, the stress-provoking nature of development-related role transitions is at least partially defined by the extent to which these transitions result in difficulties within established social relationships. Here we see that the instability of friendship networks during the adolescent years may be understood as a feature of role restructuring and maturation rather than reflecting unexplicable mood and interest fluctuation. When change results in a loss of support and when youth cannot rapidly renegotiate these or other ties, we might hypothesize that these conditions are antecedent to more severe problems of loneliness and isolation.

Finally, a question should be raised concerning group differences in the nature of these processes and their salience to the youth. Although we found the girls to provide more detailed descriptions of these events, both boys and girls described similar discontinuities with similar effects on their sense of support. Because the interview instrument assessed these issues in a relatively open-ended manner, beginning with some questions about "how things are going" and "what about problems," the data show that very low-income youth residing in the dangerous city neighborhoods were preoccupied with serious family-level stressors as well as with their own difficulties with the law. When asked about "good things that have happened," many such youth pointed to relative improvements in or nonoccurrence of bad things, thus illustrating the differential salience of developmental and nondevelopmental stressors in a diverse adolescent population. Thus, although we have focused our description on the nature and impact of developmental change from stress and role perspectives, alternative frameworks might consider how youth in high-risk environments negotiate these stressors and experience developmental change.

ACKNOWLEDGMENTS

This project was supported in part by BRSG 2 S07 RR05442 awarded by the Biomedical Research Support Grant Program, Division of Research Resources, National Institutes of Health, and by research grants 5 R01 MH40831 and R01 MH42909 from the National Institute of Mental Health.

Both authors express appreciation to the W. T. Grant Foundation for supporting this collaborative project. The authors would also like to thank the UCLA field staff and Virginia MacKay for preparing the manuscript for this chapter.

REFERENCES

Achenbach, T. M. (1982). *Developmental Psychopathology* (2nd ed.). New York: Wiley.
Albert, N., & Beck, A. T. (1975). Incidence of depression in early adolescence: A preliminary study. *Journal of Youth and Adolescence, 4*, 301–306.
Aneshensel, C. S., & Pearlin, L. I. (1987). Structural contexts of sex differences in stress. In R. C. Barnett, L. Biener, & G. K. Baruch (Eds.), *Gender and stress* (pp. 75–95). New York: Free Press.
Baumrind, D. (1987). A developmental perspective on adolescent risk taking in contemporary America. In C. E. Irwin (Ed.), *Adolescent social behavior and health* (pp. 93–125). San Francisco; Jossey-Bass.
Bolger, N. Delongis, A., Kessler, F., & Wethington, E. (1990). The microstructure of daily role-related stress in married couples. In J. Eckenrode and S. Gore (Eds.), *Stress between work and family* (pp. 95–115). New York: Plenum Press.
Brooks-Gunn, J., & Petersen, A. C. (1983). *Girls at puberty: Biological and psychosocial perspectives*. New York: Plenum Press.
Brooks-Gunn, J., & Warren, M. P. (1985). The effects of delayed menarche in different contexts: Dance and nondance students. *Journal of Youth and Adolescence, 14*, 285–300.
Burke, R. J., & Weir, T. (1978). Sex differences in adolescent life stress, social support, and well-being. *Journal of Psychology, 98*, 277–288.
Bush, D. M., & Simmons, R. (1987). Gender and coping with the entry into early adolescence. In R. Barnett, L. Beiner, & G. Baruch (Eds.), *Gender and stress* (pp. 185–217). New York: Free Press.

Compas, B. E., Wagner, B. M., Slavin, L. A., & Vannatta, K. (1986a). A prospective study of life events, social support, and psychological symptomatology during the transition from high school to college. *American Journal of Community Psychology, 14,* 241–257.

Compas, B. E., Slavin, L. A., Wagner, B. M., & Vannatta, K. (1986b). Relationships of life events and social support with psychological dysfunction among adolescents. *Journal of Youth and Adolescents, 15,* 205–211.

Coleman, J. C. (1978). Current contradictions in adolescent theory. *Journal of Youth and Adolescence, 7,* 1–11.

Erickson, E. (1968). *Identity: Youth and Crisis.* New York: Norton Press.

Freud, A. (1958). Adolescence. *Psychoanalytic study of the child, 13,* 255–278.

Gad, M. T., & Johnson, J. H. (1980). Correlates of adolescent life stress as related to race, SES, and levels of perceived social support. *Journal of Clinical Child Psychology, 9,* 13–16.

Greenberger, E., Steinberg, L., & Vaux A. (1982). Person-environment congruence as a predictor of adolescent health and behavioral problems. *American Journal of Community Psychology, 10,* 511–526.

Hall, G. S. (1904). *Adolescence* (Vol. I). New York: D. Appleton.

Hamburg, B. A. (1974). Early adolescence: A specific and stressful stage of the life cycle. In G. V. Coehlo, D. A. Hamburg, & J. E. Adams (Eds.), *Coping and Adaptation* (pp. 101–124). New York: Basic Books.

Huba, G. J., & Wingard, J. A., & Bentler, P. M. (1980) Applications of a theory of drug use to prevention programs. *Journal of Drug Education. 10,* 25–38.

Kandel, D. B., & Davies, M. (1982). Epidemiology of depressive mood in adolescents. *Archives of General Psychiatry, 39,* 1205–1212.

Kaplan, S. L., Hong, G. K., & Weinhold, C. (1984). Epidemiology of depressive symptomatology in adolescents. *Journal of American Academy of Child Psychiatry, 23,* 91–98.

Kessler, R. C. (1979). Stress, social status, and psychological distress. *Journal of Health and Social Behavior, 20,* 259–272.

Kessler, R. C., Price, R. H., & Wortman, C. B. (1985). Social factors in psychopathology: Stress, social support, and coping processes. *Annual Review of Psychology, 36,* 531–572.

Klerman, G. L., & Weissman M. M. (1989). Increasing rates of depression. *JAMA, 261*(15), 2229–2235.

Langner, T. S., Gersten, J. C., & Eisenberg, J. G. (1974). Approaches to measurement and definition in the epidemiology of behavior disorders: Ethnic background and child behavior. *International Journal of Health Services, 4,* 483–501.

Magnusson, D. (1982). Situational determinants of stress: An interactional perspective. In L. Goldberger & S. Breznitz (Eds.), *Handbook of stress: Theoretical and clinical aspects* (pp. 231–253). New York: Free Press.

Murphy, G. E., & Wetzel, R. D. (1980). Suicide risk by birth cohort in the U.S. *Archives of General Psychiatry, 37,* 519–523.

Neinstein, L. S. (1984). *Adolescent health care: A practical guide.* Baltimore: Urban & Schwarzenberg.

Pearlin, L. I., & Schooler, C. (1978). The structure of coping. *Journal of Health and Social Behavior, 19,* 2–21.

Pearlin, L. I. (1983). Role strains and personal stress. In H. B. Kaplan (Ed.), *Psychosocial stress: Trends in theory and research,* (pp. 3–32). New York: Academic Press.

Pearlin, L. (1989). The sociological study of stress. *Journal of Health and Social Behavior, 30* (3), 241–256.

Petersen, A. C., & Spiga, R. (1982). Adolescence and stress. In L. Goldberger & S. Breznitz (Eds.), *Handbook of stress: Theoretical and clinical aspects* (pp. 515–528). New York: Free Press.

Robins, L. (1983). Some methodological problems and research directions in the study of the effects of stress on children. In N. Garmezy & M. Rutter (Eds.), *Stress, coping, and development in children* (pp. 335–346). New York: McGraw-Hill.

Rutter, M. (1986). The developmental psychopathology of depression: Issues and perspectives. In M. Rutter, C. E. Izard, & P. B. Read (Eds.), *Depression in young people: Developmental and Clinical Perspectives* (pp. 3–30). New York: Guilford Press.

Schoenbach, V. J., Kaplan, B. H., Wagner, E. H., Grimson, R. C., & Miller, F. T. (1983). Prevalence of self-reported depressive symptoms in young adolescents. *American Journal of Public Health, 73*, 1281–1287.

Siegel, J. M., & Brown, J. D. (1988). A prospective study of stressful circumstances, illness symptoms, and depressed mood among adolescents. *Developmental Psychology, 24*, 715–721.

Simmons, R. G., & Blyth, D. (1987). *Moving into adolescence: The impact of pubertal change and school context.* Hawthorne, NY: Aldine de Gruyter.

Simmons, R. G. (1987). Social transition and adolescent development. In C. E. Irwin (Ed.), *Adolescent social behavior and health* (pp. 33–61). San Francisco: Jossey-Bass.

Smetana, J. (in press). Adolescents' and parents' reasoning about family conflict. In M. E. Colten & S. Gore (Eds.), *Adolescent stress: Causes and consequences.* Hawthorne, NY: Aldine de Gruyter.

Sommer, B. (1984). The troubled teen: Suicide, drug use, and running away. In S. Golub (Ed.), *Health care of the female adolescent* (pp. 117–141). New York: Haworth Press.

Teri, L. (1982). The use of the back depression inventory with adolescents. *Journal of Abnormal Child Psychology, 10*, 277–284.

Thoits, P. A. (1983). Dimensions of life events that influence psychological distress: An evaluation and synthesis of the literature. In H. B. Kaplan (Ed.), *Psychological Stress: Trends in theory and research* (pp. 33–103). New York: Academic Press.

Thoits, P. A. (1982). Problems in the study of social support. *Journal of Health and Social Behavior, 23*, 145–158.

United States Department of Health and Human Services. (1986). (Centers for Disease Control: Youth Suicide in the United States, 1970–1980). Washington, DC: U.S. Government Printing Office.

Vaux, A. (1981). *Adolescent life change, work stress and social support.* Unpublished doctoral dissertation, University of California, Irvine.

Wells, V. E., & Deykin, E. Y., & Klerman, G. L. (1985). Risk factors for depression in adolescence. *Psychiatric Developments, 3*, 83–108.

Wheaton, B. (1990). Where work and family roles meet. In J. Eckenrode & S. Gore (Eds.), *Stress between work and family.* New York: Plenum Press.

5

Age Differences in Workers' Efforts to Cope with Economic Distress

KAREN ROOK, DAVID DOOLEY, and RALPH CATALANO

The idea that people of different ages may cope with stressful life events quite differently is a recurring theme in the literature on stress and adaptation. Yet neither current theories nor existing empirical evidence offer a consistent picture of such life-course variations. Some theorists, for example, argue that coping efforts in old age are marked by regression to immature, ineffective defense mechanisms (Guttman, 1964, 1974; Pfeiffer, 1977). Others argue that, as a result of lifelong experience in adapting to stressful situations, older adults exhibit equanimity and maturity in their efforts to cope with stressful events (e.g., Denney, 1982; Vaillant, 1977). Moreover, as these two examples illustrate, work on life-course variations in coping is motivated by prescriptive as well as descriptive concerns. That is, investigators have attempted not only to document and describe age differences in coping styles but also to evaluate the maturity or adequacy of various coping styles, sometimes on the basis of clinical judgment or theoretical criteria rather than empirical evidence of effectiveness (e.g., Frydman, 1981; Haan, 1977; Vaillant,

KAREN ROOK and DAVID DOOLEY • Program in Social Ecology, University of California, Irvine, California 92717.   RALPH CATALANO • School of Public Health, University of California, Berkeley, California 94720.

The Social Context of Coping, edited by John Eckenrode. Plenum Press, New York, 1991.

1977). Work in this area accordingly reflects our conceptions of what constitutes healthy adaptation at different stages of the life cycle and may also influence our models of age-appropriate interventions for individuals who experience serious losses and disruptions (Folkman, Lazarus, Pimley, & Novacek, 1987).

In this chapter we seek to contribute to a small but growing literature on life-course variations in coping with stressful events. We begin by reviewing existing theory and empirical evidence on this topic. As our review will indicate, interpretation of empirical findings has been hampered by the fact that age differences may reflect either genuine developmental changes in the manner of adapting to stressful events or age-related differences in the kinds of events that people experience (Felton & Revenson, 1987; Folkman *et al.*, 1987; McCrae, 1982). Examining age differences in how people cope with the *same* stressor represents one way of reducing this ambiguity. Therefore, in the third section of the chapter, we present data from a study of age differences in coping with financial difficulties. We conclude by offering recommendations for further research and for social intervention.

THEORETICAL PERSPECTIVES ON LIFE COURSE VARIATIONS IN COPING SKILLS

Theorists have offered three rather different versions of how coping skills may change over the life course (cf. Folkman *et al.*, 1987). One version portrays coping skills as deteriorating in old age, marked by a return to the primitive defense mechanisms of childhood and adolescence. A second version portrays coping skills as improving across the life course or even peaking in old age, as a result of increased psychosocial maturity and accumulated experience in adapting to stress. A third version predicts that coping skills will remain relatively stable across the life course, consistent with a general tendency for core aspects of personality to become "institutionalized" in early life and to exhibit little change in ensuing decades. Each of these perspectives is discussed later.

Before turning to this discussion, we should note that most work has addressed how coping efforts in late life differ from coping efforts in young adulthood or middle age. Relatively little work has contrasted coping efforts in young adulthood versus middle age, perhaps reflecting a common tendency for researchers to ignore middle age as a distinctive period of life (Perlman, 1981). In addition, the following discussion emphasizes how people cope with specific stressful events and circumstances (cf. Cornelius & Caspi, 1987; Lazarus & Folkman, 1984), rather than how they deal with long-standing internal problems (e.g., low self-esteem or persistent guilt) or with existential challenges that may emerge in a particular life stage (e.g., the struggle between generativity and self-absorption in middle adulthood, or between ego integrity and despair in late adulthood; Erikson, 1963, 1980).

Decline in Coping Skills across the Life Course

Guttman (1964, 1974) is perhaps the main proponent of the view that as people grow old, they tend to regress toward more passive and primitive modes of coping, such as magical thinking. Guttman (1970) distinguished three kinds of "ego mastery style" on the basis of his work with the Thematic Apperception Test: active mastery, passive mastery, and magical mastery. The latter refers to a tendency to distort and deny real-life problems, merely wishing them away instead. Guttman (1970) argued that shifts from active to passive to magical mastery over the life course represent a nearly universal developmental pattern, particularly among men.

Although Pfeiffer (1977) did not advocate such universal shifts toward regressive coping across the life course, he echoed Guttman in suggesting that primitive defense mechanisms predominate in old age. These early defense mechanisms that reemerge in old age include, in Pfeiffer's (1977) view, withdrawal, avoidance, denial, projection, somatization, depression, and anxiety. Pfeiffer's conclusions were derived from clinical work rather than from empirical research, however, which may partly account for his pessimistic view of coping and adaptation in late life.

Some cognitive theorists have postulated an increase in rigidity in old age that could interfere with an older adult's ability to adapt to new situations and challenges. Rigidity has been investigated primarily in studies of intellectual functioning and refers to the tendency to adhere to previous response patterns in situations in which a change would be optimal (Schultz, Hoyer, & Kay, 1980). Sensory and motor decrements in late life may make some older adults doubt their abilities, encouraging cautious or rigid patterns of responding (e.g., Langer & Benevento, 1978; Okun, 1976). Premature cognitive commitment also has been hypothesized to contribute to rigid response styles (Chanowitz & Langer, 1981). This refers to a premature tendency to judge as irrelevant information that subsequently becomes relevant to important tasks. According to Chanowitz and Langer (1981), such premature closure occurs more often in late life because the elderly are encouraged to respond passively to existing environments rather than to participate actively in constructing their own environments (see also Langer, Rodin, Beck, Weinman, & Spitzer, 1979). Although most work on ridigity has focused on cognitive performance (memory, learning, and problem solving), this work represents another pessimistic perspective on older adults' coping skills to the extent that effective adaptation to life stress requires cognitive flexibility.

Improvement in Coping Skills across the Life Course

Other theorists espouse a decidedly more optimistic view of coping styles in late life. These theorists argue that, over many years of experiencing difficult challenges and losses, adults develop highly adaptive strategies for responding to stress and learn to eliminate ineffective strategies (Denney, 1982). Lifelong observation of others' efforts to cope with stressful events should also expand one's own repertoire of coping skills (Cornelius & Caspi, 1987). Thus, as compared with younger adults, middle-aged and older adults should exhibit greater confidence, maturity, and realism in their coping efforts. On the basis of longitudinal, clinical observations, Vaillant (1977) argued that immature coping responses (e.g., acting out, escapist fantasies, hypochondriasis) decrease from late adolescence through middle adulthood, and that mature responses (e.g., altruism, humor, sublimation) increase over the life course. Caspi and Elder (1986, p. 19) have described the Great Depression as representing for some individuals "a potential form of apprenticeship in learning to cope with the inevitable losses of old age."

Some ambiguity exists in these formulations regarding whether older adults would respond confidently and effectively only to stressful events that resemble events encountered earlier in life, or whether they would respond capably even to novel events (cf. Cornelius & Caspi, 1987). Caspi and Elder (1986, p. 25) did not emphasize the significance of similarity between previous and current stressors, but they did suggest that the "ability to cope with new situations and events is partly shaped by having had to cope with *similar* [emphasis added] events in the past." Yet many of the most stressful experiences of old age, such as widowhood and chronic disability, have little precedent in earlier life stages. The degree of similarity between the struggles of young or middle adulthood and those of old age becomes less important, however, if prior exposure to stress encourages the development of generalized resilience rather than event-specific adaptive responses.

Prior exposure to stress facilitates development of just this kind of generalized resilience, according to Eysenck (1983). He regarded prior exposure to stress as having an "inoculation effect," such that tolerance of subsequent stress increases. Eysenck derived his prediction of increased tolerance from animal studies in which prolonged exposure to experimentally induced stress has been shown to reduce reactivity to subsequent stress (e.g., Gray, 1975).

Implicit in many of these formulations is the idea that previous experiences of responding to stressful events contribute to psychological growth (Caspi & Elder, 1986), or to what some have termed *wisdom* in old age (cf., Denney, 1982; Osipow & Doty, 1985). This store of experience or accumulated wisdom presumably represents an internal resource that older adults can tap in their efforts to cope with late-life challenges and losses. Dohrenwend (1978) suggested in this regard that efforts to cope with life stress typically result in one of three outcomes: personal growth, restoration of the prestress status quo, or psychiatric disturbance. Developmental theorists who predict that older adults will exhibit superior coping skills as a result of lifelong experiences in coping with stress implicitly assume that older adults' previous coping efforts resulted in growth rather than the status quo or psychopathology. Obviously, this assumption applies only to some older adults; those whose earlier stressful experiences resulted in severe hardship or feelings of bitterness may not bring special resources to bear on the challenges of late life (Caspi & Elder, 1986).

Stable Coping Skills across the Life Course

Another perspective on life-course variations in coping styles suggests that the core aspects of personality solidify early in life and exhibit relatively little change thereafter (e.g., McRae & Costa, 1982; McCrae, Costa, & Arenberg, 1980). If effective coping requires adequate internal resources, such as self-esteem or openness (see discussions by Gore, 1985; Lazarus & Folkman, 1984; Menaghan, 1983), then coping styles should remain stable across the life course so long as these aspects of personality remain stable. In fact, Gore (1985, p. 271) argued that coping resources themselves are influenced by prior coping episodes and that "over time, these experiences become traitlike characteristics of personality." Stagner (1981) similarly suggested that specific coping tactics become integrated into generalized, traitlike patterns of responding to stressful events.

After reviewing the available empirical evidence, Lazarus and Folkman (1984) concluded that aging *per se* probably brings few changes in coping. In their view, if older adults do exhibit regressive patterns of coping, it is likely to reflect deteriorating physical and mental health or efforts to adapt to unfavorable environmental conditions.

EMPIRICAL WORK ON LIFE COURSE VARIATIONS IN COPING

A small body of empirical work has addressed life-course variations in coping. This work typically has been cross-sectional in nature, requiring researchers to infer developmental changes from comparisons of the coping responses of different age groups (Lazarus & DeLongis, 1983; Lazarus & Folkman, 1984). Several major longitudinal studies of personality, however, have examined the extent to which important personality traits and internal resources (e.g., self-esteem, assertiveness, openness) change or remain stable over the life cycle. In this section, we discuss studies that have found age differences in coping as well as those that have found few such differences.

Studies That Have Found Age Differences in Coping

In an early and influential study of coping, Pearlin and Schooler (1978) examined age as a correlate of coping styles in a representative sample of 2,300 urban residents (ages 18–65). The researchers found substantial age variation in coping responses but no consistent evidence of superior coping by either younger or older adults. For example, younger adults were more self-denigrating than older adults, but younger adults also were more likely to report a sense of control or mastery over their lives. In coping with marital problems, older adults tended more often to rely on their own resources (rather than seeking advice) and to respond with controlled reflection on their marital problems (rather than emotional discharge). These responses proved to be beneficial in limiting emotional distress (Pearlin & Schooler, 1978). But older adults also were more likely to report selective ignoring of their marital difficulties, which proved to be a counterproductive coping strategy (Pearlin & Schooler, 1978). Older adults and younger adults also responded somewhat differently to economic stress, with older adults making fewer optimistic projections about their financial prospects, engaging in less selective ignoring of their financial difficulties, and devaluing the significance of money to a greater extent. In general, however, older adults and younger adults employed coping strategies that seemed to be balanced with respect to overall effectiveness; neither age group enjoyed a clear advantage (Pearlin & Schooler, 1978).

Modest evidence of age differences in coping emerged in a study by McCrae (1982) of 255 community-residing adults, ages 24 to 91. Initial comparisons of three age groups (24 to 49, 50 to 64, and 65 to 91) revealed some differences in use of the 28 coping mechanisms investigated, although the results did not suggest a pattern of superior coping by a particular age group. McCrae (1982) recognized that coping responses could be influenced by the types of stress that people encounter at different points in the life cycle. To take this into account, McCrae examined how younger, middle-aged, and older respondents coped with stressors in each of three relatively homeogeneous categories. The analyses yielded no support for the view that older adults make greater use of primitive coping mechanisms and, indeed, revealed a greater tendency for younger adults to use such mechanisms. McCrae (1982) replicated these results in a different sample of 150 adults (ages 21 to 90). Specifically, younger persons were significantly more likely than middle-aged and older persons to report escapist fantasies and hostile reactions. In most other respects, however, members of the three age groups coped with stress in much the same way.

The coping strategies of 75 middle-aged couples (mean age of approximately 40 years) and 141 older adults (mean age of approximately 68 years) were contrasted in a study by Folkman *et al.* (1987). As compared with the older age group, the younger group reported greater use of active, interpersonal, problem-focused coping strategies (confrontive coping, seeking social support, planful problem solving). Older adults, in contrast, used more passive, emotion-focused methods of coping (distancing from the threat, acceptance of responsibility, and positive reappraisal of the situation). This pattern emerged both when a general measure of stressful events was used and when the events were grouped into homeogeneous clusters defined in several different ways (e.g., content, perceived changeability, degree of threat to self-esteem). The sole exception to this consistent pattern of results occurred in analyses of participants' efforts to cope with health threats; in response to these threats, older participants coped more actively than did younger participants.

Evidence that coping skills may improve with increasing age emerged from a study of 100 males and females (ages 10 to 77) by Labouvie-Vief, Hakim-Larson, and Hobart (1987). The authors developed a composite index of the maturity of participants' coping and defense strategies, as reported in response either to a recent stressful experience or to hypothetical conflict situations. The results revealed a curvilinear association between age and mature coping/defense strategies, such that maturity increased steadily with age and then eventually leveled off. Additional analyses substituted ego level, defined in terms of developmental complexity, for age as a predictor of coping maturity. These analyses revealed a positive linear association between ego level and coping maturity. Both patterns support the idea that coping strategies improve rather than deteriorate with increasing age and developmental maturity. Consistent with this, Cornelius and Caspi (1987) found in a sample of 126 adults (ages 20 to 78) that middle-aged and older participants performed at least as well, if not better, than younger participants on a test of practical problem solving.

Similar results were reported by Vaillant (1977) in one of the few longitudinal studies of coping. In a 30-year study of male college graduates, Vaillant (1977) abstracted from participants' case files vignettes reflecting their use of adaptive strategies in various life situations. Raters subsequently scored the psychological maturity of these adaptative strategies using criteria derived from ego-psychology formulations. The results suggested that aging was accompanied by increasingly mature adaptive processes. Specifically, the men exhibited fewer immature responses and a greater number of mature responses as they aged, although most subjects were middle-aged at the conclusion of the study, limiting generalizability to late life.

The studies described thus far focused on coping with stressors of everyday life. A few studies have examined age differences in coping with nonnormative stressors, such as serious illness. Among cancer patients, Cassileth, Zupkis, Sutton-Smith, and March (1980) found that younger patients sought more detailed medical information and advice and wanted more active involvement in their health care. Older patients recovering from colostomy surgery in another study (Keyes, Bisno, Richardson, & Marston, 1987) similarly used less active behavioral coping responses. For example, older patients were less likely to have made and followed a specific plan of action or to have talked to a professional. Their less active coping style did not make the older patients more prone to depression, however. Felton and Revenson (1987) similarly found that older participants (particularly those over age 75) were less likely to engage in information seeking in a study of 151 adults (ages 41 to 89) who were coping with one of four chronic illnesses (hypertension, diabetes, rheumatoid arthritis, or systemic blood cancer). In addition, older participants were less likely to report emotional expression and self-blame.

The finding that older adults used less active forms of coping in these studies of health threats contradicts the finding by Folkman *et al.* (1987) that older adults used more active coping strategies in response to health-related stressful events. It is unclear how to interpret these divergent findings, although the health problems examined in the study by Folkman *et al.* (1987) may have been less serious than those examined by the other researchers.

Studies That Have Not Found Age Differences

Several studies have failed to find age differences in coping patterns. In a study of 424 depressed adults (average age of 41 years),

Billings and Moos (1984) found that age was generally unrelated to the method of coping (appraisal-focused, problem-focused, or emotion-focused). The only association with age that emerged for both men and women was a modest association with emotional discharge, with younger adults tending to make somewhat greater use of this coping response. Folkman and Lazarus (1980) studied 100 adults (ages 45 to 64) and found no age differences in either problem-focused coping or emotion-focused coping.

The studies by Billings and Moos (1984) and by Folkman and Lazarus (1980) used samples with a fairly narrow age range, which may have limited the opportunity to identify changes in coping that occur late in life. Two studies by McCrae (1982) described earlier included a much broader age range, however, and similarly found only a few age differences in coping.

Research on the stability of personality over the life course offers insights about life-course variations in coping, despite the fact that this work has not focused explicitly on coping. Several large, longitudinal studies have found that key dimensions of personality (such as neuroticism, extraversion, and openness) tend to be quite stable over a period of many years (e.g., McCrae et al., 1980; Thomae, 1980). For example, the test–retest correlations of personality measures administered over a span of several decades have been found to be quite high, in some cases approaching the short-term retest reliabilities of the measures. This evidence led McCrae and Costa (1982, p. 296) to conclude that "the cardinal feature of personality in adulthood is the stability of a number of its major dimensions."

Summary

Considered as a group, the studies reviewed in this section offer little support for the idea that, with increasing age, people adapt to life stress by reverting to the primitive defense mechanisms of early life. Researchers who have attempted to evaluate the maturity of participants' coping responses generally have found greater rather than less maturity with increased age (e.g., Cornelius & Caspi, 1987; Labouvie-Vief et al., 1987; Vaillant, 1977). Some researchers have found few age differences (Billings & Moos, 1984; Folkman & Lazarus, 1980; McCrae, 1982) or have found age differences that do not clearly favor one age group over another (e.g., Pearlin & Schooler, 1978). Perhaps the most consistent difference is that older adults appear to engage in less vigorous forms of coping than younger adults (Cassileth et al., 1980; Felton & Revenson, 1987; Folkman et al., 1987; Keyes et al., 1987), although the specific stressful events to which this generalization applies remains unclear.

Thus, this body of research suggests the tentative conclusion that age exerts a modest effect on one's choice of coping strategies, but no one age group can be considered to employ consistently superior coping strategies.

Several limitations of previous studies warrant comment, however, as they point to the need for further investigation of the nature and consequences of life-course variations in coping. First, some studies have used a rather restricted age range, which may have masked age changes that occur after the age of 70 or 75. In addition, as mentioned earlier, most studies have been cross-sectional rather than longitudinal in nature, making it difficult to disentangle age differences from cohort effects (Lazarus & Folkman, 1984; Shenfeld, 1984–1985). Cross-sectional studies can be useful in generating hypotheses about the nature of age differences in coping, but supplementary longitudinal and historical data are needed to help sort out the roles of developmental and historical changes in shaping coping (Felton & Revenson, 1987; Folkman *et al.*, 1987; Lazarus & Folkman, 1984). Ambiguity surrounding the interpretation of age differences can also be reduced by studying efforts to cope with a particular stressor (Felton & Revenson, 1987; Keyes *et al.*, 1987). Finally, previous investigations of age differences in coping have not always controlled for the possible influence of age-related differences in socioeconomic status and health (Lohr, Essex, & Klein, 1988). Our study sought to respond to these latter two concerns—the need to consider age differences in coping in the context of a common stressor and the need to control for factors other than age *per se* that might influence coping.

AGE DIFFERENCES IN COPING WITH ECONOMIC DISTRESS: EVIDENCE FROM A METROPOLITAN SAMPLE

Our study focused on two basic questions: Do people of different age groups make use of different strategies in attempting to cope with economic distress? Does the effectiveness of specific coping strategies differ across age groups? Our analyses focused on the problem of economic distress for several reasons. First, economic difficulties are ubiquitous at all stages of the adult life cycle and have been linked to vulnerability to emotional disorders (see review by Dooley & Catalano, 1986). In addition, how people cope with financial difficulties has implications for other stressors they may experience, such as family conflict, loss of housing, and compromised health care (e.g., Catalano,

Dooley, & Rook, 1987; Kessler, House, & Turner, 1987; Pearlin, Lieberman, Menaghan, & Mullan, 1981). Finally, as noted, focusing on a common stressor reduces ambiguity in the interpretation of age differences.

The Sample

The data for this study (described more fully in Catalano & Dooley, 1983; Catalano, Rook, & Dooley, 1986; Dooley, Catalano, & Rook, 1988) were obtained through telephone interviews with adults (aged 18 years and over) sampled by random-digit dialing in the Los Angeles–Long Beach Metropolitan area (coterminous with Los Angeles County) from 1978 to 1982. In all, 16 fresh samples (minimum $N = 500$ per sample) were contacted at quarterly intervals, yielding a total of 8,376 respondents. Respondents were interviewed in either English (93%) or Spanish (7%). Up to 12 calls were made to reach and complete the interview: 4 to get an answer at the number, 4 more to reach a randomly chosen respondent from among the household's adult members, and 4 more to complete the interview if it was refused or terminated initially. These procedures resulted in a completion rate of 76%.

Panel data were also available for a subset of respondents from the primary sample who were recontacted after a 3-month interval. Approximately 40 respondents from each of the first 15 quarterly samples were reinterviewed (total reinterviewed = 604, 63% completion rate). The 40 reinterviewees from each survey wave consisted of 10 chosen randomly from four groups defined by the life events they reported in the first interview: high or low economic events by high or low noneconomic events.

Because many of the economic stressors that we investigated were related to changes in respondents' work situations (e.g., decline in wages or job layoff), we confined our analyses to reinterviewees who either were currently employed or were unemployed but considered themselves to be in the labor force (i.e., were actively seeking employment). A total of 388 reinterviewees met these criteria and were included in our primary analyses. Of this group, 44% were men, 53% were married, and 66% were of Anglo ethnicity.

We distinguished three age categories in our sample: younger workers (ages 18–34, $N = 195$), middle-aged workers (ages 35–59, $N = 158$), and older workers (age 60 and over, $N = 35$). Although the cutpoints used to define age categories ultimately are somewhat arbitrary, these cutpoints are consistent with those used in previous studies (e.g., Cornelius & Caspi, 1987). In addition, our selection criteria resulted in a rather small group of older workers, necessitating caution in generalizing from our age-group comparisons. Nevertheless, although the older subgroup is small, it has the advantage of having been drawn from a large probability sample of metropolitan residents who were interviewed at two time points.

Measures of Economic Distress, Coping, and Psychological Functioning

Economic Distress. Information about economic distress was obtained from responses to 10 questions that assessed the presence or absence of various sources of financial strain in the respondent's life. Respondents indicated which, if any, financial stressors they had experienced in the preceding 3 months. The specific financial stressors investigated were: difficulty paying bills, foreclosure of a home mortgage, repossession of personal property (e.g., a car or furniture), job demotion, reduction of wages/salary not related to a job demotion *per se,* financial loss not related to one's job, business loss or failure, being unemployed for more than 30 consecutive days, being laid off from a job, and being fired from a job.

Coping. Lazarus and Folkman and their colleagues (e.g., Folkman & Lazarus, 1980; Folkman, Lazarus, Dunkel-Schetter, DeLongis, & Gruen, 1986; Lazarus & Folkman, 1984) have distinguished two fundamentally different types of coping: problem-focused coping and emotion-focused coping. Problem-focused coping refers to active efforts to alter the stressful situation, such as seeking information and advice, constructing and implementing an appropriate plan of action, or developing new skills. Emotion-focused coping, in contrast, refers to attempts to manage one's emotional reactions to a stressor. Emotion-focused coping includes such strategies as reappraising the seriousness of the situation, trying to avoid thinking about the situation, and focusing on positive aspects of one's life. A similar distinction appears in the conceptual frameworks of other coping theorists (see reviews by Haan, 1977; Lazarus & Folkman, 1984; Menaghan, 1983; Pearlin & Aneshensel, 1986), and the usefulness of the distinction has been demonstrated in numerous empirical studies. We accordingly assessed both problem-focused and emotion-focused strategies of coping with financial difficulties.

We obtained our information about coping through the reinterviews of our panel sample. A total of 38 items in the reinterview focused on various ways that respondents might have attempted to cope with economic distress in the 3 months prior to the interview. Nineteen items asked about problem-focused coping, and these items were grouped into three categories that reflected efforts to (1) cut back on one's expenses or personal belongings (to generate a source of cash); (2) increase funds by borrowing money, refinancing loans, or dipping into personal savings; and (3) improve one's skills in order to obtain a better job. The specific items included in each category are summarized in Table 1.

Our approach to the assessment of emotion-focused coping was guided by the work of Pearlin and his colleagues (e.g., Pearlin et al., 1981; Pearlin & Schooler, 1978). Pearlin and Schooler (1978) distinguished several largely cognitive strategies for coping with stressful events, including economic stressors (see also Menaghan & Merves, 1984). These coping strategies included efforts to ignore selectively the stressful situation, to engage in favorable comparisons of one's current situation with one's past situations or with the situations of others (cf. downward social comparison; Wills, 1981), to devalue the importance of the threatened resources (such as money), to substitute alternative rewards for the threatened rewards, and to rely on sheer faith or optimism that the stressful situation will have a positive resolution. The necessarily time-limited nature of the telephone interview in our study precluded inclusion of items that represented the full range of cognitive coping responses identified by Pearlin and Schooler (1978). Nevertheless, the survey included a series of items adapted from their work that represented three kinds of emotion-focused coping: (1) engaging in positive comparisons with others or with one's past, (2) passively waiting for things to improve and selectively ignoring or minimizing the stressors, and (3) projecting a more optimistic future. The items included in each of the emotion-focused coping scales are given in Table 1.[1]

The six measures appeared to capture relatively independent dimensions of coping. Intercorrelations among the measures ranged from .01 to .31.

Finally, we wished to capture the overall intensity of respondents' coping efforts as well as the specific type of coping strategies they pursued. That is, even if the three age groups did not differ in the use of specific coping strategies, they might have differed in how vigorously they attempted to cope in general. To explore this possibility, we constructed a measure of *coping intensity* based on the number of times that the respondent's score on a specific coping measure fell above the median for the full sample. Thus scores on this measure could range from 0 to 6, with high scores indicating above-average use (relative to other workers in the sample) of multiple coping strategies.

[1]The 68-item Ways of Coping Scale (Folkman & Lazarus, 1980; Folkman et al., 1986) had not been published at the time that the survey began and would have been difficult to incorporate in the time-limited telephone interview.

Table 1. Items in Coping Variables

	Problem-focused coping		
Cutting back on expenses, personal belongings	Increasing funds	Improving one's status
Decided not to buy something that respondent or household members had planned to buy	Borrowed money from friends or relatives	Sought training to improve job status
Postponed nonemergency medical or dental treatment	Borrowed money from a financial institution	Sought an additional job to increase income
Cut back on customary purchases considered nonessential	Refinanced a mortgage	
Cut back on purchases considered necessary to respondent's health or well-being	Used credit cards or installment purchase plans more than usual	
Sold or pawned household or personal items	Drew from savings more heavily than usual	
Sought another residence to lower rent, mortgage, or real estate taxes		

	Emotion-focused coping	
Positive comparisons	Passive acceptance and selective focus	Optimistic projections
View one's current economic situation as better than earlier situation	Just sit back and wait for things to work out	Expect much better standard of living in the future
View one's work life as better now than earlier	Concentrate on more important things in life	Expect much better work life in the future
View one's family income as higher than others with comparable education	Pay little attention to money problems	
View one's family income as higher than one's friends	Tell oneself that jobs are unimportant	
View oneself as less adversely affected than others by price increases	Just wait for job difficulties to work themselves out	

Psychological Functioning. Because one goal of our study was to investigate whether the effectiveness of specific coping strategies varied across age groups, we needed a criterion by which we could gauge effectiveness. Although some researchers have approached this issue by asking respondents themselves to rate the efficacy of their coping efforts (e.g., McCubbin, 1979), we elected to evaluate the relationship between respondents' use of various coping strategies and their psychological functioning (cf. Felton & Revenson, 1984; Menaghan, 1982; Pearlin & Schooler, 1978). Symptoms of psychological distress were measured with a 25-item inventory adapted for telephone use from the PERI (Psychiatric Epidemiology Research Instrument) scales (Dohrenwend, Shrout, Egri, & Mendelsohn, 1980; Tanaka & Huba, 1984). Items asked, for example, how often respondents had experienced nervousness or shakiness, frightening thoughts, uncontrollable temper outbursts, and extreme restlessness.

One disadvantage of this symptom scale is that item recall extended up to 3 months. Although this recall period poses no problem in estimating a baseline level of disorder, it is not optimal for estimating recent changes in disorder. In the reinterview, therefore, the 20-item CES–D (Center for Epidemiologic Studies—Depression Scale) was utilized as the dependent variable because it is based on symptoms experienced during the past week (Radloff, 1977). Sample items asked respondents how often in the past week they had felt depressed or inadequate compared to others, had experienced crying spells, or had difficulty eating or sleeping.

We should note that we made no *a priori* assumptions that each of the coping strategies we investigated would be effective in the sense of reducing respondents' vulnerability to psychological distress. Some coping responses may have salutary effects, whereas others may have no effects or may even have adverse effects (Aldwin & Revenson, 1987). Indeed, researchers have found some types of emotion-focused coping to be associated with worse rather than better psychological functioning (e.g., Felton & Revenson, 1984; Folkman & Lazarus, 1980; Keyes *et al.*, 1987). We expected the effectiveness of the coping responses we studied to vary, and we recognized that this variation could encompass negative as well as positive effects.

Results

Age Differences in the Use of Specific Coping Strategies. Our initial analyses focused on the extent to which members of the three age groups used different kinds of strategies for coping with economic stress. To examine this issue, we conducted a multivariate analysis of covariance in which age group was the independent variable, and the six coping strategies (three problem-focused and three emotion-focused) were dependent variables. Several factors that might independently have influenced the respondent's choice of coping strategies were included as covariates, including the respondent's sex, ethnicity (Anglo versus non-Anglo), socioeconomic status, health status, and Time 1 level of psychological distress. Thus the influence of age *per se* was estimated after taking into account these other influences.

The analysis revealed an overall effect of age group on three coping strategies: cutting back on one's expenses and personal belongings, making optimistic projections about the future, and attempting to improve one's job status. Multivariate contrasts indicated that the younger workers were significantly more likely than middle-aged workers to have cut back on their expenses, to have attempted to improve their job status, and to have made optimistic projections about the future. Identical patterns were observed when younger workers and older workers were compared, although the difference in "cutting back" did not achieve statistical significance. Middle-aged and older workers differed significantly only with respect to efforts to improve their job status: The middle-aged were more likely to have adopted this strategy. Thus these analyses suggest that it is the young whose coping efforts are most distinctive; fewer differences emerged between the middle-aged and the oldest groups.

Age Differences in the Intensity of Coping Efforts. In addition to possible age differences in the use of specific coping strategies, we wished to examine the extent to which the age groups might have differed in the intensity of their coping efforts. An analysis of covariance (with sex, socioeconomic status, health status, and Time 1 level of psychological distress included as controls) revealed a significant effect of age group. Contrasts indicated that both the younger and middle-aged workers coped with greater intensity than did the older workers; the younger and middle-aged workers did not differ in coping intensity.

We also recognized that the group differences reported could reflect exposure to different economic stressors rather than age *per se.* That is, even though we sought to avoid some of the ambiguity in previous work on age differences in coping by focusing on only one kind of stressor—economic distress—the three age groups might nonetheless have differed in the specific kind of economic stressors experienced. Inspection of the stressors reported by respondents in each of the three age groups only partly supported this idea. Across age groups, the most common financial problems were difficulty paying bills, a decrease in wages, a financial loss not related to one's job, and being unemployed for more than 30 days (being laid off or fired *per se* occurred quite infrequently). These common stressors were distributed evenly among younger and middle-aged workers, as were the rarer stressors. Thus, at least with respect to comparisons of younger versus middle-aged workers, differences in coping do not appear to reflect exposure to different kinds of economic stressors. The older workers, in contrast, tended to experience fewer economic stressors overall and appeared less vulnerable even to the most common stressors (difficulty paying bills, etc.). Thus the less vigorous coping efforts of the older workers could reflect fewer or less difficult coping demands rather than age *per se*.

Age Differences in the Effectiveness of Specific Coping Strategies. Because of the ambiguity regarding interpretation of differences between the older workers and the other workers and because the group of older workers was relatively small, we confined our analyses of the effectiveness of specific coping strategies to the younger and middle-aged groups. To examine whether different coping responses affected mental health in the younger and middle-aged groups, we conducted a series of regression analyses within each of the two age groups. We conducted hierarchical regression analyses that included, in step 1, controls for the respondent's sex, ethnicity, socioeconomic status, health status, and Time 1 level of psychological distress. This allowed us to estimate the effects of respondents' coping strategies independent of their prior symptom levels. In step 2, we entered terms representing the main effects of financial stress and the coping strategies. In the third step, terms representing the interaction between financial stress and each of the coping strategies were entered.

The analyses involving the younger workers revealed significant main effects of two of the coping strategies—attempting to increase one's funds (e.g., by borrowing money or refinancing a loan) and passively waiting for the situation to improve. Respondents who reported using these coping strategies experienced higher levels of depression, controlling for Time 1 levels of psychological distress. Two interaction terms also were significant. Cutting back on one's expenditures in the context of financial strain was associated with less depression, whereas borrowing money and other attempts to increase one's funds in this context were associated with greater depression.

A different pattern emerged in the analyses involving the middle-aged workers. With respect to main effects, middle-aged workers who reported having made efforts to curtail expenses in recent months were more depressed. In contrast, middle-aged workers who had made efforts to improve their status (e.g., by obtaining job training) were less depressed. There were no main effects of borrowing or of passively waiting for things to improve, as there had been among the younger workers. Nor were any of the individual interaction terms significant.

Thus the coping strategies investigated in this study appeared to differ in adaptive significance for younger and middle-aged workers. Some of the coping strategies that benefited younger workers appeared to distress middle-aged workers. Some strategies that aided one age group had little effect, positive or negative, in the other age group.

Discussion of Findings

Considered together, our analyses of the choice and effectiveness of respondents' strategies for coping with economic strain revealed some notable age differences. First, younger workers had to resort more often than other age groups to cutting back on expenses or personal belongings as a means of weathering financial difficulties. This strategy appeared to serve younger workers well, in that it was associated with less depression. In contrast, the quite different financial tactic of taking on greater debt was associated with increased depression among younger workers. These patterns are not surprising if one assumes that a modest standard of living and a certain amount of belt tightening are common in young adulthood. Although having to postpone desired purchases or otherwise cut back on expenses may cause disappointment among younger workers, it does not appear to be psychologically devastating. Moreover, if having to curtail one's expenses is more common among younger workers than among middle-aged workers, as our data suggest, then unflattering comparisons with one's peers may be less common, perhaps sparing younger workers one source of threat to their self-esteem.

For middle-aged workers, in contrast, the emotional significance of having to curtail expenses appears to be quite different. Such curtailment may represent a retreat from a hard-won standard of living, prompting feelings of despair and perhaps, inadequacy. A sense of inadequacy (and concomitant depression) may be particularly likely to develop among middle-aged workers who do not witness their peers having to take such actions. Borrowing money did not appear to threaten the middle-aged workers as it did the younger workers, perhaps because the middle-aged workers have had greater experience in managing debt or have greater resources to muster (e.g., home equity) should a debt crisis emerge. What appeared to benefit middle-aged workers the most (and not solely in the context of financial strain) were efforts to improve their job status. Such efforts were more common among the younger workers but appeared to have greater psychological significance for the middle-aged workers.

Our finding of an inverse relationship between age and the intensity or vigor of coping efforts is consistent with previous research (Cassileth *et al.,* 1980; Felton & Revenson, 1987; Folkman *et al.,* 1987; Keyes *et al.,* 1987). The less vigorous efforts of the middle-aged and particularly the older workers need not be viewed perjoratively, however. As Folkman *et al.* (1987) noted, age differences in coping efforts may simply reflect the choice of coping styles that are appropriate to the unique challenges that each age group faces. Thus, the more active coping responses of the younger workers may have provided a good match with the numerous life demands they faced in attempting to build their careers, launch families, achieve financial security, and the like. Indeed, for younger workers, a passive coping style of simply waiting for the situation to improve was associated with greater depression.

Although our findings suggest a fairly coherent story regarding the way workers at different life stages attempt to cope with economic strain, our study suffered from several limitations that warrant comment. First, although we sought to reduce some of the ambiguity surrounding previous findings of age differences in coping by controlling for the kind of stressor experienced, a more fine-grained approach would have been beneficial. For example, financial strain that stems specifically from a jeopardized job situation may elicit quite different coping responses from younger, middle-aged, and older workers. Financial strain that does not stem from the job may elicit more similar coping responses. Our three age groups were too small to permit such disaggregation by type of economic stressor, but future studies might seek to include finer distinctions among economic stressors.

In addition, our measures of coping were not as extensive as measures that have been published since the start of the survey (e.g., the Ways of Coping Scale; Folkman & Lazarus, 1980, 1985; Folkman *et al.,* 1986). For example, our measures did not capture coping in the form of emotional expression (e.g., venting one's feelings, taking anger out on someone) or self-blame (internalization of responsibility for the situation). Further age differences might have emerged had we assessed a broader range of coping responses, although it is important to bear in mind that the length of some popular coping measures limits their use in telephone surveys.

Finally, our study was not designed in a way that would allow us to distinguish age differences that reflect cohort effects from those that reflect developmental changes (cf. Felton & Revenson, 1987; Folkman *et al.*, 1987). To detect cohort effects requires very long-term studies, coupled with collection of appropriate information regarding historical conditions and shifts in behavior patterns (e.g., Elder & Caspi, 1988). In their discussion of previous research on age differences in coping, Felton and Revenson (1987) noted that commonly observed age differences in information seeking and help seeking may reflect cohort factors, as evidence suggests that recent generations of Americans have become more receptive to interpersonal approaches to problem solving. Disentangling the respective roles of cohort factors and developmental changes in influencing coping patterns represents an important challenge for further research.

CONCLUSION

That age may influence the choice and effectiveness of responses for coping with economic distress should not surprise us. Such age effects may stem from many factors, including age differences in resources, social role demands, or time horizons. In attempting to cope with job and financial stressors, older adults may enjoy greater material assets (e.g., accrued pensions, home equity) and fewer obligations to dependents, coupled with shorter time to retirement. To unemployed individuals who are nearing retirement age, job improvement strategies such as retraining or relocation become less attractive psychologically and financially as the ratio of time in the new job to time spent retraining or in relocation shrinks. Recent research has found a curvilinear relationship between age and well-being among the unemployed, with less deterioration among those over 60 (and those under 20) compared to those between 20 and 59 (Warr, Jackson, & Banks, 1988). Of course, such age differences in emotional health do not necessarily reflect differences in coping style or coping effectiveness; they may reflect differences in the impact of stressors that overwhelm differences due to coping style or coping effectiveness.

Such research is complicated by the need to consider two potential conditioning variables: cohort and economic context. As indicated earlier, the cross-sectional design used in this study cannot distinguish developmental effects from cohort effects. Although research is sparse, we have reason to expect significant cohort effects in the realm of work and consumption attitudes. Elder's work on the children of the Great Depression has shown that growing up deprived can lead to lowered aspirations and that understaffed households can lead to undersocialization of young family members (Elder & Caspi, 1988).

As a more current example, we are witnessing a generational

change in expectations for living standards (e.g., differences in the prospects of home ownership between those over versus under 40). Erosion of a generation's belief that it will be better off than its parental generation can be expected to influence the choice of problem-focused coping responses (such as striving for better jobs) versus emotion-focused coping (such as focusing on parallel struggles experienced by one's peers).

In addition to cohort differences, the prevailing economic situation at the time of measurement must be considered. Our own research has indicated that the current state of the local economy affects well-being even after controlling for personal economic events such as job loss (Dooley, Catalano, & Rook, 1988). Consider a specific instance in which the larger economic climate modifies a particular experience of job loss. In cyclic industries, workers become accustomed to periodic layoffs and recalls. The decision to cope with a layoff by passively waiting for recall rather than more actively seeking retraining or relocation is, naturally, shaped by the past experience of such layoffs. Workers in relatively high-paying industries such as automobile manufacturing obviously would prefer to be recalled to their familiar and well-paid positions rather than start all over in an unfamiliar and, initially, less lucrative field. However, the economic situation of the 1980s contradicted earlier experiences. Car makers in this country lost a substantial share of the market to foreign manufacturers, permanently closed some older plants, and shifted some remaining jobs to other countries. Workers were forced to acquire new coping responses that would have seemed inappropriate in earlier decades: accept lower-paying jobs (e.g., in retail food services) and a permanently lowered standard of living, or greatly upgrade their skills in an effort to approximate their old salaries in new industries (e.g., computer industry). Such a situational change must appear rather different to workers of different ages, such as 22 versus 45 versus 64.

Research on age differences in coping would do well to focus on specific events, such as job loss or occupational stress. Such specificity should help to separate developmental effects from cohort effects and to evaluate the situational factors that may modify the meaning of events among different age groups.

Implications for Intervention

National and state unemployment policies have concentrated on job training and, most recently, early warning of plant closures (Hansen, 1988). Such policies necessarily fail to deal with the economic stressors felt by many people. For example, workers who lose jobs from small employers or for reasons other than plant closure are not guaranteed early warning under present law. For other workers, it is not job loss but continuation in a stressful job that causes distress, and an aggregate rise in unemployment only measures the extent of their frustration in seeking improved working conditions. Still others never enter the job market or are counted as nonparticipants in the labor force because they have become discouraged by their job prospects. A glance at a typical month's unemployment statistics identifies the most chronically underemployed group as minority youth.

The apparent failure of social policies to address the needs of such groups of workers implies a possible age bias in which governmental action is responsive largely to the economic needs of the most effective political constituencies (e.g., the highly organized elderly mobilizing around their social security benefits versus the politically disorganized inner-city unemployed youth). Without governmental programs, many unemployed or distressed workers will have to cope with their difficulties largely on their own.

The optimal coping responses of such individuals may be highly idiosyncratic to their age, their cohort, and the prevailing economic climate in their region of the country. Unfortunately, such individuals are likely to receive little in the way of assistance or only the most generic types of guidance. Research is needed on how to customize counseling for groups defined by specific combinations of stressor, age, cohort, and economic climate variables. Or, revising the question, research is needed on the potentially harmful effects of uncustomized, generic interventions.

As an example, suppose an elderly worker, without modern work skills, is laid off in a terminal plant closure. If the region is experiencing massive unemployment, the prospects that this individual will ever be recalled may be vanishingly small. In such a situation, active coping efforts that are appropriate for some younger workers (e.g., enrolling in classes to learn job interviewing skills and resume preparation) may only produce repeated humiliations for the displaced older worker and a measurable decline in psychological well-being. A few such individuals may adapt successfully on their own, but research has yet to identify how this adaptation may be optimized (Warr et al., 1988).

We largely lack intervention mechanisms that can be tailored suitably to the person's age, cohort, and economic prospects, and the daunting complexity of developing cost-effective interventions is apt to discourage many researchers and service providers. But such efforts to develop interventions assume great urgency at a time when deep recessions appear to be beyond political control and, indeed, when policymakers continue to talk of induced unemployment as an antidote to inflation (Johnston, 1989). Even modest accomplishments in the design of interventions would help to mitigate the human costs of economic stress.

ACKNOWLEDGMENTS

This research was supported by a grant (#MH 39463-02) from the National Institute of Mental Health. The authors appreciate the assistance of Randy DeWeerd in data management and analysis.

REFERENCES

Aldwin, C. M., & Revenson, T. A. (1987). Does coping help? A reexamination of the relation between coping and mental health. *Journal of Personality and Social Psychology, 53*(2), 337–348.

Billings, A. G., & Moos, R. H. (1984). Coping, stress, and social resources among adults with unipolar depression. *Journal of Personality and Social Psychology, 46,* 877–891.

Caspi, A., & Elder, G. H., Jr. (1986). Life satisfaction in old age: Linking social psychology and history. *Psychology and Aging, 1,* 18–26.

Cassileth, B. R., Zupkis, R. V., Sutton-Smith, K., & March, V. (1980). Information and participation preferences among cancer patients. *Annals of Internal Medicine, 92,* 832–836.

Catalano, R., & Dooley, D. (1983). The health effects of economic instability: A test of the economic stress hypothesis. *Journal of Health and Social Behavior, 24,* 46–60.

Catalano, R., Rook, K. S., & Dooley, D. (1986). Labor markets and help-seeking: A test of the employment security hypothesis. *Journal of Health and Social Behavior, 27,* 277–287.

Catalano, R., Dooley, D., & Rook, K. S. (1987). A test of reciprocal risk between undesirable economic and noneconomic life events. *American Journal of Community Psychology, 15,* 633–651.

Chanowitz, B., & Langer, E. J. (1981). Premature cognitive commitment. *Journal of Personality and Social Psychology, 41,* 1051–1063.

Cornelius, S., & Caspi, A. (1987). Everyday problem-solving in adulthood and old age. *Psychology and Aging, 2,* 144–153.

Costa, P. T., Jr., & McCrae, R. R. (1980). Still stable after all these years: Personality as a key to some issues in adulthood and old age. In P. B. Baltes & O. G. Brim, Jr. (Eds.), *Life-span development and behavior* (Vol. 3, pp. 65–102). New York: Academic Press.

Denney, N. W. (1982). Aging and cognitive changes. In B. B. Wolman (Ed.), *Handbook of developmental psychology* (pp. 807–827). Englewood Cliffs, NJ: Prentice-Hall.

Dohrenwend, B. S. (1978). Social stress and community psychology. *American Journal of Community Psychology, 6,* 1–14.

Dohrenwend, B. P., Shrout, P. E., Egri, G., Mendelsohn, F. (1980). Nonspecific psychological distress and other dimensions of psychopathology. *Archives of General Psychiatry, 37,* 1229–1236.

Dooley, D., & Catalano, R. (1986). Do economic variables generate psychological problems? Different methods, different answers. In A. J. McFadyen & H. W. MacFadyen (Eds.), *Economic psychology: Intersections in theory and application* (pp. 503–546). Amsterdam: North-Holland.

Dooley, D., Catalano, R., & Rook, K. S. (1988). Personal and aggregate unemployment and psychological symptoms. *Journal of Social Issues, 44*(94), 107–123.

Elder, G. J., Jr., & Caspi, A. (1988). Economic stress in lives: Developmental perspectives. *Journal of Social Issues, 44,* 25–45.

Erikson, E. H. (1963). *Childhood and society* (2nd ed.). New York: Norton.

Erikson, E. H. (1980). *Identity and the life cycle.* New York: Norton.

Eysenck, H. J. (1983). Stress, disease, and personality: The "inoculation" effect. In C. J. Cooper (Ed.), *Stress research* (pp. 121–146). New York: Wiley.

Felton, B. J., & Revenson, T. A. (1984). Coping with chronic illness: A study of illness controllability and the influence of coping strategies on psychological adjustment. *Journal of Consulting and Clinical Psychology, 52.* 343–353.

Felton, B. J., & Revenson, T. A. (1987). Age differences in coping with chronic illness. *Psychology and Aging, 2,* 164–170.

Folkman, S., & Lazarus, R. S. (1980). An analysis of coping in a middle-aged community sample. *Journal of Health and Social Behavior, 21,* 219–239.

Folkman, S., & Lazarus, R. S. (1985). If it changes it must be a process: Study of emotion and coping during three stages of a college examination. *Journal of Personality and Social Psychology, 48,* 150–170.

Folkman, S., Lazarus, R. S., Dunkel-Schetter, C., DeLongis, A., & Gruen, R. (1986). The dynamics of a stressful encounter: Cognitive appraisal, coping, and encounter outcomes. *Journal of Personality and Social Psychology, 50,* 992–1003.

Folkman, S., Lazarus, R. S., Pimley, S., & Novacek, J. (1987). Age differences in stress and coping process. *Psychology and Aging, 2,* 171–184.

Frydman, M. I. (1981). Social support, life events and psychiatric symptoms: A study of direct, conditional, and interaction effects. *Social Psychiatry, 16,* 69–78.

Gore, S. (1985). Social support and styles of coping with stress. In S. Cohen & L. Syme (Eds.), *Social support and health* (pp. 263–278). New York: Academic Press.

Gray, J. (1975). *Elements of a two process theory of learning.* London: Academic Press.

Gutmann, D. L. (1964). An exploration of ego configurations in middle and later life. In B. L. Neugarten & Associates (Eds.), *Personality in middle and later life* (pp. 114–148). New York: Atherton Press.

Gutmann, D. L. (1974). The country of old men: Cross-cultural studies in the psychology of later life. In R. A. LeVine (Ed.), *Culture and personality* (pp. 95–127). Chicago: Aldine.

Haan, N. (1977). *Coping and defending: Processes of self-environment organization.* New York: Academic Press.

Hansen, G. B. (1988). Layoffs, plant closings, and worker displacement in America: Serious problems that need a national solution. *Journal of Social Issues, 44,* 153–171.

Johnston, O. (1989, April 7). Inflation seen spreading to wages. *Los Angeles Times,* p. 2.

Kessler, R. C., House, J. S., & Turner, J. B. (1987). Unemployment and health in a community sample. *Journal of Health and Social Behavior, 28,* 51–59.

Keyes, K., Bisno, B., Richardson, J., & Marston, A. (1987). Age differences in coping, behavioral dysfunction and depression following colostomy surgery. *The Gerontologist, 27,* 182–184.

Labouvie-Vief, G., Hakim-Larson, J., & Hobart, C. J. (1987). Age, ego level, and the lifespan development of coping and defense processes. *Psychology and Aging, 2,* 286–293.

Langer, E. J., & Benevento, A. (1978). Self-induced dependence. *Journal of Personality and Social Psychology, 36,* 886–893.

Langer, E. J., Rodin, J., Beck, P., Weiman, C., & Spitzer, L. (1979). Environmental determinants of memory improvement in late adulthood. *Journal of Personality and Social Psychology, 37,* 2003–2013.

Lazarus, R. S., & DeLongis, A. (1983). Psychological stress and coping in aging. *American Psychologist, 38,* 245–254.

Lazarus, R. S., & Folkman, S. (1984). *Stress, appraisal, and coping.* New York: Springer.

Lohr, M. J., Essex, M. J., & Klein, M. H. (1988). The relationships of coping responses to physical health status and life satisfaction among older women. *Journal of Gerontology: Psychological Sciences, 43,* P54–60.

McCubbin, H. I. (1979). Integrating coping behavior in family stress theory. *Journal of Marriage and the Family, 41,* 237–244.

McCrae, R. R. (1982). Age differences in the use of coping mechanisms. *Journal of Gerontology, 37,* 454–460.

McCrae, R. R., & Costa, P. T., Jr. (1982). Aging, the life course, and models of personality. In T. M. Field, A. Huston, H. C. Quay, L. Troll, & G. E. Finley (Eds.), *Review of human development* (pp. 292–303). New York: Wiley.

McCrae, R. R., Costa, P. T., Jr. & Arenberg, D. (1980). Constancy of adult personality structure in males: Longitudinal, cross-sectional and times-of-measurement analyses. *Journal of Gerontology, 33* 877–883.

Menaghan, E. G. (1982). Measuring coping effectiveness: A panel analysis of marital problems and coping efforts. *Journal of Health and Social Behavior, 22,* 220–234.

Menaghan, E. G. (1983). Individual coping efforts: Moderators of the relationship between life stress and mental health outcomes. In H. B. Kaplan (Ed.), *Psychosocial trends in theory and research* (pp. 157–191). New York: Academic Press.

Mehaghan, E. G., & Merves, E. S. (1984). Coping with occupational problems: The limits of individual efforts. *Journal of Health and Social Behavior, 25,* 406–423.

Okun, M. A. (1976). Adult age and cautiousness in decision: A review of the literature. *Human Development, 19,* 220–233.

Osipow, S. H., & Doty, R. E. (1985). Occupational stress, strain, and coping across the life span. *Journal of Vocational Behavior, 27,* 98–108.

Pearlin, L. I., & Aneshensel, C. S. (1986). Coping and social supports: Their functions and applications. In L. H. Aiken & D. Mechanic (Eds.), *Applications of social science to clinical medicine and health policy* (pp. 417–437). New Brunswick, NJ: Rutgers University Press.

Pearlin, L. I., & Schooler, C. (1978). The structure of coping. *Journal of Health and Social Behavior, 19,* 2–21.

Pearlin, L. I., Lieberman, M. A. Menaghan, E. G., & Mullan, J. T. (1981). The stress process. *Journal of Health and Social Behavior, 22,* 337–356.

Perlman, H. H. (1981). Forward. In N. Golan (Ed.), *Passing through transitions* (p. xv–xvi). New York: Free Press.

Pfeiffer, E. (1977). Psychopathology and social pathology. In J. E. Birren & K. W. Schaie (Eds.), *Handbook of psychology and aging* (pp. 650–671). New York: Van Nostrand Reinhold.

Radloff, L. S. (1977). The CES-D Scale: A self-report depression scale for research in the general population. *Applied Psychological Measurement, 1,* 385–401.

Schultz, N. R., Hoyer, W. J., & Kay, D. B. (1980). Trait anxiety, spontaneous flexibility and intelligence in young and elderly adults. *Journal of Consulting and Clinical Psychology, 48,* 289–291.

Shenfeld, M. E. (1984–1985). The developmental course of defense mechanisms in later life. *International Journal of Aging and Human Development, 19,* 55–71.

Stagner, R. (1981). Stress, strain, coping, and defense. *Research on Aging, 3,* 3–32.

Tanaka, J. S., & Huba, G. J. (1984). Confirmatory hierarchical factor analyses of psychological distress measures. *Journal of Personality and Social Psychology, 467,* 621–635.

Thomae, H. (1980). Personality and adjustment to aging. In J. E. Birren & R. B. Sloane

(Eds.), *Handbook of mental health and aging* (pp. 285–309). Englewood Cliffs, NJ: Prentice-Hall.

Vaillant, G. E. (1977). *Adaptation to life.* Boston: Little, Brown & Co.

Warr, P., Jackson, P., & Banks, M. (1988). Unemployment and mental health: Some British studies. *Journal of Social Issues, 44,* 47–68.

Wills, T. A. (1981). Downward comparison principles in social psychology. *Psychological Bulletin, 90,* 245–271.

6

Gender Differences in Coping with Emotional Distress

PEGGY A. THOITS

The finding that women report and exhibit higher levels of psychological distress than men has puzzled stress researchers for years (Dohrenwend & Dohrenwend, 1976; Gove & Tudor, 1973; Kessler & McRae, 1981; Link & Dohrenwend, 1980). Three major explanations have been offered. The methodological artifact explanation suggests that women are socialized to be more expressive and therefore will admit more emotional symptoms than men in response to standard psychological distress scales (e.g., Newmann, 1984). The stress-exposure argument suggests that women face more stressors in general or more severe, persistent stressors than men (e.g., Gove, 1972; Kessler & McLeod, 1984; Aneshensel & Pearlin, 1987). The vulnerability argument suggests that women lack coping resources, such as high self-esteem, a sense of mastery, or appropriate coping strategies for handling the stressors to which they are exposed (Kessler & Essex, 1982; Pearlin & Schooler, 1978; Turner & Noh, 1983).

At present, the evidence for each explanation is mixed. For example, Newmann's (1984) analyses suggest that women overreport minor symptoms that inflate their overall distress scores, whereas in contrast, Gove and Geerken (1977) have demonstrated that women's responses to distress scales are not biased by response set or the perceived social

PEGGY A. THOITS • Department of Sociology, Vanderbilt University, Nashville, Tennessee 37235.

The Social Context of Coping, edited by John Eckenrode. Plenum Press, New York, 1991.

desirability of symptoms. Similarly, stress researchers have reported that women are exposed to significantly fewer, significantly greater, or equivalent numbers of negative life events and ongoing strains compared to men (Kessler, 1979; Kessler & McLeod, 1984; Pearlin & Johnson, 1977; Markush & Favero, 1974; Thoits, 1984b, 1987). And vulnerability researchers have demonstrated that coping resources (e.g., low self-esteem, low sense of mastery) either do or do not adequately account for women's higher emotional reactivity to stress exposure (Kessler & Essex, 1982; Thoits, 1984b, 1987; Turner & Noh, 1983).

In this chapter I take a more agnostic and exploratory stance toward these issues. I ask instead whether there are systematic differences in the ways women and men perceive the stressors to which they are exposed and systematic differences in the ways women and men cope with these stressors. My emphasis is especially on coping responses and their relationships to *perceived* dimensions of stressful events, because there are relatively few detailed explorations in the literature of gender differences in this domain.

GENDER DIFFERENCES IN COPING

Our cultural imagery portrays men as rational problem solvers and women as emotional, dependent, and helpless. Given this imagery, it is curious to note that relatively few investigators have examined gender differences in coping responses, even when large numbers of both sexes are included in a study sample (e.g., Billings *et al.*, 1983; Caplan *et al.*, 1984; Folkman & Lazarus, 1985, 1986; Folkman *et al.*, 1986; Holahan & Moos, 1987; Miller & Kirsch, 1987). However, in some studies, stereotypical notions find support when questions about coping responses are not tied to specific stressful experiences. For example, Veroff *et al.* (1981) asked a large national sample of adult respondents how they handled worries and periods of unhappiness. Men were significantly more likely than women to report doing nothing or not thinking about it, but men also were more likely to cite problem-solving efforts. Women, on the other hand, were more likely to seek help from others or to turn to prayer as ways of coping with worries or unhappiness. Similarly, aggregating over 2,368 reported daily problems, Stone and Neale (1984) found that men were often reported taking direct action, whereas women endorsed more passive strategies, such as distraction, catharsis, tension release, and prayer. However, women were more likely to seek social support, which can be considered an active strategy. Folkman and her colleagues (1987) studied two samples of adults stratified by age and life-cycle stage: 35- to 45-year-olds with a child living at home and 65- to 74-year-olds who had retired. To cope with hassles, men in both age groups reported using emotional self-control and planful problem solving. Women were more likely to seek social support and engage in positive reappraisal to cope with hassles.

When questions are asked about coping with specific difficulties, however, a more complex picture emerges. Gender differences are relatively infrequent, yet when they occur, they emerge *within* specific problem contexts. For example, Folkman and Lazarus (1980) found no gender differences in the use of *emotion*-focused coping responses for work, health, and family problems. But in this and other studies, men were more likely to use more *problem*-focused coping strategies than women in response to work problems (Folkman & Lazarus, 1980; Pearlin & Schooler, 1978), whereas women were more likely to use problem-solving strategies (e.g., negotiation) within marriage and parenting contexts (Menaghan, 1982; Pearlin & Schooler, 1978). Further, women were more likely than men to cognitively reinterpret the situation[1] when facing marital, parental, and work problems (Fleishman, 1984; Menaghan, 1982). Women also were more likely than men to seek advice or support when facing marital and parental difficulties (Fleishman, 1984).

There is a hint in these disparate findings that problem-solving efforts are more likely to be used when individuals perceive that they have more control, power, or responsibility in a particular role domain (e.g., men in the occupational arena, women in the family arena). Conversely, when individuals perceive uncontrollability, they are more likely to use strategies to alter the meaning of the situation or change their emotional states. Folkman (1984) recently has argued this pattern explicitly: Objectively controllable stressors, when appraised as controllable, should more often result in problem-focused coping efforts; objectively uncontrollable stressors, when appraised as uncontrollable, should more often result in emotion-focused coping efforts (which include cognitive reinterpretations of situational meaning). Mismatches between the objective nature and subjective appraisal of a stressor should result in inappropriate (and thus less effective) coping attempts. Folkman has reviewed the results of several studies that are consistent with this reasoning. However, Stone and Neale (1984) and Thoits (1991) found no relationship between the perceived controllability of a stressor and the likelihood of taking direct action to cope with it. This may have been due to the differential tendency of men (also observed by Folkman &

---

[1]Example items: Looking on the bright side, telling yourself that it is not really important, comparing to others who are worse off.

Lazarus, 1980 and Folkman *et al.*, 1987) to engage in problem-solving even when a situation is appraised as one that has to be accepted or that is unchangeable. Obviously, further explorations of gender differences in perceptions and coping strategies are needed.

This study examines the perceived qualities of the stressors faced by young women and men and the relationship of those perceptions to their choice of coping strategies. Although the objective nature of the stressors they face cannot be assessed with these data, the relative frequency with which women and men perceive controllability and the differential use of problem solving versus other coping strategies can be explored.

Because it is well established that men have a stronger internal locus of control orientation, or sense of personal control, than women (Lefcourt, 1981; Pearlin & Schooler, 1978; Wheaton, 1980), I expected this tendency to be reflected in respondents' perceptions of controllability and causal responsibility for events. Specifically, I expected to find that, compared to men, women are more likely to perceive events as uncontrollable and thus to choose other than problem-solving responses to events. These choices, in turn, should be related to the perceived satisfactory or unsatisfactory outcome of the event, with women less likely to perceive satisfactory outcomes.

The model of coping that undergirds this exploration borrows from previous work by Lazarus and his colleagues (e.g., Lazarus & Folkman, 1984) and Pearlin and Schooler (1978) but is elaborated further by my own work on the nature of emotion (Thoits, 1984a). Following Lazarus, the model assumes that individuals must cope with two sources of difficulty when facing an environmental demand—somehow solving or adjusting to the demand itself and regulating the emotional distress engendered by the threat to well-being that it represents (Lazarus & Folkman, 1984). In Lazarus and Folkman's terms, both "problem-focused" and "emotion-focused" coping are usually required (see Folkman & Lazarus, 1980, for relevant evidence). Following Lazarus and Folkman (1984) and Pearlin and Schooler (1978), I further assume that there are two basic modes of changing the problem or the emotional reaction: behavioral and cognitive. Behavioral responses consist of actions taken to confront or avoid a stressful situation or to alter directly an undesired emotional state. Cognitive responses consist of efforts to change the *meaning* of the situation or the *meaning* of the emotional reaction. Thus, a fourfold table of coping responses is implied: Situations can be altered behaviorally or cognitively, and emotional reactions can be altered behaviorally or cognitively (or, of course, several or all of these responses might be used).

However, the literature on emotion indicates that emotions themselves are complex, consisting of a number of associated components.

These include, in addition to situational antecedents, physiological changes, expressive gestures, and the cultural labels used to identify emotional states (Thoits, 1984a). Because each of these latter components is amenable to both behavioral and cognitive manipulation for the purpose of changing feelings, a more complicated model of coping responses is implied (see Figure 1). Thus, I argue that there are seven distinguishable types of coping responses (seven because it is not possible to behaviorally alter an emotional label)—behavioral or cognitive manipulations of the problematic situation and/or *components* of the problematic emotional reaction. Specific examples of techniques that might be used in each category are indicated in Figure 1.

This model includes virtually all of the coping techniques that have been identified by previous researchers. For example, Pearlin and Schooler (1978) identify three basic strategies: changing the situation, managing the emotional distress, and reinterpreting the meaning of the situation. Stone and Neale (1984) identify eight modes of coping—direct action, seeking social support, situation reinterpretation, distraction, acceptance, tension release, catharsis, and prayer. Factor analyses of the Ways of Coping Checklist developed by Lazarus and his colleagues (Aldwin *et al.*, 1980; Folkman *et al.*, 1987; Vitaliano *et al.*, 1985) have revealed five to eight coping factors, depending on the analytic strategy that is employed. These include confrontive coping, planful problem solving,

Target	Mode	
	Behavioral	Cognitive

Situation-focused strategies	Act, confront
	Seek information,
	   advice, practical aid
	Withdraw, leave
		Reinterpret situation
		Distraction
		Thought stopping
		Accept the situation
		Fantasize solution or
		   escape

Emotion-focused strategies		
(A) Physiology	Hard exercise Use drugs/alcohol Relaxation techniques	Biofeedback Meditation Progressive desensitization Hypnosis
(B) Expressive gestures	Catharsis Hide feelings	Fantasy release Prayer
(C) Emotional label	(N.A.)	Reinterpret feelings

Figure 1.   More complex model of coping.

support seeking, positive reappraisal, distancing, accepting responsibility, self-control, and escape/avoidance. Thus, my exploratory model is compatible with previous inductive and empirical work on coping responses.

METHODS

Procedures

Two hundred undergraduates at Indiana University were asked to write (for introductory psychology course credit) detailed descriptions of two emotional experiences that were important to them, one negative emotional experience and one positive. (The protocols were counterbalanced; half asked for the positive experience first, half for the negative experience first.) Within each situation, respondents were asked to describe how they handled the situation, how they handled their feelings, and how the situation turned out. These descriptions were coded independently for content by two research assistants and myself. The protocol included a number of closed-ended questions about those experiences as well, including probes for perceived expectedness, preventability, controllability, responsibility for causing, and responsibility for solving the situation. Respondents also indicated on a subsequent closed-ended checklist of 19 coping items (derived from the coping model already discussed) whether they *usually* try each strategy when handling a stressful situation, and if so, how well that strategy usually works for them. Respondents' sociodemographic characteristics were the final items assessed in the protocol. For the purpose of this chapter, only the content of the negative-experience descriptions are analyzed.

The Sample

Out of 200 protocols, only one, containing obviously facetious responses, was unusable, resulting in a sample N of 199. The sample consisted of 106 women (53.3%) and 93 men (46.7%). The mean age was 19; freshmen or sophomores comprised 91% of the sample. Ninety-two percent were white, reflecting the predominantly white racial composition of this midwestern university. Ninety-seven percent had never been married; 1.5% were married, and 1.5% were divorced. Protestants were in the majority (48%); Catholics composed 29.6% of the sample; Jews, 8.7%; other religions, 3.6%, and 10.2% claimed no religious affiliation. Respondents' fathers had completed college, on average; their mothers had some years of college education, on average. In short, this was a predominantly white, Protestant, middle-class sample of unmarried college students.

Coding Procedures

A preliminary content-coding scheme was devised based on recurrent themes in the first 50 protocols; then existing codes were refined or new codes were added as other categories emerged during the coding process. Each protocol was coded independently for content by two out of the three raters. For each batch of 10 protocols, disagreements between coders were discussed and resolved prior to the next round of coding. Before resolutions were made, interrater agreements were at or above 79.9% on all variables, with the exception of "how the situation turned out," which had an interrater agreement of 67% prior to resolution.

Negative Events

Respondents' situational descriptions were first coded into three categories: the situation described an event, an ongoing strain, or both. A situation was categorized as an event if it represented the onset of a major change in the individual's life circumstances (e.g., parents announce that they will seek a divorce, a sibling is diagnosed as having cancer, a lover decides to end their relationship). A situation was categorized as an ongoing strain if no change onset was described and if the difficulty had persisted for longer than 1 week (e.g., continuous conflicts with a parent, continuous conflicts with a roommate, continued illness of a loved one). If a situation included both an event and an ongoing strain (e.g., the respondent had repeated fights with his/her lover and eventually decided to end the relationship), then it was coded as a strain plus an event. The majority of descriptions referred to an event (72.9%); 22.6% included both an event and a strain, whereas 4.5% described only an ongoing strain. The analyses described will exclude respondents ($N = 9$) who described only an ongoing strain.

Situations then were coded for the specific events that were described. Fifty event categories were used (see Appendix 1 for a list of all described events). Many situational descriptions referred to more than one discrete event;[2] up to four events were coded per situation described. The mean number of discrete events coded for the sample as a

[2]Multiple events were described because many key or focal events had antecedents or consequences. For example, discovering a lover's infidelity frequently was followed by a major quarrel, which in turn resulted in the relationship being ended.

whole was 1.6. Analyses here are based on the initial or key event in each description—that which caused subsequent events to occur (for example, being raped is an initial event, which might be followed by pregnancy and then an abortion).

The number of lines written to describe each emotional experience also was counted as a rough indicator of the expressivity (or motivation or verbal skills) of each respondent. Respondents wrote a mean of 26 lines (range from 3 to 99) to describe their negative experience. As expected, the order in which these descriptions were requested affected the number of lines written; respondents wrote a mean of 29 lines if they described their negative experience first and a mean of 22 lines if second ($p = .001$). Because respondents worked steadily on the protocol for an hour to an hour and a half, these order effects likely reflect fatigue.

Women wrote significantly more lines than men for each requested experience. For the negative experience, females wrote a mean of 30.3 lines, whereas males wrote a mean of 20.7 ($p < .001$). This gender difference held regardless of the order in which the negative and positive emotional experiences were requested. Although gender differences in expressivity (or motivation or verbal skills) may have biased our coding of respondents' negative event experiences, there were no significant gender differences in the mean numbers of discrete events or strains that were coded. Differences in expressivity (or motivation or verbal skills) also might affect the number of coping strategies that were spontaneously mentioned by respondents. Because preliminary analyses revealed significant sex differences in the number of coping strategies reported, the number of lines written by each respondent (and order effects) are controlled in each equation reported.

Respondents were asked "how long ago" the negative situation they described had happened. Described situations occurred an average of 1.7 years ago. There were no significant gender differences in time since the situation had occurred, nor was there an association between "time ago" and the number of lines written by the respondent to describe the situation.

Obviously, given the characteristics of the sample, the negative emotional experiences described by these respondents will be restricted in range. In particular, negative reactions due to financial difficulties are rare in the protocols, as, of course, are descriptions of marital, parental, or occupational difficulties. On the other hand, and unexpectedly, academic difficulties do not predominate in their protocols (only five respondents described reactions to academic problems). Rather, 15% of all described events were what Kessler and McLeod (1984) have called "network events"—that is, reactions to problems experienced by loved ones such as family members and friends (see Appendix 1). The other 85% were what can be termed "personal events"—that is, reactions to their own problems. The bulk of these personal events were interpersonal problems—events experienced in relationships with other people—family members, friends, and especially lovers (see Appendix 1). There were no significant gender differences in the frequency of these subgroups of events, with one exception: Women more frequently described the death of a family member or friend.

It will be important to bear in mind that the stressful experiences described by these respondents are not representative of all possible stressors. However, for the purpose of exploring the theoretical relationships between perceived controllability and coping, and between coping and outcomes, these data are still useful.

Described events ranged in severity. Some were highly traumatic—such as witnessing a close friend's fatal accident, finding the body of a parent who had committed suicide, and having been raped. Others were major events—such as the death of a close relative, family member seriously ill, or parents' divorce. Others were moderately stressful events—such as having been arrested or caught in the act of wrongdoing, having a love relationship end, and having been expelled from a team or fraternity house. Still others were relatively minor and common events—such as leaving home to come to college, experiencing a temporary separation from a lover, and having an argument with a family member or friend. (Relatively minor events that were infrequently described [e.g., being the subject of gossip, losing a game to an opposing team, moving residence] fell into the "other problem" category.) Because all respondents were asked to write about a negative experience that was important to them, the perceived stressfulness of that experience was not directly assessed in the protocol. Given the range of experiences described, it would be useful to have some indicator of perceived event severity. For example, more stressful events might have affected the number and types of coping strategies that respondents reported (presuming that more severe events require more, and more varied, coping efforts). To examine this possible bias, some analyses control for the key event experienced by each respondent.[3]

---

[3]Students' events were compared with those on the PERI life events checklist (Dohrenwend, Krasnoff, Askenasy, & Dohrenwend, 1978) and the Social Readjustment Rating Scale (Holmes & Rahe, 1967). There was very little overlap between students' events and those on the PERI or SRRS checklists, so the normative readjustment scores developed in these previous life-events studies could not be used as indicators of event severity here.

Perceptions of Events

Closed-ended items probed for respondents' perceptions of the situations they had described. Possible responses to these questions were "no," "to some extent," and "yes." Anticipation was assessed with the following question: "At the time, did you *anticipate or expect* that the situation would happen?" (emphasis in the original). Preventability was assessed if the respondent answered "to some extent" or "yes" on anticipation: "Did you believe that you could have *prevented* the situation from happening?" Controllability was assessed with this phrasing: "At the time, did the situation seem like one that you could *control*—that is, did you think you could change the situation for the better?" Causal responsibility was indicated with "Did you believe that you were *responsible* for the event happening?" And finally, to indicate responsibility for problem solving: "Did you believe that you were responsible for *solving* the situation?"

Coping Strategies

Respondents were asked how they handled the situation that they had described and in a second question, how they handled their feelings. The open-ended responses to both questions were content-coded first into 37 distinguishable coping strategies. Up to 7 strategies were coded for each respondent. These then were collapsed into 18 subtypes of coping, based on the coping model outlined in the introduction (see Figure 1 and Appendix 2). To these were added three "miscellaneous" strategies; these types of coping emerged from the content coding and could not be reliably classified as to their target and mode (see Appendix 2).

A reader might wonder why the 37 initial coded strategies were not grouped into the broader 18 categories shown in Appendix 2 on the basis of a factor analysis of the items. Exploratory work indicated that a coping typology could not be derived from factor analysis for several reasons. First, coping strategies are complexly interrelated. Some strategies are used in conjunction with others; some are used to the exclusion of others; and some regularly follow others in chronological sequence. Consequently, no clear typology emerges, even from an oblique rotation that allows for correlations among coping factors.

Second, several strategies within a theoretical category often do not "hang together" because individuals select only one of those strategies to achieve the same implicit function. For example, talking to family, to friends, or to authority figures are alternative ways of seeking social support, at least theoretically. Yet these strategies do not correlate highly because individuals tended to report using one support source in preference to others.

Third, a single strategy can serve several latent functions simultaneously or can serve different latent functions for different people. For example, going for a drive correlated with spending time alone, thinking through a situation, leaving a situation permanently (i.e., a decision was apparently made during the drive), trying not to think about the situation, engaging in strenuous exercise, and using drugs or alcohol! In other words, going for a drive can help a person make decisions, can distract the person from the problem, or can exhaust or deaden feelings. For some, driving may serve all of these functions; for others, driving may serve one function and not others.

For these several reasons, no further attempt was made to construct coping factors empirically. Instead, strategies were grouped on theoretical grounds, and these groupings were modified only slightly on the basis of an inspection of their intercorrelations. No attempt was made to classify strategies on the basis of the underlying functions they served (e.g., problem solving, escape/avoidance) because explicit probes for the perceived functions of each strategy were not asked (see Stone & Neale, 1984). Strategies were grouped only on the basis of their mode of action (behavioral or cognitive) and the apparent target of those actions (the situation, components of feelings).

Outcomes

Respondents were asked in the protocols to report how the negative situation that they described had turned out. Two dimensions emerged from the content coding of their replies: The valence of the outcome was positive, negative, or had mixed positive and negative aspects, and the effects of the situation had ended or were continuing. Outcome valence was coded ordinally: 1 if negative, 2 if mixed negative and positive, and 3 if positive. Whether the effects of the event had ended or were continuing was indicated by a dummy variable, 1 if ended, 0 if continuing.[4]

[4]The effects of a situation were coded as ended if the respondent indicated that the experience was over, or behind him/her. A situation was coded as having continuing, persistent effects if the respondent said that he/she still thinks or worries about it, or that the described event had further positive and/or negative consequences (e.g., "now my mother has remarried and although I don't like my new step-father, I'm pleased for my mother"). If the respondent said he/she had become resigned or had accepted the situation, this was coded as "situational effects ended, with mixed positive and negative aspects." Some respondents' replies were too ambiguous or vague to code, and these were treated as missing.

RESULTS

Gender Differences in Coping Strategies

Table 1 reports the frequency with which respondents used each type of coping, arrayed in order of frequency.

The five most frequent types of coping were letting out feelings (catharsis), taking direct action, hiding feelings, reinterpreting the situation, and seeking social support. Note that the top 10 types of coping used by these respondents come exclusively from three cells in Figure 1: behavioral situation-focused, cognitive situation-focused, and behavioral expression-focused strategies.

Table 1. Strategies Used to Cope with Negative Events (Percent of Sample Mentioning Strategy)

Strategy	Total sample (N=188)	Women (N=100)	Men (N=88)	F–M differences (CHI-SQ)
Catharsis	64.4	76.0*	51.1	.001
Direct action	39.9	36.0	44.3	ns
Hide feelings	38.8	42.0	35.2	ns
See it differently	38.3	44.0*	31.8	.08
Seek support	34.0	43.0*	23.9	.01
Leave the situation	20.7	22.0	19.3	ns
Think it through	15.4	10.0	21.6*	.03
Thought stopping	13.8	11.0	17.1	ns
Distraction	7.5	8.0	6.8	ns
Accept it	7.5	4.0	11.4*	.06
Exercise	5.9	2.0	10.2*	.02
Prayer	5.9	7.0	4.6	ns
Use drugs/alcohol	4.8	5.0	4.5	ns
Fantasy expression	4.3	3.0	5.7	ns
Fantasy solution	4.3	5.0	3.4	ns
Wait	4.3	5.0	3.4	ns
Write about it	4.3	8.0*	0.0	.01
Other physiological	3.2	2.0	4.6	ns
Desensitization	1.1	1.0	1.1	ns
Music	1.1	1.0	1.1	ns
Redefine feelings	0.0	0.0	0.0	—
Mean strategies used	3.7	4.0*	3.3	.003

Note. Percentages are based on dummy variables indicating whether each type of coping was used by the respondent or not. Means are based on the number of strategies actually coded for each respondent.

As shown in Table 1, females and males differed significantly in the likelihood of using several types of coping. Women were more likely than men to express their feelings freely, try to see the situation differently, seek social support, and write about the situation. Men were more likely than women to analyze (think through) the situation, accept the situation, and engage in strenuous exercise. Contrary to expectation, there were no gender differences in taking direct action to change the situation (a problem-focused tactic). Similarly, women and men did not differ in the likelihood of leaving the situation (which might be considered another problem-focused tactic). However, women were more likely to seek social support, whereas men were more likely to analyze the situation (two other techniques that might be considered problem focused). In general, there was little in these patterns to support a stereotyped image of men as problem solvers. However, consistent with gender stereotypes, men's coping choices suggest a rational and stoic style; women's suggest an expressive style.

Most notable in Table 1 were significant gender differences in the total number of strategies that respondents mentioned; women reported using more coping strategies than men—four strategies versus three, on average. Because earlier it was shown that women wrote longer responses than men in this sample, this finding potentially could be explained by differential expressivity (or motivation or verbal skills). However, three additional pieces of evidence suggest that the finding is valid. First, after respondents had written detailed event descriptions (which included their descriptions of coping efforts), they responded to a closed-ended checklist of 19 coping items. (Items were similar in content to the types of coping shown in Table 1.) Respondents were asked to indicate whether they usually tried each type of coping during times of emotional stress. On average, females endorsed 11.6 items, whereas males endorsed 10.3 ($p < .001$). Because these items were closed ended and answered by all respondents, differential expressivity (or motivation) was less likely to have been an influence (although social desirability might still have affected these responses). The results for the closed-ended items supported the gender difference found in the open-ended responses.

Second, the number of strategies mentioned (spontaneously) by each respondent was regressed on gender, the number of lines he/she had written, the order in which the negative experience was described in the protocol, and the number of discrete events the respondent had described within the experience. The "female" coefficient remained positive and significant despite these controls ($b = .69$, $p < .01$).

Finally, because the number of coping strategies mentioned might have been due to the nature of the events women and men described, in particular, due to their severity, the mean number of strategies cited by subgroups of respondents who had experienced the same key event was calculated. Mean strategies for the key event were added to the previous equation as a control for the nature of the event that the respondent had experienced. (This procedure amounts to an analysis of covariance design.) The "female" coefficient remained positive and significant ($b = .55$, $p = .01$). Consequently, it seems appropriate to conclude that, on average, women employed more strategies than men in coping with an emotionally distressing situation. This was an unexpected finding. Its implications are discussed later.

Gender Differences in Event Perceptions

As described earlier, closed-ended alternative responses for each perception question were "no," "to some extent," and "yes." For the next analysis, responses of "to some extent" and "yes" were collapsed, creating dummy variables for each perception (0 = no, 1 = yes). The majority of respondents perceived their described event as unanticipated (61.6%), not preventable (79.6%), and uncontrollable (66.8%). Slightly over half regarded their event as one for which they were not causally responsible (56.3%), and as one they were not responsible for solving (54.5%). Gender differences in these situational perceptions are reported in Table 2.[5]

Women were more likely to have anticipated the situation and to have viewed it as preventable. Unexpectedly, there were no gender differences in perceptions of controllability, responsibility for causing, and responsibility for solving the situation.

These findings were unexpected for two reasons. First, as mentioned earlier, men have a stronger internal locus-of-control orientation, or sense of personal control, than women; I expected this tendency to be reflected in respondents' perceptions of controllability and causal responsibility for the events that they chose to describe. Second, given the cultural stereotype of men as active problem solvers, it is surprising to find that male respondents did not differ from females in the belief that they were responsible for solving the situation. Perhaps these perceptions were more a function of the events respondents chose to describe than a reflection of their orientations to life experiences in general.

[5]Table 2 also reports the intercorrelations among event perceptions. The correlation of .44 between anticipation and preventability reflects the skip pattern for these two questions. Preventability was asked only if the respondent had anticipated the event at least "to some extent"; otherwise the event was assumed to be and coded as nonpreventable.

Table 2. Perceptions of Events by Gender

	Percentage answering "yes"			
Perception	Women	Men	F–M difference	N (F/M)
Was situation anticipated?	45.3*	30.4	.03	(106,92)
Was situation preventable?	20.4*	9.7	.04	(103,93)
Was situation changeable?	36.0	30.1	ns	(100,93)
Was R responsible for it happening?	43.4	44.1	ns	(106,93)
Was R responsible for solving it?	45.7	45.2	ns	(92,84)

	1.	2.	3.	4.	5.
1. Anticipation	—				
2. Preventability	.44***	—			
3. Changeability	.15*	.27***	—		
4. Causal respon.	−.01	.23***	.31***	—	
5. Respon. for solv.	.13#	.20**	.09	.23**	—

#$p < .10$; *$p < .05$; **$p < .01$; ***$p < .001$.

Note. Female–male differences were determined by chi-square tests. Responses of "to some extent" and "yes" were treated as "yes" responses for this analysis. N's vary due to missing values on some variables. Intercorrelations among perceptions also are reported.

To test this possibility, I calculated mean event perceptions for each subgroup of respondents who had experienced the same key event (i.e., I computed each subgroup's mean on anticipation, on preventability, etc.). Then I regressed each respondent's actual event perception (now coded ordinally, 0 = no, 1 = to some extent, 2 = yes) on gender, controlling for the mean perception of the particular event that was experienced by the respondent. The results (not shown) indicated that the gender difference in event anticipation was not due to the nature of the event described. However, females' greater propensity to view the situation as preventable *was* a function of the event described. No other gender differences in event perceptions were revealed. Subsequent exploratory analyses indicated that "other" personal events were the primary sources of differential perceptions of preventability.

In sum, these findings do not support the hypothesis that females and males differ in their perceptions of stressful events with respect to preventability, controllability, causal responsibility, and responsibility for solving the situation. Females were simply more likely than males to report having anticipated or expected a negative event.

Event Perceptions and Coping

The next issues are (1) whether event perceptions influence the number and types of coping strategies that individuals use and (2) whether the relationships between event perceptions and coping differ by gender. These issues were explored simultaneously by regressing each of the coping strategies (each coded as a dummy variable, 1 = strategy used, 0 = not used) that were mentioned by 5% or more of the sample on anticipation, preventability, controllability, causal responsibility, and solution responsibility (coded ordinally); these regressions were estimated separately by gender. Each equation also controlled for the number of lines written by the respondent and the order in which the event description was requested. The results of these analyses are shown in Table 3.[6]

It is clear from these results that there are significant interactions of event perceptions with gender on the choice of particular coping strategies. Reading down the columns, although women more frequently anticipated a negative situation (see Table 2), anticipation did not affect their choice of strategies at all. In contrast, men were more likely to accept the situation and to hide their feelings when they anticipated or expected it. When women viewed a negative event as having been preventable, they were more likely to employ distraction, whereas men's use of coping strategies was unaffected by this perception. When women perceived a situation as controllable or changeable, they were more likely to leave the situation (at least temporarily) and to try not to think about it. Men tried to distract themselves from a controllable situation. Perceiving oneself as responsible for causing a negative event did not affect women's coping strategies at all, whereas men were more likely to take direct action, to think through the situation, and *not* to express their feelings. When women believed they were responsible for solving the situation, they used more strategies overall and tried not to think about the situation; men instead took direct action and expressed their feelings.

These results again yielded a mixed and confusing picture of styles of coping by gender. On the one hand, one might be tempted to describe men as problem solvers and as stoics, given their tendencies to confront a situation they believe themselves responsible for causing or solving, to think through situations that they believed that they had caused, and to hide their feelings and accept negative situations that they anticipated. One might be tempted, too, to describe women as escape-avoidant, given their tendencies to try not to think about controllable and solvable situa-

---

[6]Replications with probit analysis indicated that the coefficients reported in Table 3 are more conservative estimates of effects. That is, marginally significant regression coefficients were significant at acceptable levels in the probit results.

tions and to leave controllable ones. On the other hand, women engage in more coping efforts when they view themselves as responsible for solving the situation, and men try to distract themselves from ones they might control or change. Gender stereotypes in patterns of coping are only weakly supported by these findings.

Perhaps most interesting in Table 3 is the notable *lack* of association between the perceived controllability of an event and attempts at problem solving, for both genders. Considerable theoretical attention has been given to the controllability dimension of events; controllable events should predict active problem solving; uncontrollable events should predict emotion-focused coping—or at worst, helplessness and passivity (e.g., Folkman, 1984; Abramson *et al.*, 1978). The results in Table 3 indicate that perceptions of controllability do not significantly increase active problem-solving attempts for either gender; attributions of responsibility for causing and for solving a problem are more closely associated with active coping (at least for men).

Outcomes

An obvious question is whether the number and types of coping strategies used by men and women influenced their event outcomes. Based on the repeated finding in the literature that women have higher distress levels than men overall, one might expect women more frequently to report continuing consequences and/or negative (or mixed) outcome valences.

These expectations were confirmed. Males were more likely than females to report that their situation had ended (56% vs. 43%, respectively, $p < .10$). Males also were more likely than females to report a positive outcome of the experience (45% vs. 36%, respectively, $p < .05$). Further analysis (not shown) indicated that women were far more likely than men to report continuing outcomes with mixed positive and negative aspects (33% vs. 13%, respectively, $p < .001$). Other combinations of event ended/continuing and outcome valence did not differ significantly by gender.

The relationship between the number of coping strategies used and event outcomes was examined next. Because previous results indicated a three-way interaction (gender by situation ended/continuing by outcome valence), analyses were conducted separately by gender and situation ended/continuing. Outcome valence (1 = negative, 2 = mixed negative and positive, 3 = positive) was regressed on the number of strategies used, with number of lines written and order of event description controlled. The results are summarized in Table 4.

For men, event outcomes were unrelated to the number of strat-

Table 3. The Effects of Event Perceptions on the Use of Coping Strategies, by Gender

	Anticipation	Preventability	Controllability	Causal responsibility	Responsible for solving	R^2
Females (N=84)						
Number of strategies	-.14	.05	.19	-.12	.25*	.17
Direct action	-.05	.18	.16	-.10	.17	.15
Leave the situation	-.13	-.04	.23#	-.15	-.03	.10
Seek support	-.06	.07	-.000	.09	.07	.07
Think it through	-.05	.09	-.18	-.09	.11	.10
See differently	.15	-.20	-.13	.07	.14	.07
Accept it	-.02	-.004	-.07	-.02	-.11	.08
Thought stopping	-.19	-.05	.42***	-.12	.21#	.20
Distraction	-.13	.26#	.12	-.18	.01	.09
Exercise	.13	-.21	.13	-.03	.11	.05
Use drugs/alcohol	-.06	.21	-.09	-.06	.14	.11
Catharsis	-.06	.02	.18	-.13	.04	.04
Hide feelings	-.002	-.17	.01	-.03	.10	.05
Prayer	.12	-.01	-.15	-.03	-.08	.05

Males (N=78)

Number of strategies	.04	-.04	.03	.03	-.01	.11
Direct action	.17	.06	.11	.20#	.27*	.24
Leave the situation	-.17	-.01	-.04	.16	-.09	.14
Seek support	-.16	.07	.15	-.16	.13	.07
Think it through	-.11	.08	-.16	.27*	-.09	.11
See differently	-.09	-.18	.01	.20	-.14	.12
Accept it	.26*	.002	-.19	-.09	-.12	.14
Thought stopping	.17	-.13	.10	.03	.08	.08
Distraction	-.19	-.08	.28*	-.13	.02	.11
Exercise	-.02	.18	-.13	-.13	.12	.10
Use drugs/alcohol	-.13	.01	-.20	.11	-.06	.12
Catharsis	.002	.01	.14	-.24*	.19#	.15
Hide feelings	.39**	-.13	-.01	.08	-.18	.19
Prayer	-.10	.001	-.13	.06	-.07	.04

#p < .10; *p < .05; **p < .01; ***p < .001.

Note. Standarized coefficients are presented. Respondents who described only an ongoing difficulty are excluded from analysis. N's are lower in this analysis due to missing values on the event-perception variables. All equations include controls for the number of lines written by the respondent and the order in which the negative-experience description was elicited.

Table 4. Event Outcomes Regressed on Number of Coping Strategies Used, by Gender and Situation

	Situation continuing	Situation ended
Women		
Number of strategies	.09#	−.34*
R^2	.08	.15
N	53	39
Men		
Number of strategies	.13	.14
R^2	.10	.03
N	37	45

$\#p < .10$; $*p < .05$.

Note. Standarized coefficients are presented. Outcome valence is coded 1 = negative, 2 = mixed negative and positive, 3 = positive. Number of lines written and order of event description are controlled in each equation, but not shown.

egies used. For women, the relationship between number of coping strategies used and outcomes depended on whether the situation had ended or was continuing. If the situation had continuing consequences, more strategies were associated with better outcomes. If the situation had ended, more strategies were associated with worse outcomes. Unfortunately, the interpretation of these findings is ambiguous because outcomes—particularly continuing outcomes—and coping efforts are likely to be reciprocally related. It seems reasonable that a situation that ends negatively elicits more coping attempts than a situation that ends positively. But a situation with continuing consequences might elicit more coping attempts, or more coping attempts might result in better continuing outcomes. In other words, it is not clear whether coping efforts resulted in certain outcomes or certain outcomes elicited variations in coping attempts.

To assess the influence of particular coping strategies on outcome valence, valence was regressed (by gender and situation ended vs. continuing) on all strategies employed by 5% or more of the sample (see Table 1). Each strategy was represented by a dummy variable (1 = strategy used, 0 = not used by the respondent). Again, number of lines written and order-of-event description were controlled in each equation. The results of these analyses are shown in Table 5.

Coping strategies primarily affected the valence of event outcomes in situations with persisting effects, for women *and* men. For women,

Table 5.
The Effects of Different Coping Strategies on Event Outcomes,
by Gender and Situation

Strategy	Women continuing	Women ended	Men continuing	Men ended
Direct action	.19	−.15	.08	.15
Leave the situation	−.11	−.15	−.23	.18
Seek support	−.11	−.07	−.15	−.02
Think it through	−.06	.15	.08	.20
See it differently	.42**	−.02	.28	−.05
Accept it	−.03	−.20	.40*	.08
Thought stopping	.004	−.40	−.17	.11
Distraction	.02	−.15	.15	.05
Exercise	—	−.21	.29	.05
Use drugs/alcohol	.25	.05	.06	—
Catharsis	.28#	.25	.52*	−.01
Hide feelings	.11	−.10	−.07	−.01
Prayer	.31#	—	—	.20
R^2	.34	.32	.46	.15
N	53	39	37	45

Note. Standarized coefficients are presented. Outcome valence is measured ordinally (1 = negative, 2 = mixed negative and positive, 3 = positive outcome). Situation continuing or ended refers to the respondent's report that the distressing situation had continuing effects or consequences or was over. Number of lines written and order of event description also are controlled in each equation, but are not shown, A missing coefficient indicates that not respondent in the analysis group used the strategy indicated.

trying to see the situation differently, letting out feelings, and prayer were associated with more positive continuing outcomes. For men, accepting the situation and letting out feelings were associated with positive continuing outcomes. For women, "trying not to think about it" also was associated with situations that ended negatively. Interestingly, direct action, leaving the situation, seeking social support, and thinking through the situation (each of which might be considered problem-focused strategies) were unrelated to outcome valence for both males and females. Other strategies did not influence outcome valence.

Although four strategies were associated with persistent and more positive outcomes, they cannot be described as effective coping techniques on the basis of these findings. Trying to see the situation differently, letting out feelings, engaging in prayer, and accepting the situation may have been responses to the perception that the effects of the situation would persist, rather than the causes of that persistence. In further support of this cautionary statement, the persistence of event effects was positively related to the number of coping strategies used ($r = .19$, $p <$ .01), further suggesting that more consequential situations elicit more attempts at coping.

Although effective and ineffective coping strategies cannot be identified from these findings, *perceptions* of the relative efficacy of these strategies could be explored. Respondents were asked whether any of their attempts to handle the situation or their feelings were more successful than others, and if so, which ones. Women more frequently believed that one or two of their coping strategies were more successful than others (50% of the women vs. 31.8% of the men who answered this question responded "to some extent" or "yes," $p = .01$). Table 6 shows the percentages of women and men citing particular coping strategies as more successful.

There were few gender differences in perceiving particular strategies as more efficacious. Women more frequently cited writing about the situation, whereas men cited strenuous exercise. Note that the top five preferences in *choice* of strategy (see Table 1) were reflected in *perceptions* of efficacy as well. Although there were gender differences in the *choice* of these top five strategies (Table 1), men and women were equally likely to perceive them as efficacious (Table 6).

Interestingly, perceptions of efficacy were related to event outcomes for women but not for men. Among women, believing one or more coping strategies were successful was significantly related to a positive, continuing outcome ($r = .25$, $p < .10$). But once again, coping and outcomes may be reciprocally related—perceived efficacy may influence outcomes, but outcomes also may affect perceptions of coping efficacy. Unfortunately, because the data are cross-sectional (and retrospective), these reciprocal influences cannot be further disentangled.[7]

DISCUSSION AND CONCLUSIONS

I began this chapter with three expectations. First, I expected women more frequently to perceive their negative experiences as uncontrollable. Second, I expected perceptions of uncontrollability to influence the choice of coping strategies, and that, therefore, women would use more emotion-focused coping strategies and men more prob-

---

[7]Perceptions of events (in terms of controllability, responsibility for causing, and so on) were unrelated to outcomes for both women and men, with one exception: Men who believed that they could have prevented a situation were more likely to report that the situation had ended negatively.

Table 6. **Percentages of Respondents Citing Particular Coping Strategies as More Successful in Handling the Situation**

Strategy	Total sample (N=69)	Women (N=43)	Men (N=26)	F–M difference (p)
Catharsis	21.7	20.9	23.1	ns
Seek support	20.3	23.3	15.4	ns
See it differently	20.3	18.6	23.1	ns
Hide feelings	13.0	14.0	11.5	ns
Direct action	10.1	9.3	11.5	ns
Leave the situation	8.7	9.3	7.7	ns
Thought stopping	8.7	9.3	7.7	ns
Write about it	7.3	11.6*	0.0	.07
Exercise	7.3	2.3	15.4*	.04
Distraction	5.8	9.3	0.0	ns
Use drugs/alcohol	4.4	2.3	7.7	ns
Prayer	2.9	2.3	3.9	ns
Think it through	1.5	0.0	3.9	ns
Wait	1.5	2.3	0.0	ns
Other physiological	1.5	0.0	3.9	ns

Note. Only respondents who indicated that a strategy was successful, or successful to some extent, are included in this analysis. Percentages do not sum to 100% because more than one strategy could be cited.

lem-focused strategies. Third, I expected problem-solving efforts to be associated with more positive outcomes, and thus that women would experience less satisfactory outcomes than men. Each of these expectations was disconfirmed. Perceptions of controllability did not differ by gender; perceptions of controllability were not associated with problem-solving efforts for either gender; and problem-solving efforts were not related to event outcomes for either gender. These results call into question the utility of focusing on the perceived controllability of negative events as predictors of active coping efforts and positive coping outcomes.

However, three cautions need mention: First, previous research shows that middle-class, highly educated individuals are more likely to have an internal locus-of-control orientation or a high sense of personal control over life circumstances (Lefcourt, 1981; Pearlin & Schooler, 1978; Wheaton, 1980). Consequently, perceptions of event controllability may not have differed by gender because men *and* women selected into a middle-class college sample hold similar beliefs about personal control. Second, some problem-solving efforts may be needed to determine that an event is indeed uncontrollable, and thus, one might not obtain a strong positive relationship between perceived controllability and problem solving.[8] Third, negative emotional experiences may have been memorable and thus described *because* they were problem-solving failures. Events that were averted or reversed through successful problem solving may not have been recalled by respondents as negative emotional experiences. Thus recall bias might account for the lack of relationship between active coping efforts and positive coping outcomes. On the other hand, even controllable events often turn out badly despite individuals' best efforts at problem solving. There is sufficient qualitative support for this possibility in the data (see Thoits, 1991) to suggest that coping researchers might need to rethink their presumption that positive outcomes typically follow from active coping efforts.

The key unexpected finding of the research was that women used more coping strategies than men when handling a distressing event. This effect was not a spurious product of differences in expressivity (or motivation or verbal skills), differences in the events described, or differences in event perceptions by gender. One might be tempted to conclude that women have more flexible coping styles or broader coping repertoires. However, it is also plausible to argue that women use more strategies because (1) the techniques they use are less effective (see Pearlin & Schooler, 1978; Menaghan, 1982), or (2) they are already more distressed than men. Consistent with the first possibility, among women, coping efforts were associated with situations that ended negatively and with persistent situations that had mixed positive and negative aspects. However, effectiveness could not be assessed definitively here, due to the potentially reciprocal influences of event outcomes and coping efforts. Consistent with the second possibility, other studies have reported a positive relationship between symptoms of depression and the number of coping techniques individuals use (Billings & Moos, 1984; Coyne *et al.*, 1981; Folkman & Lazarus, 1986). Thus women's greater use of coping strategies in specific situations may reflect their higher levels of emotional distress in general.

To some extent, the analysis supported stereotypes of gender differences in coping styles. Women were more likely to use expressive strategies, whereas men's strategies were more likely to be rational and stoic. When events were perceived as controllable, women were more likely to use escape/avoidant strategies; men responded with problem-solving efforts to events for which they perceived themselves responsi-

---

[8]I am grateful to David Dooley and Susan Folkman for these two cautionary observations.

ble. However, because many exceptions to expectations were observed, support for gender-stereotyped coping styles must be considered fairly weak.

In terms of the three explanations for women's higher distress relative to men offered at the outset of this chapter, it appears that differential expressivity may be a factor—women were certainly more verbose than men in their event description and in describing their coping strategies. Greater exposure to structural stress or to severe, persistent stressors among women could not be assessed, given the format of the study—only one negative event was examined here. The vulnerability argument—that women lack coping resources for dealing with the stressors they face—was partially disconfirmed, at least in terms of the number of coping strategies women use and the similarity of men's and women's attributions for events. But because women's use of more coping strategies was not associated consistently with more satisfactory event outcomes than men's, one must speculate that women's techniques generally may be less effective in eliminating problems or alleviating distress. It should be clear from this analysis that detailed longitudinal data will be necessary to further disentangle the reciprocal influences of coping attempts and event outcomes by gender and to explain adequately women's use of more coping strategies.

ACKNOWLEDGMENTS

An earlier version of this paper was presented at the American Public Health Association, New Orleans, Louisiana, October 1987. I thank Kris Baughman and Lori Sudderth for their careful research assistance on this project and Larry Griffin for his helpful comments and suggestions regarding analysis. Members of the Consortium for Research in Stress-Buffering Processes (CRISP), funded by the William T. Grant Foundation, provided valuable feedback on this chapter.

REFERENCES

Aldwin, C., Folkman, S., Schaefer, C., Coyne, J. C., & Lazarus, R. S. (1980). *Ways of Coping: A Process Measure*. Paper presented at the meetings of the American Psychological Association, Montreal, September.

Abramson, L. Y., Seligman, M. E. P., & Teasdale, J. D. (1978). Learned helplessness in humans: Critique and reformulation. *Journal of Abnormal Psychology, 87,* 49–74.

Aneshensel, C. S., & Pearlin, L. I. (1987). Structural contexts of sex differences in stress. In R. Barnett, L. Biener, & G. Baruch (Eds.), *Women and Stress.* (pp. 75–95). New York: Free Press.

Billings, A. G., & Moos, R. H. (1984). Coping, stress, and social Resources among adults with unipolar depression. *Journal of Personality and Social Psychology, 46,* 877–891.

Billings, A. G., Cronkite, R. C., Moos, R. H. (1983). Social-environmental factors in unipolar depression: Comparisons of depressed patients and nondepressed controls. *Journal of Abnormal Psychology, 92,* 119–33.

Caplan, R. D., Naidu, R. K., & Tripathi, R. C. (1984). Coping and defense: Constellations vs. components. *Journal of Health and Social Behavior, 25,* 303–320.

Coyne, J. C., Aldwin, C., & Lazarus, R. S. (1981). Depression and coping in stressful episodes. *Journal of Abnormal Psychology, 90,* 439–447.

Dohrenwend, B. P., Dohrenwend, B. S. (1976). Sex differences in psychiatric disorders. *American Journal of Sociology, 81,* 447–459.

Dohrenwend, B. S., Krasnoff, L., Askenasy, A. R., & Dohrenwend, B. P. (1978). Exemplification of a method for scaling life events: The PERI Life Events Scale. *Journal of Health and Social Behavior, 19,* 205–229.

Fleishman, J. A. (1984). Personality characteristics and coping patterns. *Journal of Health and Social Behavior, 25,* 229–244.

Folkman, S. (1984). Personal control and stress and coping processes: A theoretical analysis. *Journal of Personality and Social Psychology, 46,* 839–852.

Folkman, S., & Lazarus, R. S. (1980). An analysis of coping in a middle-aged community sample. *Journal of Health and Social Behavior, 21,* 219–239.

Folkman S., & Lazarus, R. S. (1985). If it changes it must be a process: A study of emotion and coping during three stages of a college exam. *Journal of Personality and Social Psychology, 48,* 150–70.

Folkman, S., & Lazarus, R. S. (1986). Stress processes and depressive symptomatology. *Journal of Abnormal Psychology, 95,* 107–13.

Folkman, S., Lazarus, R. S., Dunkel-Schetter, C., DeLongis, A., & Gruen, R. J. (1986). The dynamics of a stressful encounter: Cognitive appraisal, coping, and encounter outcomes. *Journal of Personality and Social Psychology, 50,* 997–1003.

Folkman, S., Lazarus, R. S., Pimley, S., & Novacek, J. (1987). Age differences in stress and coping processes. *Psychology and Aging, 2(2),* 171–184.

Gove, W., and Tudor, J. F. (1973). Adult sex roles and mental illness. *American Journal of Sociology, 78,* 50–73.

Gove, W. (1972). The relationship between sex roles, mental illness, and marital status. *Social Forces, 51,* 34–44.

Gove, W., & Geerken, M. (1977). Response bias in surveys of mental health: An empirical evaluation. *American Journal of Sociology, 82,* 1289–1317.

Holahan, C. J., & Moos, R. H. (1987). Personal and contextual determinants of coping strategies. *Journal of Personality and Social Psychology, 52,* 946–955.

Holmes, T. H., & Rahe, R. H. (1967). The Social Readjustment Rating Scale. *Journal of Psychosomatic Research, 11,* 213–218.

Kessler, R. C. (1979). Stress, social status, and psychological distress. *Journal of Health and Social Behavior, 20,* 259–272.

Kessler, R. C., & Essex, M. (1982). Marital status and depression: The importance of coping resources. *Social Forces, 61,* 484–507.

Kessler, R. C., & McLeod, J. (1984). Sex differences in vulnerability to undesirable life events. *American Sociological Review, 49,* 620–631.

Kessler, R. C., McRae, Jr., J. A. (1981). Trends in the relationship between sex and psychological distress: 1957–1976. *American Sociological Review, 46*, 443–452.

Lazarus, R. S., & Folkman, S. (1984). *Stress, appraisal, and coping.* New York: Springer.

Lefcourt, H. M. (1981). Locus of control and stressful life events. In B. S. Dohrenwend & B. P. Dohrenwend (Eds.), *Stressful life events and their contexts* (pp. 157–166). New York: Prodist.

Link, B. & Dohrenwend, B. P. (1980). Formulation of hypotheses about the true prevalence of demoralization in the United States. In B. P. Dohrenwend, B. S. Dohrenwend, M. Schartz-Gould, B. Link, R. Neugebauer, R. Wunsch-Hitzig (Eds.), *Mental Illness in the United States: Epidemiological Estimates,* (pp. 114–132). New York: Praeger.

Markush, R. E., & Favero, R. V. (1974). Epidemiological assessments of stressful life events, depressed mood, and psychophysiological symptoms—A preliminary report. In B. P. Dohrenwend & B. S. Dohrenwend (Eds.), *Stressful Life Events: Their Nature and Effects* (pp. 171–190). New York: Wiley.

Menaghan, E. (1982). Measuring coping effectiveness: A panel analysis of marital problems and coping efforts. *Journal of Health and Social Behavior, 23*, 220–234.

Miller, S. M., & Kirsch, N. (1987). Sex differences in cognitive coping with stress. In R. C. Barnett, L. Biener, & G. K. Baruch (Eds.), *Gender and Stress,* (pp. 278–307). New York: Free Press.

Newmann, J. P. (1984). Sex differences in symptoms of depression: Clinical disorder or normal distress? *Journal of Health and Social Behavior, 25*, 136–159.

Pearlin, L. I., & Johnson, J. S. (1977). Marital status, life strains, and depression. *American Sociological Review, 42*, 704–715.

Pearlin, L. I., & Schooler, C. (1978). The structure of coping. *Journal of Health and Social Behavior, 19*, 2–21.

Stone, A. A., & Neale, J. M. (1984). New measure of daily coping: Development and preliminary results. *Journal of Personality and Social Psychology, 46*, 892–906.

Thoits, P. A. (1984a). Coping, social support, and psychological outcomes: The central role of emotion. In P. Shaver (Ed.), *Review of Personality and Social Psychology, Vol. 5,* (pp. 219–238). Beverly Hills, CA: Sage.

Thoits, P. A. (1984b). Explaining distributions of psychological vulnerability: Lack of social support in the face of life stress. *Social Forces, 63*, 452–481.

Thoits, P. A. (1987). Gender and marital status differences in control and distress: Common stress versus unique stress explanations. *Journal of Health and Social Behavior, 28*, 7–22.

Thoits, P. A. (1991). Patterns in coping with controllable and uncontrollable events. In E. M. Cummings, A. L. Greene, & K. H. Karraker (Eds.), *Life-span developmental psychology: Perspectives on stress and coping* (pp. 235–258). Hillsdale, NJ: Lawrence Erlbaum.

Turner, R. J., & Noh, S. (1983). Class and psychological vulnerability among women: The significance of social support and personal control. *Journal of Health and Social Behavior, 24*, 2–15.

Veroff, J., Kulka, R. A., & Douvan, E. (1981). *Mental health in America: Patterns of help-seeking from 1957 to 1976.* New York: Basic.

Vitaliano, P. P., Russo, J., Carr, J. E., Maiuro, R. D., & Becker, J. (1985). The ways of coping checklist: Revision and psychometric properties. *Multivariate Behavioral Research, 20*, 3–26.

Wheaton, B. (1980). The sociogenesis of psychological disorder: An attributional theory. *Journal of Health and Social Behavior, 24*, 208–229.

Appendix 1.   All Negative Events Described by Respondents

	Frequencies		
	Total sample	Women	Men
Network events			
Family network events			
1. Parents had major fight	6	2	4
2. Parents plan/get divorce	7	3	4
3. Parent(s) have onset of financial problems/lose job	4	2	2
4. Parent has onset/hospitalized for serious illness	7	3	4
5. Family member attempted suicide	2	2	0
6. Family member (other than parent) has onset/hospitalized for illness	3	2	1
Subtotal	29	14	15
Friend network events			
7. Friend has onset/hospitalized for serious illness	2	1	1
8. Friend attempted suicide	1	0	1
9. Friend engages in behavior that is disapproved of by R (e.g., drug use, repeated abortions)	11	7	4
10. Friend was a victim of injustice	2	2	0
Subtotal	16	10	6
Personal events			
Deaths			
11. Family member committed suicide	3	2	1
12. Parent died (causes other than suicide)	4	1	3
13. Other family member died (causes other than suicide)	13	9	4
14. Friend committed suicide	3	3	0
15. Friend died (causes other than suicide)	8	6	2
Subtotal	31	21	10
Family related			
16. Parent assaulted R (sexually or aggressively)	3	2	1
17. Parent(s) refused economic support to R	3	0	3

(*continued*)

Appendix 1. (*Continued*)

	Frequencies		
	Total sample	Women	Men
18. Parent(s) reveal disapproval of R's lover/friends/lifestyle	9	6	3
19. Parent(s) and R have major fight	9	3	6
20. Other family members and R have major fight/entire family have fight	3	1	2
Subtotal	27	12	15
Friend related			
21. R witnessed friend injured/killed	2	2	0
22. Friend betrayed R's trust	4	3	1
23. R and friends are parted (due to trips, college)	3	1	2
24. R had major fight with friend	6	2	4
25. Friend hurt R's feelings	3	2	1
Subtotal	18	10	8
Lover related			
26. Lover ended the relationship	19	12	7
27. R ended the relationship	13	6	7
28. Lover was unfaithful	16	5	11
29. R was unfaithful	8	6	2
30. R and lover were separated	6	5	1
31. R got lover pregnant	3	–	3
32. R got pregnant	1	1	–
33. Major fight with lover	15	8	7
Subtotal	81	43	38
Other personal events			
34. R was injured/became ill	2	1	1
35. R attempted suicide	4	4	0
36. R realized had drinking/drug problem	3	2	1
37. R had misarriage/abortion	2	2	–
38. R was raped/physically assaulted	5	5	–
39. R "came out" as gay/lesbian	2	1	1
40. R was approached by gay person	1	0	1
41. R was victim of injustice	7	3	4

(*continued*)

Appendix 1. (*Continued*)

		Frequencies		
		Total sample	Women	Men
42.	R was caught/arrested in act of wrongdoing	9	3	6
43.	R was rejected from job/team/fraternity/sorority	6	3	3
44.	R voluntarily quit job/team	1	0	1
45.	R lost scholarship	1	0	1
46.	R received failing grade(s)	4	1	3
47.	R experienced major failure (other than listed)	6	4	2
48.	R had negative revelation about another person	9	4	5
49.	R left home to come to college	5	2	3
50.	Miscellaneous other events	29	16	13
	Subtotal	96	51	45

Appendix 2.   Coping Strategies

Behavioral strategies, situation as target

Direct action	Acted on situation to try to change it, confronted or discussed the problem with person involved, gathered information for solving the problem, read books about the situation
	Substituted new situation for the old (e.g., found another lover, another job)
Seek social support	Talked to family member(s) for advice/help
	Talked to friends(s) for advice/help
	Consulted therapist/minister/other authority figure
Leave the situation	Left the situation permanently
	Left or avoided the situation temporarily
	Went off by self for long walks or drives
	Withdrew from contact with others

(*continued*)

Appendix 2. (*Continued*)

Cognitive strategies, situation as target

Think it through	Analyzed the situation, thought through the situation, analyzed the alternatives, made a plan of action, made a decision
See it differently	Saw the situation in a new way, reinterpreted the meaning of the situation, tried to see the positive side, had a realization or told self something about the situation
	Compared self to others who were worse off
Accept it	Accepted the situation, became resigned
Thought stopping	Tried not to think about it, refused to think about it
Distraction	Kept busy doing useful things to distract self, distracted self by watching TV/socializing/reading novels
Fantasy solution	Fantasized a magical solution to the situation, wished for a magical resolution or reversal of circumstances

Behavioral strategies, physiology as target

Use drugs/alcohol	Took pills (legal or illegal), smoked marijuana, drank alcohol
Exercise	Engaged in hard physical exercise
Other physiological	Used muscle-relaxation techniques, broke things to exhaust self, ate, slept

Cognitive strategies, physiology as target

Desensitization	Used progressive desensitization techniques, hypnosis

Behavioral strategies, expressive gestures as target

Catharsis	Expressed emotion freely when alone, expressed emotion with/to others who were involved in the situation, expressed emotion freely with/to others who were not involved in the situation, expressed emotion freely (context unknown)
Hide feelings	Controlled expressive behaviors (tried not to cry, hid feelings from others, went on as usual, acted as if nothing had happened), suppressed the emotion (method unspecified)

(*continued*)

Appendix 2. (*Continued*)

Cognitive strategies, expressive gestures as target	
Fantasy expression	Fantasized expressing true feelings, wanted to aggress or visualized aggression against someone
Prayer	Prayed, spoke to God
Cognitive strategies, emotion label as target	
Redefine	Reinterpreted existing feelings as different ones, told self I wasn't feeling what I was
Miscellaneous strategies	
Write	Wrote in journal, wrote a letter that was never sent, wrote a poem about it
Music	Listened to music, played an instrument
Wait	Waited for situation or feelings to pass, let time pass, endured it

7

Gender, Stress, and Distress

Social–Relational Influences

SUSAN GORE and MARY ELLEN COLTEN

One of the most frequently asked questions in research on the social sources of psychological distress is why there is a higher prevalence of depressive symptoms from adolescence all through adulthood among women as compared to men. The problem is a significant one, not only because it suggests something distinctive about the mental health of women but also because it provides the opportunity to examine how well major conceptual and analytic frameworks for explaining health and behavior contribute to our understanding of an important empirical problem.

This chapter discusses the two major approaches that have guided study of this problem—the stress/coping and illness paradigm and the sex differences/gender role paradigm—considers their weaknesses as well as strengths for contributing to an understanding of the etiology of depression in both men and women, and identifies various points of intersection. Because the guiding framework for most current thinking about gender and distress is the stress/coping and illness paradigm we begin by describing the analytic approaches that are now well established, emphasizing their benefits as well as inherent constraints. Next we turn to the contributions of the sex differences/gender role tradition of research, fo-

SUSAN GORE • Department of Sociology, University of Massachusetts–Boston, Boston, Massachusetts 02125.   MARY ELLEN COLTEN • Center for Survey Research, University of Massachusetts–Boston, Boston, Massachusetts 02116.

The Social Context of Coping, edited by John Eckenrode. Plenum Press, New York, 1991.

cusing on the study of intrapsychic processes and social–relational ties, factors that are "outcome" variables in research on sex differences but that are seen as mediating variables in the stress process. Here we emphasize the pivotal role that both self-esteem and social relationships play in shaping the stress process for women. We conclude with a consideration of directions that should enhance the study of gender differences in distress and inform a more general theory of depression.

Before turning to this discussion, the stress and gender role frameworks should be characterized in a very general sense; the particulars will become apparent as the chapter evolves. In contrasting the two approaches, we have in mind the conceptual tools and analytic frameworks widely adopted by researchers who contribute to these bodies of knowledge. First, regarding the stress paradigm, we are referring here to the very specific frameworks that have been advanced for investigating the effects of life stress on physical and mental status. For example, B. S. and B. P. Dohrenwend (1981, p. 20) have detailed six models of the stress process that have more or less guided research in this field to date. Among these models is what they call the "vulnerability hypothesis," an understanding of stress that underlies most research on the importance of coping efforts and social supports in offsetting the harmful consequences of stressful life events. Although the five alternative models posit very different stress processes, all share a concern with three classes of variables: life stress or adversity, mental and physical health changes (for the worse), and interpersonal and personal "individual difference" variables that act in conjunction with stressors or independently affect health status.

Similarly, there is a vast body of research on gender differences. In characterizing the sex differences/gender role paradigm, we are concerned not with gender differences in role occupancy *per se* but with sex differences in personality and orientation that appear to be a consequence of the "social organization of gender" (Chodorow, 1978), acquired through socialization processes and continuously reinforced over the life span, and that may be both the cause and consequence of gender-linked role behavior. In addition to an earlier interest in masculinity, femininity, and psychological androgyny as well as sex differences in instrumentality and expressiveness, considerable attention has been given to the question of sex differences in intraindividual characteristics such as self-esteem, sense of mastery, dependence on others, and assertiveness, and more recently, to differences in cognitive and especially attributional processes that may shape mental health and adjustment. However, even when aspects of mental health are a substantive focus of gender research, the research questions and approaches that guide these investigations as a whole do not conform to the formal features of stress research that are dictated by the models of vulnerability noted.

GENDER DIFFERENCES IN DEPRESSION, DISTRESS, AND EXPOSURE TO STRESS

The higher rates of current and lifetime depressive disorder and incidence of reports of depressive symptoms among women is a well-documented phenomenon (Brown & Harris, 1978; Gove, 1978; Myers *et al.*, 1984; Radloff, 1977; Robins *et al.*, 1984; Weissman & Klerman, 1977; Weissman, Leaf, Holzer, Meyers, & Tischler, 1984). Studies of adolescents, typically using the Beck Depression Inventory, the CDI, and the Center for Epidemiologic Studies Depression Scale (CES-D), also tend to reveal an overall picture of more depressive symptomatology among adolescent and young adult women (Albert & Beck, 1975; Dean & Ensel, 1983; Kandel & Davies, 1982; Lin, Dean, & Ensel, 1986; Rutter, 1986). Finally metanalyses of large numbers of studies conducted with varying instruments have established (Boyd & Weissman, 1981; Weissman & Klerman, 1977) that there are meaningful gender differences in depression.[1]

[1]Clearly, there are significant methodological issues in this research area, and these also reflect underlying critical issues in the conceptualization of illness. A number of articles have questioned whether gender differences in depressive symptoms are substantively as well as statistically important. For example, Newmann (1984) has argued that major screening instruments, such as the PERI (Psychiatric Evaluation Research Interview; Dohrenwend *et al.*, 1980) do not distinguish between mild feelings of dysphoric mood, such as sadness, that are fairly common in a normal population, and symptoms that reflect a true, abnormal depressive reaction. A different critique of widely used nondiagnostic screening instruments has been presented by Golding (1988) who examined the distribution of male and female cases at various levels of symptom severity on three major inventories: the CES–D, the PERI, and the SCL–90. Her analysis of seven different studies indicated that a handful of women reporting extremely high levels of depression produce statistically significant mean differences that are taken to represent a general pattern for the sexes. She suggests that extreme scores can be accounted for by the demographic disadvantages of women, concluding that, at best, "the effect of gender on depression can be understood as indirect, i.e., as mediated by gender differences in rate of employment, job status, education and income."

Others (Cooperstock, 1971; Phillips & Segal, 1969) suggest that the observed differences in reporting of symptoms are simply differences in reporting due to the greater willingness of women to admit to symptoms and do not reflect an actual difference in incidence or intensity of morbidity. Similarly, reliance on treatment statistics, an alternative basis for determining morbidity, confounds the presence of illness with help-seeking behavior, also possibly contributing to spuriously high estimates of illness among women. However, a series of studies that addressed sex differences in reporting behavior

Early studies that addressed explanations for apparent gender differences in depressive symptoms and nonspecific psychological distress
considered the beneficial impact of working for adult women, and
whether distress among married women could be linked to the stress of
domestic roles. The logic of such analyses should be credited to Gove
and colleagues who argued that the relatively similar distress profile of
single men and women in contrast to the discrepancies among the married reflects the nature of the sex-linked roles associated with marital
status and, particularly, the disadvantaged social situation of the married
woman (Gove & Tudor, 1973).

Research of this nature addresses the question of whether there is
differential exposure to role-related stressors by sex and advances the
fundamental hypothesis that the more similar men and women are with
respect to their social roles, the less of a gender gap there will be in
psychological distress. An important distinction in this line of research is
whether the benefits and liabilities of social roles are the same, regardless of the gender of the role occupant, or whether they differ by
gender because role expectations and involvements are gender specific.
Whereas the former possibility reflects an additive model of social role
effects that is essentially gender neutral, the latter interactive model of
sex-role effects assumes that the content of roles even in like statuses
greatly differs for men and women (Gore & Mangione, 1983).

Following this line of thinking, tests of whether women's roles and
role configurations are more stressful than men's are based upon analyses that address whether social statuses determined by employment, parental, and marital roles account for both within- and between-sex variation in distress (Aneshensel, Frerichs, & Clark, 1981; Gore & Mangione,
1983). Kessler and associates have referred to this research tradition as
providing at best indirect or inferential data about gender, social roles,
and distress because the research depends upon "gross comparisons of

---

failed to confirm a significant role for these types of illness behaviors in accounting for
the picture of greater affective disorder among women. (Gove & Geerkin, 1977; Gove,
1978).

Finally, some researchers are concerned about the generalization that women are
overall less mentally healthy than men that arises from investigations of illness etiology
that focus almost exclusively on depression, distress, or a generalized sense of demoralization. When community-based assessments of antisocial personality and abuse of alcohol
and drugs are included in addition to the affective disorders, men and women are found
to have similar overall rates of psychiatric disorder (Cleary, 1987). Moreover, because
there is some basis for thinking that men cope with depression through use of alcohol and
drugs, the use of these diagnostic categories may mask the true prevalence of depressive
disorder among males.

psychological distress across different role statuses and combinations," and there is no focus on the actual content of role experiences (Bolger, DeLongis, Kessler, & Wethington, 1990).

The major strategy for obtaining these more direct assessments of role content and role strain permitting examination of the interactive effects of gender and social roles has been the use of life events inventories (Dohrenwend, Krasnoff, Askenasy, & Dohrenwend, 1978; Holmes & Rahe, 1967) in which stress is operationalized as the occurrence of an acute stressor.[2] The life events approach has been the major conceptual orientation and methodology in stress research and, as such, it has shaped epidemiological investigations of depression and distress in the general population and in particular subgroups. As we will see, this approach relegates problems of gender to the realm of "individual differences," which limits the range of questions that can be asked about the role of gender in the stress process. We now briefly review the life events framework so as to understand the components of a prototypical investigation of gender, stress, and distress.

Readers are probably familiar with the instruments measuring the occurrence of acute life events that have come to be the dominant means for operationalizing the stressor construct in most epidemiological research on life stress and its effects (Dohrenwend et al., 1978; Holmes & Rahe, 1967). Readers are perhaps also familiar with the numerous critiques of the validity and reliability of such inventories (Rabkin & Struening, 1976), and some may wonder why these instruments continue to be used. Their strength is fourfold. First, the operational definition of stress as inherent in acute life changes has strong theoretical underpinnings in the life crisis tradition of prevention research (Caplan, 1986). Such life crises are understood as breaches in the continuity of previous routines that are imposed by forces outside the individual and that require coping efforts to master the challenges of transition. Reflecting this understanding of stress, events inventories assess changes in life situation and have been seen as a reasonable means for assessing the acute change dimension of stressful experience.

Second, in studying the etiological role of stressful experiences, it is important to establish whether stressful experiences are in fact indepen-

---

[2]The other two primary strategies are (1) measurement as a continuous variable of on-going role strain in major life roles, a strategy developed by Pearlin and colleagues that reflects a markedly different view of stress (Pearlin & Schooler, 1978; Pearlin & Lieberman, 1979; Pearlin, Lieberman, Menaghan, & Mullan, 1981); and most recently (2) use of daily diaries, which take a short term, yet longitudinal snapshot of daily stressful experiences as well as the coping and health responses to them (Bolger et al., 1989; Gortmaker, Eckenrode, & Gore, 1982).

dent of and responsible for changes in mental health status. For example, having arguments with one's spouse may reflect rather than cause psychological distress, so the etiological role of continued marital fighting in bringing about depression is more difficult to determine than is the influence of time-anchored episodes of fighting, due to the reverse causation issue. Thus stress inventories provide a way of recording new experiences and their timing and establishing whether they occurred prior to the onset of the symptoms being studied.

Third, as described earlier, stressors are actual life occurrences and are more proximal influences of behavior and health status than the more abstract social statuses that are studied in the Gove tradition. A focus on these events is essential to the situational or process orientation that is increasingly called for in stress research.

Finally, life events instruments are meant to be applicable to all populations. The events themselves are often characterized as "fortuitous" or "fateful," that is, not brought on by the individual's own actions, suggesting an accidental or random patterning of events that would make all populations potentially equally exposed to stress. Of course, because many events are indeed not truly fortuitous nor are they randomly distributed across age groups, distinct instruments have been developed for different groups within the general population.

The view that events are socially structured experiences rather than isolated occurrences (Pearlin & Lieberman, 1979) presents an important challenge to the validity of these measures and especially to their value in considerations of gender-linked outcomes. Gender researchers have, for example, questioned the exhaustiveness of these inventories and their appropriateness for various groups within the population. Belle (1982) and Makosky (1980) have pointed to the omission from such lists critical stressors in the lives of women, such as being victims of sexual abuse, discrimination, and violence.

Beyond the problems of content, Eckenrode and Gore (1981) have challenged the individualistic view of stressors as undesirable events that directly affect a single individual. Within a broader critique of the "events paradigm," they maintained that if social support should be viewed as a set of social–relational resources available through networks, then exposure to life stress should also be viewed as a network level phenomenon.[3] This position highlights two problems in models of the

[3]Data to support the idea that the problems of close ties have a significant impact on the mental health of individuals was first presented by Brown and colleagues in their landmark study *Social Origins of Depression* among London women (Brown & Harris, 1978). Following this lead, Eckenrode and Gore (1981) surveyed a sample of Boston women and,

stress process that are especially salient when gender differences are discussed. The first pertains to the wide range of empirical situations that could constitute exposure to stress. As researchers depart from the use of fixed checklists to determine exposure, defining the range of exposure experiences becomes more difficult. We would think that the problems of other people would be more likely to feature in women's stress "exposure" than in men's. Thus, fine-tuning the content of stress inventories only partially addresses the problem of exposure even in this method of assessment. Second, a consideration of the stressors happening in the lives of others draws attention to the fact that the social support system, its nature and availability, will be constrained by the level of stress and adaptive work that already occupies it. This interrelatedness of exposure to stress and the availability of coping resources such as social support has been a thorny problem in stress research because the central feature of the dominant "stress-buffering" model is the joint influence of stress and social support (or other coping variables) on health status outcomes. Whether stressors imply anything about coping resources has not traditionally been a central question in epidemiologic research on stress, although this is changing as the increased concern with understanding the transactional character of stress has brought forward a host of new conceptual and empirical problems for research on stress. In the next sections, we consider how these unresolved issues concerning stress exposure and the relatedness of stress and resource variables complicate the study of gender differences in depressive responses to stress.

DIFFERENTIAL VULNERABILITY TO STRESS: SOCIAL SUPPORT, PERSONALITY, AND COPING

In stress research, the concept of *vulnerability* refers to the "force with which stress impacts on the distress of an individual" (Kessler, 1979, p. 100), and it is assessed as a difference among individuals in their physical and mental health responses to stressful stimuli. It is commonly observed, as well as documented in the stress literature, that some individuals are virtually unaffected by undesirable events and adversities,

---

using an expanded version of a life events inventory that included questions about events occurring to significant others, found that fully 70% of the total events reported by respondents were events experienced by others around them. In other words, respondents reported as stressful more than twice as many events happening in the lives of other people as themselves.

whereas other individuals in the same circumstances experience a significant negative health impact. Because the effects of stressors are not uniform across all individuals or groups, the task of "stress-buffering" research is to identify factors and processes that make for "vulnerable" versus "resilient" individuals. How individuals cope with life stress, including the availability and use of social supports, is seen as a key to understanding vulnerability and resilience.

Thus, research on sex differences in vulnerability to stress moves a step beyond documenting differential exposure to life events or to ongoing strains in major life roles. A model of greater female vulnerability to the effects of stress predicts an interaction between sex and exposure, indicating that women are more highly affected by the stressful situations to which they and men are similarly exposed. The task then is to examine the factors contributing to this heightened reactivity.

Although most research demonstrates higher levels of distress and depression among women, the extent to which these gender differences are due to differences in stress exposure or to greater responsiveness or reactivity has become a significant issue, but there is much speculation and very little data. Kessler and associates have led the way with a series of innovative secondary analyses. Using a number of major data sets, they (Kessler, 1979; Kessler & McLeod, 1984; Kessler, McLeod, & Wethington, 1984; Wethington, McLeod, & Kessler, 1987) have examined gender differences in vulnerability to stressors that were disaggregated into particular clusters of negative experience (e.g., undesirable economic events, social losses). As other investigators have also found (Newmann, 1986; Thoits, 1982), there appears to be no empirical support in the Kessler *et al.* data for the idea of a generalized vulnerability to stress among women, which would be the case if they were more reactive than men to all or most classes of stressful experiences. Instead, their data pinpoint a greater degree of exposure to the problems of other people and suggest that an orientation to the problems of others and, possibly, involvement in supportive activities on their behalf may be responsible for gender differences in depression due to stress reactivity.

In addition to social support processes, much research has focused on a number of intraindividual characteristics that might account for gender differences in distress and in reactivity or vulnerability to stress. Both stress theory and theories of gender and depression share a concern with cognitive attributional or explanatory styles, problem-solving versus inactive coping styles, and sense of self-efficacy (or internal locus of control). These factors are most often viewed as causal explanations for the excess of depression among women but are modeled as moderating or mediating variables in models of stress, coping, and depression. This distinction, we will see, is a critical one because, although the strength of the gender or sex roles approach lies in establishing sex differences in these individual variables and their association with differential socialization experiences, the person–situation models that are characteristic in stress research provide a dynamic approach to understanding processes leading to depression. Later, we detail some issues regarding the study of gender differences in cognitive and other intraindividual variables.

An hypothesized gender difference in learned helplessness has for some time been regarded as a possible mechanism accounting for the excess of depression among women (Radloff & Monroe, 1978), and the current view of helplessness as integral to a broader maladaptive attributional style (Abramson, Seligman, & Teasdale, 1978) has received particular attention given the recent surge of interest in cognitive theories of depression (Beck, 1976). The Reformulated Learned Helplessness model of depression posits that individuals who are prone to self-blaming depressions tend to make internal (self-blaming), stable, and global attributions for failure experiences, whereas success experiences are seen as due to external, unstable, and specific factors. This attributional style reinforces the acceptance of and expectation for failure, while minimizing positive self-statements in the face of success. Although the theory is intuitively appealing, given its obvious linkages to sex role socialization data and particularly in light of the effectiveness of cognitive therapies in treating some depressions, it has not received strong empirical support as an explanation for gender differences in depression (Hammen, Krantz, & Cochran, 1981; and see Hammen, 1982, who reports other negative findings).

Most often cited in support of attributional differences and effects is evidence from a series of field and laboratory experiments conducted by Dweck and associates (Dweck & Bush, 1976; Dweck & Repucci, 1973; Dweck, Goetz, & Strauss, 1980). Their data indicate that girls generalize expectations for failure from old to new situations, whereas boys' expectations do not carry over in a like manner. Moreover, girls attribute achievement-related failure to internal factors such as lack of ability, in contrast with boys who use external rationale, such as teacher variables. However, a meta-analysis of 28 studies dealing with gender differences in attributions for success and failure found only two consistent sex differences in causal attributions of success and failure: Males make stronger ability attributions and are less likely to make attributions to luck irrespective of whether the outcome is success or failure (Whitley, McHugh, & Frieze, 1986). In sum, most studies of adults have failed to find any sex differences in expectations of future success and failure (Miller & Kirsch, 1987).

More important than the relative lack of sex differences identified in these studies is the difficulty the research has had in making a link between these cognitive deficits or styles and mental health variables. Although there are scattered reports of correlations between depression and cognitive style, there is virtually no evidence implicating these factors in the *etiology* of depression. In an extensive and carefully reasoned review of research that has attempted to identify psychosocial causes of depression, Barnett and Gotlib (1988) conclude with respect to attributional style, dysfunctional attitudes, and personality variables that there is little evidence that attributional style functions as a temporal antecedent to depression or is associated with increases in symptoms over time, though attributional style may play a role in recovery and predict to normal fluctuations in mood. Specifically, Barnett and Gotlib call for future research that departs from conceptualizations of cognition as "traitlike causal entities" that function independently of current life experiences in the etiology of depression. They see this more idiographic focus evidenced in an increasing literature that implicates negative life events, self-esteem, and relationships—as well as cognitions—in the onset of depression (Pyszczynski & Greenberg, 1987).

The embeddedness of intraindividual variables in a wider context of depressogenic conditions is a likely reason why empirical studies of these characteristics produce evidence that is suggestive at best both for any direct causal link between these types of variables and depression and for sex differences in the characteristics themselves. Miller and Kirsch (1988) have reviewed the evidence for gender differences in a number of cognitive variables and conclude that the evidence is weak and inconsistent regarding gender differences in positive or negative self-evaluations, negative evaluations for task performance, and perceptions of control. Although they cite some support for a relationship between gender and problem-centered versus emotion-centered coping style, systematic studies by Folkman and Lazarus (Folkman & Lazarus, 1980; Lazarus & Folkman, 1984) largely suggest otherwise. In a survey of a community population of middle-aged adults (Folkman & Lazarus, 1980), using their widely adopted "Ways of Coping" tool, analysis of coping responses aggregated across situations did reveal sex differences for both problem-centered and emotion-centered coping. However, more refined analyses showed the greater influence of situational variables.

Similarly, the locus of control construct has been studied for its relevance to the problem of sex differences in depression. Again, empirical support for direct linkages among gender, locus of control, and depression is weak and contrasts with the better established view of locus of control as a moderator variable that acts in conjunction with life stress variables and other situational and individual characteristics in shaping mental health outcomes of these processes (Lefcourt *et al.*, 1984).

In sum, it should be emphasized that the unlikely prospect of identifying one or two intraindividual variables that mediate between gender and depression in a simplistic fashion does not argue for throwing the baby out with the bath water. Rather, we see the literature as suggesting that the influence of these variables must be investigated through designs that on the one hand attend to existing knowledge about gender differences and sex roles, and on the other are informed by theories of depression that describe how these processes occur.

SOCIAL RELATIONSHIPS, SOCIAL SUPPORT, AND SELF-ESTEEM IN EXPOSURE AND VULNERABILITY TO STRESS

In this section we present a number of considerations relevant to the role of social relationships in the stress process, providing some insight into the interrelatedness of the social support and self-esteem concepts and why research on the role of social support in the stress process has been so problematic. Here we begin to examine areas in which cross-fertilization of gender research and stress research will lead to fresh understandings of stress, coping, and social support. Specifically, we point to indications that processes affecting self-esteem may be the critical intrapsychic portion of the emergent model linking stress to depression and that significant gender differences might lie in the intensity of the interplay between social ties and self esteem.

We begin this undertaking by considering the social–relational basis for self-esteem, especially among females, and the interpersonal dimensions to both stress and coping.

Interpersonal Dimensions to Self-Esteem, Stress, and Coping

In the previous section, we focused on the intrapsychic dimension of coping and research on gender differences in coping-related traits. The contrast between the wealth of research studies and the paucity of "results" with respect to gender differences is significant in that it highlights how little attention has been given both to the contexts in which these coping-related variables may operate and to the mental health outcomes they are presumed to affect. However, on the positive side, we wish to explore the research potential of one significant individual difference variable—self-esteem—in models linking the stress process to depression onset because here is an area for which there are more consistently reported sex differences and, as Barnett and Gotlib (1988) have also noted, a theoretical rationale for its relevance both to stressful experiences and depression.

Regarding the association between gender and self-esteem, a considerable literature describes feminine socialization and the resulting dependency of women on the opinions and evaluations of others in making their own judgments of how they are doing, that is, in maintaining self-image and self-esteem (Bardwick & Douvan, 1971; Bush, 1987; Chodorow, 1974, 1978; Douvan, 1978; Douvan & Adelson, 1966; Kagan, 1964; Gilligan, 1982; Miller, 1976; Rubin, 1985). Although various theorists differ in the emphasis they place on family structure, socialization practices, adult social roles, biology, and the role of women as caretakers, the general themes of this literature may be woven together into a coherent tale. At a relatively early age, boys are forced for a variety of reasons to make clear distinctions between themselves and their adult caretakers and to develop ego boundaries and an independent sense of self. Girls, on the other hand, may comfortably continue to identify with the female caregiver and other adults and continue to be dependent and rely on adults for information about self-worth at a time when boys are building boundaries between themselves and others and turning to real world achievements as criteria for forming judgments about the value of the self. In addition, as Kagan (1964) notes, sex role norms demand interpersonal success from females but other, more concrete, achievements from males, so affirmation of a feminine sex role identification demands an audience, whereas a masculine identification may be derived from objective information not dependent on the responses of others. In sum, without these independent sources of esteem, girls remain more vulnerable to loss of love and more attuned and sensitive to the vicissitudes of the interpersonal world, the world of connectedness and emotional ties on which they rely for a core sense of self.

This arena of research has been largely overlooked by students of stress, despite its obvious significance to understanding the profoundly interpersonal nature of stressful experiences for women. Here we mean two things. First, the most potent stressors involve losses, disruptions, or conflicts with significant others because these interpersonal breaches threaten the ties that are the primary basis for women's judgments of their own adequacy, that is, for their self-esteem and identity. Although studies of stress make clear that women are more exposed to interpersonal conflicts and that these in turn are highly significant influences on distress (Kandel & Davies, 1982), they tend to locate the source of such gender effects in differential exposure to and investment in family roles rather than the more fundamental differences in the meaning of all relational ties and, we emphasize, their relevance to self-esteem. Research on adolescent populations also establishes that girls' self-esteem is more contingent upon relationships and that girls are more reactive in terms of diminished self-esteem to interpersonal threats ranging from dating pressure to changes in the school environment that may jeopardize these ties (Bush & Simmons, 1987; Douvan & Adelson, 1966; Simmons & Blyth, 1987). Thus data of this nature on youth, who do not yet occupy adult roles, provide additional evidence linking women's self-esteem to relational contexts rather than to particular configurations of work and family roles.

The second interpersonal aspect to stressful experiences pertains to the coping process. Over the past few years, stress researchers have been struggling to conceptualize the roles of both social and intraindividual mediators in the stress process, and particularly, to specify the relationship between reliance on social support and other coping efforts (cf. Thoits, 1984). Although research on stress and its mediators has tended to focus on social support or coping-related traits such as self-esteem or sense of competency, the few studies of depressive symptomatology that report on gender differences in stress mediators and moderators note that for women social support has greater importance as a coping device than sense of personal competency, whereas for men the sense of competency is essential, and social support in the absence of competency increases vulnerability to stress (Husaini, Neff, Newbrough, & Moore, 1982). Consistent with this view, Dean and Lin (1977) found that social support is a more central stress-mediating variable for women than men.

This interpersonal dimension to both stress and coping is relevant to depression in that recent understandings of depression highlight the etiologic role of major losses or disappointments, either interpersonally or in other domains, that directly jeopardize the sense of self-worth (Arieti & Bemporad, 1980; Brown & Harris, 1978). Of particular interest is the work of Brown and associates in that they consider the interrelationships among stressors, social support, and self-esteem in their intensive studies of working-class married and unmarried women (Brown & Bifulco, 1985; Brown & Harris, 1978). In their general model, onset of depression is directly preceded by provoking events that involve loss of some kind and that give rise to interpretations of failure and inadequacy. For the married women in the sample, ongoing low marital support and long-term difficulties with their husbands seem to have reduced self-esteem long before the occurrence of a final, provoking stressful event, and the poor fabric of the marriage is associated with the increased chance of such events occurring. For these women, individuals outside the home identified as "very close" appear not to be able to interrupt the generalization of hopelessness that is triggered by the provoking agent, and depression, therefore, follows quite swiftly. For the unmarried women, having "very close" others does function to reduce the risk of depression, and having these relationships is highly correlated with higher levels of self-esteem.

Although Brown recognizes that effective coping with living alone may heighten self-esteem and encourage building close relationships, he is more inclined to think that the major pathway of influence, at least for the married women, is from relational deterioration to loss of self-esteem, an interpretation that underscores the point that we emphasize about coping: The "coping process" cannot be understood apart from the social–relational context that provides not only a distinct class of "social support resources" but that also supports the mobilization of psychological resources and protects those resources from diminution. Although this linking of esteem to the relational context appears particularly applicable to women, the findings of Pearlin and associates (1981) on responses to stress of job loss and other negative job events also demonstrate this social basis for self-esteem in men.

Problems in Social Support Research

Despite the clear implication that these social ties are important multifunction environmental resources—as a basis for identity, in exposure to stress, in coping, and most generally in structuring the conduct of daily living—it is only very recently that researchers have begun to argue that research on social relationships should be systematically integrated with research on the stress process (Gottlieb, 1985; Hirsch & Renders, 1986). This task and the challenge it poses should not be confused with the well-established field of study that focuses on social supports. In fact, it is the sense of paradox that arises from research on the "stress-buffering" properties of social support that we believe is a key impetus for refocusing to a more general concern with social relationships of all kinds for investigations of gender, stress, and depression. The specific problem with current models of stress and stress-buffering resources is that despite the seemingly greater potential of women's support systems—that is, women's more extensive social ties, greater ease with intimacy, involvement in helping interactions, and the use of talking with others in coping with stress—the mental health and well-being of women does not seem to benefit from these interpersonal resources to the degree we might expect. How can this observation be reconciled with existing thinking about the stress process and what does this discrepancy reveal about our models and methods for studying stress?

A point of departure for obtaining perspective on this paradox is two long-standing concerns about the conceptualization and measurement of social support and its relationship to the companion concept of stress. The first pertains to the multifaceted nature of relationships and specifically to the occurrence of nonsupportive and conflictional interactions that shape the aggregate picture of support and its role in the stress process. In keeping with this first thrust, Rook (1984) has presented data to show that social network stresses are stronger negative influences of mental health status than supportive features are positive influences. And Eckenrode and Riley (Eckenrode, 1983; Riley & Eckenrode, 1986) have shown that only some women, those already evidencing significant coping resources, in fact benefit from extensive social ties. Thoits (1984) has added that attention to the stress-buffering role of social support is a narrower view still.

A second and more baffling problem in the study of support is that men and women structure their social lives differently and benefit from different types of social relational systems. Data on social support from middle childhood through adolescence and adulthood indicate that boys and men appear to benefit from having extensive casual involvements in contrast to girls who prefer fewer, more intimate ties (Bryant, 1985; cf. Belle, 1987; Miller & Ingham, 1976). Notwithstanding, this variability in social–relational styles and support requirements, researchers continue to favor measurement of one or another aspect of support. Lin and associates (Lin, Dean, & Ensel, 1981), for example, used a measure of "close-ties" support for their analyses of the stress/depression relationship and found that the effects of stress were mediated through the support variable for women only, suggesting that social support is fairly extraneous to the coping behavior of men. Although a support effect in this direction seems intuitively correct, the conclusion is unwarranted if measures of support fail to capture the essence of relationship functions and the support process for men.

Exposure and Reactivity to Stress: Problems of Meaning and Context. The problem of identifying social assets and disentangling them from social liabilities has been well recognized in stress research, but whether it should be considered a measurement caveat or a paradigm weakness is a question that might well be answered differently by gender and stress researchers. Earlier in this chapter we described the dominant vulnerability model of stress and its mental health effects and distinguished among its three analytic components: life stresses, moderating characteristics, and health outcomes. Recent papers on women and stress dig deeper into the field of gender studies than ever before and emphasize the role of social structure in shaping sex differences relevant to the key aspects of stress exposure and response: (1) one's "eligibility" to be exposed to a range of stressors (Aneshensel & Pearlin, 1987); (2) variability in the meaning of stressors (Barnett, Biener, & Baruch, 1987; Bush & Simmons, 1987; Kessler & McLeod, 1984); and (3) variability in coping resources (Bush & Simmons, 1987). Although not working explicitly within a stress/distress framework, Bush and Simmons discuss their evidence of girls' greater difficulty in early adolescence in terms of the unique configuration of vulnerability that is crystallized at this time. They argue that the social organization of gender becomes personally immediate for the first time during early adolescence and shapes the stressors to which girls are exposed (e.g., sexual pressures, socially devalued adult roles) as well as their coping resources (e.g., self-esteem). Regarding the latter, they emphasize that in this period of development characterized by stresses of changing roles and relationships as well as physical change, girls' greater dependency on the evaluations of others for their self-regard undermines their ability to cope with these sex-specific adolescent pressures.

These discussions of gender-specific stresses and coping liabilities and of the role of social structure in shaping exposure, meaning, and responses to stress are beginning to receive a good deal of empirical support. Two examples of recent data documenting gender differences in distress responses to social–relational stressors point to the differences in the determinants of stress exposure and vulnerability for men and women. Both focus on the stress process for married individuals. In the first study, Cronkite and Moos (1984) measured undesirable life change, each spouse's level of depressed mood, physical symptoms and alcohol consumption, as well as type of coping—either avoidance or approach. In general, they found that models of the stress process differed for men and women and that there was "a greater responsiveness among women to environmental influences, irrespective of whether they are beneficial or detrimental" (p. 387). For example, in the case of the detrimental, their data show that the occurrence of undesirable life events and husbands' alcohol consumption are related to wives' depressed mood. In contrast, the depressed mood of husbands was found to be determined primarily by their own experiences and problems. In addition, the primary determinant of husbands' avoidance coping was their own depressed mood, but the wives' avoidance coping was primarily determined by their own undesirable events plus their husbands' physical symptoms. Regarding responsiveness to the positive features of the environment, they summarize: "Women who reported more family support relied less on avoidance coping and showed less depressed mood and physical symptoms while similar effects were not observed for their husbands" (p. 387).

An entirely different approach to exploring gender differences in the dimensions of stress exposure and vulnerability is taken by Wheaton (1990) in testing a more general model that considers ongoing stress context as a key influence of the meaning and therefore effects of undesirable life changes. In one set of analyses, he considers whether basically positive or negative experiences in work or marriage serve to exacerbate or ameliorate the effects of negative life changes in one or the other of these roles. The case of divorce is particularly interesting: Here we see that for women, increases in the level of prior marital problems serve to decrease the effects of divorce on psychological distress, but for men, there is no relationship between context of prior problems and mental health effects of divorce. Wheaton concludes that the findings show a general pattern of "context dependence" for women; that is, because the nature of the ongoing stress context conditions the relationship between acute stressors and mental health outcome for women but not for men, it appears that women and not men seek meaning from these contexts in appraising the significance of stressors more currently experienced.

Findings such as these are richly illustrative of gender differences in the stress process, and they also raise two questions about the major conceptual and analytic frameworks that both generate and make sense out of these data. First, our distinction between stress exposure and vulnerability, although useful, has been reified in that it has been taken to mean that there are distinctly separate, isolable components of stress exposure and reactivity. Second, and related, is the view of vulnerability as a composite of individual (or group) differences, such that resources and responses to stress are located at the individual level and thus not seen in their relationship to the same social forces that shape exposure. The earlier discussion of social–structural determinants of both stress exposure and coping resources would suggest that this model is not totally appropriate for theoretically guided research into gender differences in stressful antecedents to depression.

The research by Kessler and associates (Kessler & McLeod, 1984) is interesting in this regard because, although groundbreaking in its attention to sex differences across many different types of stressful life events, the arbitrary line between exposure and vulnerability to stress is highlighted. As described earlier, their secondary analysis of data from thousands of men and women sampled in a large number of community studies disaggregated reports of undesirable life events into the following types of experience: income losses, separation and divorce, death of loved ones, other love losses, and physical illness and injuries. They also distinguished whether these events had occurred to respondents personally, to individuals within their more immediate families, or within more distant social networks. Analyses revealed two types of

sex differences in events exposure. Men reported more events of income loss, and women reported many more network events and deaths
of loved ones. Analyses conducted separately for men and women
showed that women were distressed by events that happened both to
family and to distant network members, whereas men were distressed
only by events that occurred to close family members, even if these
were relatively minor. The significance of these differentials was born
out in the models accounting for the overall vulnerability differential:
The sex difference in vulnerability to distress associated with undesirable life events was more pronounced at the edges of the caring network than at its center (Wethington, McLeod, & Kessler, 1987, p. 150).
In other words, the view that women have a generalized vulnerability
to stress, as implied by concepts such as "learned helplessness," was not
borne out. Nor was it the case that women were any more reactive than
men to the stresses in family life. Rather, it seems that women had
more involvements outside the immediate family and that their psychological well-being was more affected than that of men by aspects of
these interactions.

Although data that might account for this negative effect on women
of network involvement are limited, it is believed that some type of
caregiver liability is involved here and that the quality of women's socialization and adult roles that require this attentiveness and responsiveness to the needs of others is a more distal, yet significant underlying
thread of the "vulnerability" dynamics. This being the case, it is difficult
to reconcile the observation that "women's roles obligate them to care
more" (Wethington, McLeod, & Kessler, 1987, p. 145), which appears to
be a problem of socially structured exposure, with the relegation of this
variable to the vulnerability component to the stress process.

The blurred line between exposure and vulnerability is a specific
instance of the larger problem of meaning that comes up in stress research with great regularity. That is, assessments of stress exposure are
problematic in that there is a tremendous variability in the meaning that
these stimuli have for the individuals experiencing them. In addressing
this problem, stress researchers usually pare down lists of events to include only those that a priori would appear to have an unequivocally
negative connotation. But even doing so, upon closer examination, the
stressors have vastly different intrinsic meanings across individuals.
Some researchers, such as Brown, have abandoned altogether what he
calls this "dictionary" (Brown, 1984, p. 187) approach to stress measurement, whereas others, following Lazarus and associates (Lazarus &
Folkman, 1984), have advanced transactional frameworks in which the
concept of exposure takes on less conceptual and empirical significance.

For example, when a loss of a loved one means loss of a sole supportive tie, versus when it means the end of a stressful caretaking, these differences will be accounted for in the cognitive appraisal process. Although this formulation solves the problem of meaning by blurring the lines around the "stress exposure" construct, this conception of stress takes what is really a finetuning of the exposure construct and places it within the individual difference domain, making it, in effect, a personal vulnerability factor.

A further complicating issue is raised by Brown and Bifulco (1985) who, in describing the chain of events leading to onset of depression in their sample of low-income London women, point to the fact that the *provoking agent* or stressor and the *vulnerability* factor, in this case the availability of support, seem to be one and the same, as evidenced by the correlations between marital support and the rate of provoking agents (stressors) concerning the husband. Thoits (1982) also has pointed to the probability that stressors will affect both the character and levels of coping resources because many undesirable life events are themselves social support losses, and such events and others may produce a chain of changes within the individual support system. She presents data to show that in quantitative studies of stress exposure and vulnerability, subgroups evidencing the greatest effects of stress on their support system will appear to be more vulnerable to stress than they in fact are. Thoits sees a need to address this methodological problem before further study of the vulnerability (stress-buffering) model can proceed.

TOWARD INTEGRATING STRESS AND GENDER RESEARCH

From the perspective of stress research, problems of this nature are rightly characterized as methodological. The theme on which we shall close this chapter is that, from the perspective of gender research on stress, this issue, among others identified here, may indeed be the very focus of new investigations that promise to cross the boundaries of these two fields.

In taking a brief look at the major models of stress, we have examined how well these frameworks incorporate understandings of gender identity and roles that have been generated from a different research tradition. In specific, we have discussed two issues pivotal to understanding the relationships among stress, gender, and depression. First, there is the link between coping variables, especially self-esteem, and social relationships. Here we suggest that isolated attention to either self-esteem or social support as mediating constructs fails to grasp the underlying role of relationships for women in shaping coping abilities and efforts. Second, we see that the categoric concepts of exposure and vulnerability are problematic in that vulnerability differences between men and women are in part socially structured differences in the nature of stressors. We have emphasized that the problem of meaning remains a critical, unresolved issue in stress research.

In an important sense, the difficulties we have highlighted extend earlier discussions of the need for a contextual approach to the stress process. There is little doubt that a significant impetus for the wealth of research on sex differences in distress and depression derives from a need to give substantive flesh to an overall very abstract body of knowledge about stress and its mental health effects. Cross-fertilization of research on stress with studies of gender identity and gender role behavior can only benefit research in the latter tradition because that field is already moving away from the study of sex differences *per se* to a consideration of the contexts in which sex differences take on critical significance.

ACKNOWLEDGMENT

Work on this chapter was supported in part by a grant from the National Institute of Mental Health (MH-42909).

REFERENCES

Abramson, L. Y., Seligman, M. E. P., & Teasdale, J. (1978). Learned helplessness in humans: Critique and reformulation. *Journal of Abnormal Psychology, 87,* 49–74.
Achenbach, M., & Edelbrock, C. S. (1984). Psychopathology of childhood, *Annual Review of Psychology, 35,* 227–256.
Albert, N., and Beck, A. T. (1975). Incidence of depression in early adolescence: A preliminary study. *Journal of Youth and Adolescence, 4,* 301–306.
Aneshensel, C. S., Frerichs, R. R., & Clark, V. A. (1981). Family roles and sex differences in depression. *Journal of Health and Social Behavior, 22,* 379–93.
Aneshensel, C. S., & Pearlin, L. I. (1987). Structural contexts of sex differences in stress. In R. C. Barnett, L. Biener, & G. K. Baruch (Eds.), *Gender and stress* (pp. 75–95). New York: Free Press.
Arieti, S., & Bemporad, J. (1980). Depression-prone personality in women. *American Journal of Psychiatry, 136,* 1369.
Bardwick, J. M., & Douvan, E. (1971). Ambivalence: The socialization of women. In V. Gornick & B. K. Moran (Eds.), *Women in sexist society.* New York: Basic Books.
Barnett, P. A., & Gotlib, I. H. (1988). Psychosocial functioning and depression: Dis-

tinguishing among antecedents, concomitants, and consequences. *Psychological Bulletin, 104,* 97–126.

Barnett, R. C., Biener, L., & Baruch, G. K. (Eds.). (1987). *Gender and stress.* New York: Free Press.

Beck, A. T. (1976). *Cognitive therapy and the emotional disorders.* New York: International Universities Press.

Belle, D. (1987). Gender differences in the social moderators of stress. In R. C. Barnett, L. Biener, & G. K. Baruch (Eds.), *Gender and stress* (pp. 257–277). New York: Free Press.

Belle, D. (1982). The stress of caring: Women as providers of social support. In L. Goldberger & S. Breznitz (Eds.), *Handbook of stress: Theoretical and clinical aspects.* New York: Free Press.

Berndt, T. (1982). The features and effects of friendship in early adolescence. *Child Development, 53,* 1447–1460.

Bolger, N., DeLongis, A., Kessler, R. C., & Wethington, E. (1990). The microstructure of daily role related stress in married couples. In J. Eckenrode & S. Gore (Eds.), *Stress between work and family* (pp. 95–105). New York: Plenum Press.

Boyd, J. H., & Weissman, M. M. (1981). Epidemiology of affective disorders—A reexamination and future directions. *Archives of General Psychiatry, 38,* 1039–1046.

Brown, G. N. (1984). Contextual measures of life events. In B. S. Dohrenwend & B. P. Dohrenwend (Eds.), *Stressful life events and their contexts* (pp. 187–201). New Brunswick, NJ: Rutgers University Press.

Brown, G. N., & Harris, T. (1978). *Social origins of depression: A study of psychiatric disorders in women.* London: Tavistock Publications.

Brown, G. W., & Bifulco, A. (1985). Social support, life events, and depression. In I. G. Sarason & B. R. Sarason (Eds.), *Social support: Theory, research and applications.* The Hague: Martinus-Nijhoff.

Bryant, B. K. (1989). The need for support in relation to the need for autonomy. In D. Belle (Ed.). *Childrens Networks and Social Supports* (pp. 332–351). New York: Wiley.

Bush, D. M. (1987). The impact of family and school on adolescent girls' aspirations and expectations: The public-private split and the reproduction of gender inequality. In J. Figueira-McDonough & R. Sarri (Eds.), *The trapped women* (pp. 258–295). Beverly Hills, CA: Sage.

Bush, D. M., & Simmons, R. (1987). Gender and coping with the entry into early adolescence. In R. C. Barnett, L. Biener, & G. K. Baruch, (Eds.), *Gender and stress* (pp. 185–218). New York: Free Press.

Caplan, G. (1986). Recent developments in crisis intervention and the promotion of support services. In M. Kessler & S. Goldston (Eds.), *A decade of progress in primary prevention* (pp. 235–260). Hanover, NH: University Press of New England.

Chodorow, N. (1974). Family structure and feminine personality. In M. Rosaldo & L. Lamphere (Eds.), *Women, culture and society* (pp. 43–66). Palo Alto, CA: Stanford University Press.

Chodorow, N. (1978). *The reproduction of mothering.* Berkeley: University of California Press.

Cleary, P. (1987). Gender differences in stress related disorders. In R. C. Barnett, L. Biener, & G. K. Baruch, (Eds.), *Gender and stress* (pp. 39–72). New York: Free Press.

Cooperstock, R. (1971). Sex differences in the use of mood-modifying drugs: An explanatory mode. *Journal of Health & Social Behavior, 12,* 238.

Cronkite, R. C., & Moos, R. H. (1984). The role of predisposing and moderating factors in the stress-illness relationship. *Journal of Health and Social Behavior, 25,* 372–393.

Dean, A., & Ensel, W. M. (1983). Socially structured depression in men and women. In R. J. R. Greenley (Ed.), *Research in community and mental health.* Greenwich, CT: JAI Press.

Dean, A., & Lin, N. (1977). The stress-buffering role of social support. *Journal of Nervous and Mental Disease, 165,* 403–417.

Dohrenwend, B. S., & Dohrenwend, B. P. (1976). Sex differences in psychiatric disorders. *American Journal of Sociology, 81,* 1447–1454.

Dohrenwend, B. S., & Dohrenwend, B. P. (1981a). Life stress and illness: Formulation of the issues. In B. S. Dohrenwend & B. P. Dohrenwend (Eds.), *Stressful life events and their contexts* (pp. 1–27). New Brunswick, NJ: Rutgers University Press.

Dohrenwend, B. P., & Dohrenwend, B. S. (1981b). *Stressful life events and their context.* New York: PRODIST, Neale Watson Academic Publications.

Dohrenwend, B. S., Krasnoff, L., Askenasy A. R., & Dohrenwend, B. P. (1978). Exemplification of a method for scaling life events: The PERI Life Events Scale. *Journal of Health and Social Behavior, 19,* 205–229.

Dohrenwend, B. P., Shrout, P. E., Egri, G., & Mendelsohn, F. S. (1980). Nonspecific psychological distress and other dimensions of psychopathology: Measures for use in the general population. *Archives of General Psychiatry, 37,* 1229–1236.

Douvan, E. (1978). Sex role learning. In J. C. Coleman (Ed.), *The school years.* London: Methuen.

Douvan, E., & Adelson, J. (1966). *The adolescent experience.* New York: Wiley.

Dweck, C. S., & Bush, E. S. (1976). Sex differences in learned helplessness. *Developmental Psychology, 14,* 268–276.

Dweck, C. S., Reppucci, N. D. (1973). Learned helplessness and reinforcement responsibility in children. *Journal of Personality and Social Psychology, 25,* 109–116.

Dweck, C. S., Goetz, T. E., & Strauss, N. L. (1980). Sex differences in learned helplessness: IV. An experimental and naturalistic study of failure generalization and its medicators. *Journal of Personality and Social Psychology, 38,* 441–452.

Eckenrode, J. (1983). The mobilization of social supports: Some individual constraints. *Journal of Community Psychology, 11,* 509–528.

Eckenrode, J., & Gore, S. (1981). Stressful events and social supports: The significance of context. In B. H. Gottlieb (Ed.), *Social networks and social support.* Beverly Hills, CA: Sage.

Folkman, S., & Lazarus, R. (1980). An analysis of coping in a middle-aged community sample. *Journal of Health and Social Behavior, 21,* 219–239.

Fox, J. W. (1980). Gove's specific sex-role therapy of mental illness: A research note. *Journal of Health and Social Behavior, 21,* 260–267.

Frerichs, R. S., Aneshensel, C. S., & Clark, V. A. (1981). Prevalence of depression in Los Angeles County. *American Journal of Epidemiology, 113,* 691–699.

Gilligan, C. (1982). *In a different voice: Psychological theory and women's development.* Cambridge, MA: Harvard University Press.

Golding, J. M. (1988). Gender differences in depressive symptoms: Statistical considerations. *Psychology of Women Quarterly, 12,* 61–74.

Gore, S., & Mangione, T. (1983). Social roles, sex roles and psychological distress: Additive and interactive models of sex differences. *Journal of Health and Social Behavior, 24*(4), 49–53.

Gortmaker, S., Eckenrode, J., & Gore, S. (1982). Stress and the utilization of health services: A time-series and cross-sectional analysis. *Journal of Health and Social Behavior, 23,* 25–38.

Gottlieb, B. H. (1985). Social support and the study of personal relationships, *Journal of Social and Personal Relationships, 2,* 351–75.

Gove, W. R. (1978). Sex differences in mental illness among adult men and women: An evaluation of four questions raised regarding the evidence on the higher rates of women. *Social Science and Medicine, 12B,* 187–198.

Gove, W., & Tudor, J. (1973). Adult sex roles and mental illness. *American Journal of Sociology, 77*, 812–835.

Gove, W., & Geerkin, M. R. (1977). Response bias in surveys of mental health: An empirical investigation. *American Journal of Sociology, 82*, 1287–1317.

Hammen, C. L. (1982). Gender and depression. In I. Al-Issa (Ed.), *Gender and psychopathology.* New York: Academic Press.

Hammen, C., Krantz, C., & Cochran, S. (1981). Relationships between depression and causal attributions about stressful life events. *Cognitive Therapy and Research, 5*, 351–358.

Hirsch, B. J., & Renders, R. J. (1986). The challenge of adolescent friendship: A study of Lisa and her friends. In S. E. Hobfoll (Ed.), *Stress, social support, and women.* New York: Hemisphere Publishing Co.

Holmes, T. H., & Rahe, R. H. (1967). The social readjustment rating scale. *Journal of Psychosomatic Research, 11*, 213–218.

Hunter, F. T., & Youniss, J. (1982). Changes in functions of three relations during adolescence. *Developmental Psychology, 18*, 806–84.

Hussaini, B. A., Neff, J. A., Newbrough, J. R., & Moore, M. C. (1982). The stress buffering role of social support and personal competence among the rural married. *Journal of Community Psychology, 10*, 409–426.

Kagan, J. (1964). Acquisition and significance of sex typing and sex role identity. In M. L. Hoffman & L. W. Hoffman (Eds.), *Review of child development.* New York: Russell Sage Foundation.

Kandel, D. B., & Davies, M. (1982). Epidemiology of depressive mood in adolescents. *Archives of General Psychiatry, 39*, 1205–1212.

Kessler, R. C. (1979). A strategy for studying differential vulnerability to the psychological consequences of stress. *Journal of Health and Social Behavior, 20*, 100–108.

Kessler, R. C., McLeod, J. D., & Wethington, E. (1984). The costs of caring: A perspective on the relationship between sex and psychological distress. In I. Sarason & B. Sarason (Eds.), *Social support and health.* The Hague: Martinus Nijoff.

Kessler, R. C., & McLeod, J. D. (1984). Sex differences in vulnerability to undesirable life events. *American Sociological Review, 49*, 620–631.

Lazarus, R. S., & Folkman, S. (1984). *Stress, appraisal and coping.* New York: Springer.

Lefcourt, H. M., Martin, R. A., & Salch, W. E. (1984). Locus of control and social support: Interactive moderators of stress. *Journal of Personality and Social Psychology, 47*, 378–389.

Lin, N., Dean, A., & Ensel, W. M. (1981). Support methodology from the sociological perspective. *Schizophrenia Bulletin, 7*(1), 73–90.

Lin, N., Dean, A., & Ensel, W. M. (1986). *Social support, life events and depression.* New York: Academic Press.

Maccoby, E. & Jacklin, C. (1974). *The psychology of sex differences.* Stanford: Stanford University Press.

Makosky, V. P. (1980). Stress and the mental health of women: A discussion of research and issues. In M. Guttentag & D. Belle (Eds.), *The mental health of women.* New York: Academic Press.

Miller, J. B. (1976). *Toward a new psychology of women.* Boston: Beacon Press.

Miller, P. M., & Ingham, J. G. (1976). Friends, confidants, and symptoms. *Social Psychiatry, 11*, 51–58.

Miller, S. M., & Kirsch, N. (1987). Sex differences in cognitive coping with stress. In R. C. Barnett, L. Biener, & G. K. Baruch (Eds.), *Gender and stress* (pp. 278–307). New York: Free Press.

Myers, J. K., Weissman, M. M., Tischler, G. L., Holzer, C. E., III, Leaf, P. J., Orvaschel, H.,

Anthony, J., Boyd, J. H., Burke, J. D., Kramer, M., and Stoltzman, R. (1984). Six month prevalence of psychiatric disorders in three communities, 1980 to 1982. *Archives of General Psychiatry, 41*, 959–967.

Newmann, J. P. (1984). Sex differences in symptoms of depression: Clinical disorder or normal distress. *Journal of Health and Social Behavior, 25*, 136–159.

Newmann, J. P. (1986). Gender, life strains, and depression. *Journal of Health and Social Behavior, 27*, 161–178.

Pearlin, L. I., & Schooler, C. (1978). The structure of coping. *Journal of Health and Social Behavior, 19*, 2–21.

Pearlin, L. I., & Lieberman, M. A. (1979). Social sources of emotional distress. In R. Simmons (Ed.), *Research in Community and Mental Health, 1*, Greenwich, CT: JAI Press.

Pearlin, L. I., Lieberman, M. A., Menaghan, E., & Mullan, J. E. (1981). The stress process. *Journal of Health and Social Behavior, 22*, 337–356.

Phillips, D., & Segal, B. (1969). Sexual status and psychiatric symptoms. *American Sociological Review, 34*, 58–72.

Pyszczynski, T., & Greenberg, J. (1987). Self-regulatory perseveration and the depressive self-focusing style: A self-awareness theory of reactive depression. *Psychological Bulletin, 102*, 122–138.

Rabkin, J. G., & Struening, E. (1976). Life events, stress, and illness. *Science, 194*, 1013–1020.

Radloff, L. S. (1977). The CES-D. A self report depression scale for research in general population. *Applied Psychological Measurement, 3*, 385–401.

Radloff, L. S., & Monroe, M. M. (1978). Sex differences in helplessness: with implications for depression. In L. S. Hansen & R. S. Rapoza (Eds.), *Career development and counseling of women.* (pp. 199–221). Springfield, IL: Charles C Thomas.

Riley, D., & Eckenrode, J. (1986). Social ties: Subgroup differences in costs and benefits. *Journal of Personality and Social Psychology, 51*, 770–778.

Robins, L. N., Helzer, J. E., Weissman, M. M., Overaschel, H., Gruenberg, E., Burke, J. D., & Reigier, D. (1984). Lifetime prevalence of specific psychiatric disorders in three sites. *Archives of General Psychiatry, 38*, 381–389.

Rook, K. S. (1984). The negative side of social interaction: Impact on psychological well-being. *Journal of Personality and Social Psychology, 46*, 1097–1108.

Rubin, L. (1985). *Just friends: The role of friendship in our lives.* New York: Harper & Row.

Rutter, M. (1986). The developmental psychopathology of depression: Issues and perspectives. In M. Rutter, C. E. Izard, & P. B. Read (Eds.), *Depression in young people* (pp. 3–30). Guilford Press.

Simmons, R. G., & Blyth, D. A. (1987). *Moving into adolescence: The impact of pubertal change and school context.* New York: Aldine de Gruyrer.

Thoits, P. (1982). Life stress, social support, and psychological vulnerability: Epidemiological considerations. *Journal of Community Psychology, 10*, 341–363.

Thoits, P. (1984). Coping, social support, and psychological outcomes: The central role of emotion. In P. Shaver (Ed.), *Review of Personality and Social Psychology, 5*, 219–238. Beverly Hills, CA: Sage.

Veroff, J., Douvan, E., & Kulka, R. A. (1981). *The inner American.* New York: Basic Books.

Warheit, G. S., Holtzer, III, C. E., Bell, R. A., & Arey, S. A. (1976). Sex, marital status, and mental health: A reappraisal. *Social Forces, 55*, 459–470.

Weissman, M. M., & Klerman, G. L. (1977). Sex differences and the epidemiology of depression. *Archives of General Psychiatry, 34*, 98–111.

Weissman, M. M., Leaf, P. J., Holzer, C. G., III, Myers, J. K., and Tischler, G. L. (1984). The epidemiology of depression. An update on sex differences in rates. *Journal of Affective Disorders, 7*, 179–188.

Wethington, E., McLeod, J. D., & Kessler, R. C. 91987). The importance of life events for explaining sex differences in mental health. In R. C. Barnett, L. Biener, & G. K. Baruch (Eds.), *Gender and stress* (pp. 144–155). New York: Free Press.

Wheaton, B. (1990). Where work and family meet: Stress across social roles. In J. Eckenrode & S. Gore (Eds.), *Stress between work and family* (pp. 153–174). New York: Plenum.

Whitley, B. E., McHugh, M. C., & Frieze, I. H. (1986). Assessing the theoretical models for sex differences in causal attributions of success and failure. In J. S. Hyde & M. C. Linn (Eds.), *The psychology of gender: Advances through meta-analysis.* Baltimore: Johns Hopkins University Press.

8

Stress and Support Processes in Close Relationships

BENJAMIN H. GOTTLIEB and FRED WAGNER

INTRODUCTION

To date, our understanding of social support has relied more strongly on people's reports of the resources they could gain from their social networks than on the study of their stress-related transactions. The measures of social support that have achieved the most popularity (Cohen *et al.*, 1985; Procidano & Heller, 1983; Sarason *et al.*, 1983) gauge the psychological sense of support that people develop but leave obscure how their experiences in particular relationships affect their receipt and provision of support. As Pearlin and McCall (1990) observe, "the social and interactional character of support has either been ignored altogether or largely taken for granted." By treating social support as a dynamic process that unfolds in particular relationships and situations, we can identify some of the contingencies governing its expression and thereby learn more about the conditions under which its protective effect is conferred (Rutter, 1987). Equally important, such a process-oriented approach can offer instruction about the circumstances in which social support miscarries.

This chapter is divided into two sections. The first section reviews

BENJAMIN H. GOTTLIEB • Department of Psychology, University of Guelph, Guelph, Ontario, Canada N1G 2W1.   **FRED WAGNER** • Community Mental Health Clinic, Guelph, Ontario, Canada N1G 2W1.

The Social Context of Coping, edited by John Eckenrode. Plenum Press, New York, 1991.

three recent studies that spotlight several interactional and social–psychological variables inhibiting or detrimental to the support process. Discussion of these studies' findings centers on the special contingencies that constrain the expression of support when the would-be provider and potential recipient are in a close relationship, and particularly when they are jointly exposed to a common stressor. The second section of the chapter presents selected data on the stress and support process drawn from a qualitative study of married couples who have a seriously ill child. These data reveal the ways in which gender, coping, and relationship issues complicate the expression of interspousal support. The chapter's general aim is to characterize social support as a social process that is shaped by the commerce occurring between people in particular relationships who are attempting to maintain their equilibrium in the face of conditions that are personally *and socially* destabilizing.

INTERPERSONAL CONTINGENCIES AFFECTING THE EXPRESSION OF SUPPORT

Research by Lehman, Ellard, and Wortman (1986) spotlights one set of interactional variables that may play a vital part in determining why potentially valuable support is not successfully channeled to its intended beneficiary. They found that people who were asked hypothetically about the kinds of support they would offer to someone who was bereaved described a cluster of strategies that those who were actually bereaved said they would find supportive. Yet reports from the bereaved respondents indicated that the support they actually received was often unhelpful. For example, they reported that some of their associates inappropriately minimized the loss, offered them unwanted advice, and pressured them to make a more rapid recovery. Why, then, would the enlightened intentions regarding support not be translated into overt behavior? Lehman *et al.* (1986) suggest that the emotional climate of the interactional milieu, combined with the stakes the providers have in their relationship with the would-be recipient of support, derail the providers from tendering those forms of support that would be most supportive. Upset by their bereaved associates' distress, the supporters become off-balanced and fall back on bromides and platitudes. In the words of one respondent quoted by the authors: "I don't know what to say—I'm not a good one for that. I know what I *want* to say, but it doesn't come out in the right way" (p. 443).

It is noteworthy that the respondents' closest associates were most prone to express such miscarried helping behaviors. The authors interpret this finding in terms of the greater sense of responsibility these people may feel or the greater investment they have in the victim's recovery because it impinges so strongly on their own daily life. However, there is a competing explanation for the miscarriage of support. It is not because distress is *transferred* from the bereaved to those close associates who have the strongest sense of responsibility and motivations to be helpful but because the bereaved's distress *hampers or disrupts* the coping efforts of these close associates. Specifically, the fact that many of the instances of support judged unhelpful by the bereaved were conveyed to them by such close relatives as spouses, aunts, mothers-in-law, and parents suggests that the support process is more likely to miscarry when the supporters are independently exposed to the same adversity occurring to the recipient. Although they are one step removed from the loss, they, too, are bereaved by the death of a loved one and therefore are also attempting to maintain their own emotional equilibrium. To accomplish this goal of safeguarding their own emotional well-being, they may offer forms of support that either minimize or attempt to improve the bereaved's emotions. But in doing so, they may inadvertently invalidate the bereaved's feelings of loss that arise from their unique privileged relationship to the deceased. Accordingly, the support the bereaved receive from their close associates is unhelpful because it invalidates both their unique feelings of mourning and their unique identities as mourners. It meets the providers' coping needs, not the bereaved's supportive needs.

For example, such emotionally minimizing statements as "It can't be that bad" figured prominently among the unhelpful types of support attributed to the bereaved's relatives. Similarly, statements that voice expectations of more rapid recovery (e.g., "They think 4 years you should be ready, but you're not always") may also better serve the emotional needs of the bereaved supporters than the would-be recipients of their support. In short, a contingency affecting the communication of support in close relationships is the extent to which the interaction is influenced by the support provider's needs to regulate his/her own emotional responses to the same stressor experienced by the recipient.

More generally, in close relationships, the potential supporters are not innocent bystanders, but by definition occupy a region of their partners' network that can expose them to the same stressors, to the distress occasioned by these stressors, to their partner's coping efforts, and to a variety of longer term consequences. Moreover, both the supporter and the would-be recipient become involved in the process of comparing their emotional reactions to the event and responding to one another's coping efforts. They must concurrently deal with the demands imposed by the stressor and those imposed by each other's coping responses. Each faces the challenge of modulating his/her own ways of coping in order to avoid disrupting the partner's coping efforts and to gain his/her support. At the same time, as providers of support, each must be careful not to allow his/her own needs for emotional regulation to dictate the types of support extended to the recipient.

There is evidence that even when the helper and recipient are not in a close relationship and do not share the same problem, certain helping behaviors prompted by the needs of the donor not only aggravate the plight of the recipient but loop back and adversely affect the provider of support. In a recent laboratory study, Notarius and Herrick (1988) examined the affective and interpersonal consequences for helpers who differed in the types of support they offered to a partner who simulated the role of a depressed person. They found that helpers who responded to the distressed confederate mainly by supportive listening, expressions of empathy, and/or encouragement were significantly less depressed themselves after the interaction than helpers who either relied on the provision of advice or who attempted to distract the confederate from focusing on the dysphoric mood. In addition, they found that the latter helpers, those who engaged in what the authors call "high-risk" responses, were significantly more negative than the supportive listeners about the prospect of interacting with the depressed confederate in a variety of hypothetical situations.

Notarius and Herrick (1988) speculate that the high-risk helpers' disinclination to share the future company of the depressed arises from the feelings of ineptitude they were left with after they tried unsuccessfully to change the depressed partner's mood. In contrast, those who offered types of support that reflected acceptance of the partner's depressed affect did not expect signs of improved mood and therefore did not come away from the exchange feeling incompetent when those signs were not communicated. In short, those who were invested in efforts to ameliorate rather than validate their partner's distress had a stake in the outcome and therefore felt more depressed after their apparent failure to have an effect, leading to reluctance to engage in future interaction with the unresponsive target of their investment. Notarius and Herrick's (1988) study has several interesting implications for the study of support seeking in close relationships. First, because people in close relationships by definition share a history of stress-related transactions, each party will have learned how the other is most likely to respond to the disclosure of certain stressful topics. Their past commerce will have taught them what kinds of appropriate and inappropriate support they can anticipate receiving for work-related problems, domestic problems, relationship problems, and problems related to their feelings about themselves. Borrowing Notarius and Herrick's term, they will have learned to predict when their partner is likely to rely on "high-risk" helping strategies and when they are likely to tender more helpful types of support. In this context, "high-risk" strategies are helping responses that are not only likely to be inappropriate in terms of the helpee's needs for support but also are likely to be rejected and in turn produce interpersonal tension or conflict. In short, support will not be sought in order to avoid probable disappointment about unmet needs for support, unpleasant feedback to the helper signaling his/her ineptitude, and the additional tension that these two outcomes might place on the relationship.

In this regard, Pearlin and McCall's (1990) study of marital support for occupational problems offers vivid testimony that job problems in particular are often not disclosed because of the risk of inviting inappropriate supportive responses. For example, one respondent does not confide in his spouse about his feelings of inferiority regarding his productivity at work because he sees his wife as "very quick when she detects a problem to offer a solution to it" (p. 10). Pearlin and McCall's (1991) interviews also reveal that couples are likely to be deterred from seeking one another's support not only when they anticipate receiving inappropriate types of helping responses but also when they anticipate criticism, hostility, and emotional overinvolvement from their partners due to the nature of the subject itself. There are several sensitive subjects that can be discussed only at certain times and in certain moods, and there are other subjects that are taboo in the sense that a deliberate effort is made to avoid raising them (Baxter & Wilmot, 1985). Because the receipt of support depends upon verbal or behavioral disclosure of problems or distress, the existence of sensitive and taboo topics reflects yet another contingency affecting the expression of social support in close relationships.

What sorts of topics preclude support seeking because they are taboo and what topics are risky in nature and therefore call for a delicate approach to their disclosure, ideally under optimal social–psychological conditions? Pearlin and McCall (1991) found that support is unlikely to be sought for problems arising from a spouse's involvement in an activity that his or her partner did not approve of in the first place. For example, if the spouse was initially opposed to the decision to take a particular job, to pursue extradomestic paid or volunteer work, or to assume caregiving responsibilities for an elderly relative, then he/she will be unreceptive to the problems arising from such unsanctioned spheres of involvement. Disclosure of problems arising from these activities must be carefully timed and expressed in a way that does not betray a high level of distress so that a contentious issue between the parties does not become an occasion for the would-be supporter to reassert his/her disapproval. However, should these activities intrude upon other roles which the partner views as more central and more legitimate, such as the marital relationship itself or the parenting role, or should they limit the partner's access to support for his/her own role-related needs, then they are likely to become taboo topics, thereby effectively precluding the possibility of obtaining any support at all.

Whether or not support is sought from a particular close relationship is therefore affected both by the nature of the help expected and by the nature of the topic itself. Some topics make support seeking hazardous, and some preclude it. Moreover, when the topic itself is not off limits or sensitive, but when unhelpful responses are anticipated, it is also likely that support seeking will be inhibited. It follows that long-term close relationships would differ from short-term relationships in several aspects of support seeking due to the learning that has taken place about the topics that are risky, taboo, and likely to engender unhelpful types of support. In fact, we know precious little about how relationships deteriorate and collapse and how they grow and endure as the partners accumulate knowledge and develop expectations about what they can disclose to one another, how much distress they can disclose to one another, and about one another's responses to distress.

If people are unlikely to seek support from sources they believe will give them inappropriate help that they will inevitably reject, they are even less likely to seek help from sources who are implicated in the cause or intensification of their distress. They may be implicated by virtue of having failed to mobilize support in the past, miscarrying their support, or blaming the help seeker for needing support in the first place or for failing to capitalize on the help he or she received. For example, an individual would be deterred from seeking help from a partner who is likely to shift attention from the recipient's distress or the circumstances occasioning it to dispositional characteristics of the recipient that prompt the need for outside support. Here, to seek help would eventually exact the admission that one's personality shortcomings, misplaced values, and misdirected commitments instigated the present difficulty and the ensuing helplessness.

In their conceptual model of the process through which support attempts can miscarry, Coyne, Wortman, and Lehman (1988) highlight a second manifestation of victim blaming. Specifically, the distressed party is not blamed for initially seeking support but for failing to profit from it. In fact, the helping process miscarries precisely because from the outset the support provider incurs significant costs that later are not repaid by the recipient in the form of signs of improvement. Over time, the increased dependency of the recipient of support and his/her impaired ability to reciprocate aid arouse feelings of resentment and reactance on the provider's part, and feelings of guilt, helplessness, and shame on the recipient's part. The provider then begins to pressure the recipient to recover more quickly, raising questions about the latter's motivation, attitude, and even appreciation of the help that is extended. In turn, the recipient exaggerates the severity of his/her condition or circumstances and feels even more constrained and derogated by the helper. Ultimately, the provider becomes so invested in the recipient's progress that its absence is interpreted as a personal affront, signaling that the provider's support is deficient and that he/she is to blame for the lack of progress. Coyne, Wortman, and Lehman's (1988) label for the final stage, "Characterological Attack and Rejection," accurately conveys the deleterious interpersonal consequences that result when this process of emotional overinvolvement is fully played out.

SUMMARY

The preceding discussion suggests that in close relationships both help seeking and the expression of support are highly subject to a number of contingencies arising during the stress process. They include the amount of distress communicated, the nature of the topic and the help expected, the impact of the stressor on both parties, and the limits that each party's ways of coping place on the other's receipt of support. These contingencies are likely to be particularly influential in close relationships because, by definition, the partners' transactions are based on a shared history and the anticipation of continued interaction in the future. Consequently, in seeking support and even disclosing distress, both parties are likely to be guided by what they have learned from their past stress-related commerce, by the stake they have in their own and their partner's well-being, and by their intentions for the relationship's future. For the partners in a close relationship, the process of seeking and gaining support must therefore be carefully managed in order to optimize their own outcomes, minimize any adverse effects of their present predicament and behavior on their partner, and safeguard the relationship's integrity. In this light, social support is as much a complex process of accommodation to the needs of close relationships as it is an accommodation to stress.

A STUDY OF INTERSPOUSAL INFLUENCES AND
IMPACTS ON COPING

In order to capture the interpersonal dynamics that affect the support exchanged between partners in a close relationship, Fred Wagner and I conducted a preliminary study among a sample of parents of children who had been diagnosed with serious illnesses (Wagner, 1986). These parents provided us with an opportunity to learn about the support process in the context of a marital relationship in which both parties face a chronic and objectively harsh stressor. Through intensive qualitative interviews, we aimed to illuminate how the various contingencies arising in the partners' stress-related transactions might impact on the expression of support. Although we selected a sample of convenience for our in-depth interviews, we deliberately recruited parents who were coping with two different chronic childhood illnesses, cystic fibrosis and juvenile diabetes, so that a broader range of caregiving demands and illness perceptions would be represented among our respondents. Both illnesses involve continuous monitoring of the child's physical functioning, a taxing daily treatment regimen, and an increased risk over time of a variety of medical complications. Cystic fibrosis is clearly the more pernicious of the two illnesses, and the more demanding for the parent due to the noxious regimen it entails, and it carries greater long-term threat because of the short life expectancy of patients. Although there is a sizable literature addressing the impact of chronic childhood illness and handicapping conditions on the family (e.g., Hymovitch & Baker, 1985; Sabbeth, 1984; Venters, 1981), there have been no empirical studies of interspousal coping processes in particular. An exceptionally insightful and moving description of parental coping dynamics in relation to the care of an autistic child is presented by Featherstone (1981).

Using a semistructured schedule, we conducted 20 interviews with 31 parents of whom 13 were fathers and 18 were mothers. Initially, we had planned to interview fathers and mothers separately, but 11 parents requested joint interviews with their spouse. More men than women wished to have their spouse present, and more mothers than fathers told us that their spouses had requested to be present during their interview. We suspected that the men either needed their wives' support during the interview, anticipated questions that might call for details known only to their wife, or wished to provide support when their wives were interviewed. Several parents told us that it was only fitting that they be interviewed together because dealing with their child's illness had always been a mutual affair. These data, then, are based on 11 joint interviews in which each question was directed at one partner and then the other, and on 2 private interviews with fathers and 7 with mothers. Interestingly, far from inhibiting their disclosures, the joint interviews generated richer information than the private ones about the interspousal coping dynamics that both amplified and moderated each parent's stress. Our respondents represented a range of occupational statuses, had been married for an average of 11.3 years, averaged 34 years in age, and cared for an ill child who averaged 7.5 years. Their participation was solicited on our behalf by the local chapters of the Cystic Fibrosis and Juvenile Diabetes Foundations.

Although we do not know how representative this small sample is of the characteristics and experiences of the local population of parents with similarly diagnosed children, our purpose was to discover whether and how the interactive aspects of coping impacted on the expression of support. Specifically, we were interested in the ways each party was affected by and in turn affected the partner's appraisals and coping responses, and more generally how they managed their stress-related transactions in order to optimize their personal well-being, their child's well-being, and the well-being of their relationship. This was accomplished by asking the respondents to reflect on the entire past course of their child's illness, and thinking in terms of a fever chart, to identify a spike representing an event, episode, or interval that was particularly stressful. We asked them to try to reanchor themselves in the experience by describing other events occurring at the time, both in their private life and in public life, and the settings in which their stressful transactions took place.

It is noteworthy that every respondent identified the period surrounding the initial diagnosis as the most stressful. Typically, they experienced a cluster of taxing events during that time, notably troubled interactions with medical personnel and with immediate family members and relatives, and changes in their daily household schedules that were necessitated by the new demands imposed by the treatment regimen. Although the average amount of time since the initial diagnosis was 6.5 years, the respondents recalled their experiences in vivid detail. With rare exceptions, spouses in the joint interviews agreed about the events and interactions occurring during this highly charged period.

Focusing on this stressful context, we began with questions about their initial thoughts and feelings at the time. We used these probes to capture their stressful primary appraisals signifying loss, harm, threat, and challenge (Lazarus & Folkman, 1984), and then we concentrated on the direct or indirect influence exerted on these appraisals by the words or deeds of their partner. For example, we asked them several questions about what their spouse did or said that added to or diminished the stress attending their initial reactions by changing the thoughts and feelings they had at that time. Next, we proceeded to a series of questions pertaining to their secondary appraisals of the personal and social resources they could marshall to deal with the event, including probes about their ability to muster these resources and their probable efficacy. Once again, we followed up with probes about the comments and actions of their spouses that were implicated in shaping or modifying these appraisals. To gauge their ways of coping, we asked them to describe what they did and thought to handle the feelings provoked by the stressful episode, following up on this topic with two types of questions about their spouse's influence: his/her reactions to these ways of emotion-focused coping, and perceptions of what he/she did or said to shape or modify them. The same sequence was repeated in relation to the parents' ways of coping with the instrumental demands they faced, if the stressful event they described offered any opportunities to do so.

Our approach, then, was not designed to capture only instances of interspousal support but invited descriptions of a much broader range of partner influences on the coping process. We viewed both parties as potential recipients and providers of support *and* as potential targets and agents of a variety of other social influences aimed to achieve adaptive outcomes for themselves, their partner, their relationship, and their child. In short, our goal was to learn how they coped with the emotional and instrumental demands of the child's illness by altering their own and their partner's ways of coping.

SELECTED FINDINGS

Our content analysis of the interview transcripts yielded a rich set of both verbal and behavioral *influences* that the spouses exerted on one another's appraisals and coping responses, and an equally rich set of descriptions of the *impacts* that they had on their stress-related cognitions and behaviors. Table 1 displays 36 categories of verbal statements made by the spouses that were perceived to have an impact on either the partner's appraisals and their emotional correlates or on the partner's ways of handling the emotional and instrumental tasks of coping. Although we were able to assign the majority of them to 5 classes on the basis of the types of verbal behaviors expressed, 11 categories appeared to be unique and are therefore listed under the label *other*. The classes of partner influences range in their overt forcefulness from leading questions to commands and in their overt evaluation from critical comments to supportive statements and offers.

Table 1.   Spouses' Verbal Influences on Appraisals and Ways of Coping

Class and category	Example
A. Issues directive to	
1. Accept situation	"He said to me that we just have to live with it, giving the best we can and carrying on"
2. Give child more attention	"He wants more attention, you have to give him more attention"
3. Spare source from further anxiety-provoking communication	"Yeah, yeah, yeah, heard it all before Julie, shut up"
4. Act more maturely	"Grow up; you have a child with this disease and you're going to have to live with it"
5. Share more caregiving responsibilities	"She has to remind me that I'm not doing my share of the physio or if I should help more"
6. Cease self-pity	"Oh cut it out; stop that; how can you feel sorry for yourself?"
7. Gain respite/distraction	"We're leaving; we have reservations; it's two blocks away, you need air, and let's go"
8. Express feelings	"Will you wake up! Will you cry, do something to show me that you care!"
9. Take problem-solving action	"He put pressure on me to go for a diagnosis"
10. Consult fellow sufferer	"She told me to ask other CF parents what they do and stuff"
B. Asks leading question about	
1. Familial commitment	"Are you going to stay or is this bothering you enough to leave your wife and kid?"
2. Depth of feeling	"She would keep asking me if I felt certain ways"
3. Adherence to regimen	"Why are you bothering with this (regimen)? She's not going to live anyway"
4. Public performance of regimen	"How can you put everybody

(continued)

Table 1.

(Continued)

Class and category	Example
	through having to watch that (physio)?"
C. Suggests options regarding	
1. Keeping or giving up child	"If you want to keep her, that's fine; but if not, you can give her up"
2. Communication with physician	"Why don't you say this or that to the Dr.?"
3. Illness management	"He would make suggestions— like he would do an arm and a leg each A.M. and I'd do . . ."
4. Child rearing	"It's little tips he offers like how to handle Halloween"
D. Offers support	
1. Affirmation of general coping ability	"You're one special gal and if anyone can handle it, you can"
2. Affirmation of illness-relevant coping	"It's because of the time and care you've given Bobby; it's the total dedication"
3. Expressing mutual emotions	"We had many a good laugh and really expressed a lot of anger to each other"
4. Offering to listen	"Making her/himself available as someone to talk to"
E. Criticizes/undermines	
1. Emotional lability	"Julie, you're overreacting and overdramatizing"
2. Disclosure of threatening information	"Your timing was all wrong; you should have never told me"
3. Degree of involvement in illness management	"There are points when I just can't do enough; she lets me know it"
4. Parenting role	"Putting his/her two cents in to let me know I'm being too harsh with the children"

(continued)

Table 1.

(*Continued*)

Class and category	Example
F. Other	
1. Forewarns about imminent stressor	"When a crisis happens, I get forewarned before I come home from work"
2. Mutual anticipatory coping	"We started planning . . . this is what we'll do, who we'll call, and how we'll take care of it"
3. Threatens to abandon partner	"Times when she's said she's had it and is going to leave"
4. Unwilling to share burdens of caregiving	"Oh no, it's OK, you go ahead and do it (physiotherapy)"
5. Refuses to argue	"I don't want to fight because when people fight they say things they don't mean"
6. Expresses hope	"She's going to live, she's not going to die because she's a fighter"
7. Ingenuinely inquires about state of affairs	"She/he will ask 'how are you today' but doesn't really want to know"
8. Encourages counting one's blessings	"She/he says it could be worse—[child] could be worse; she can run, play, do anything"
9. Avoids/postpones discussion of future threat	"He won't talk to me about what's going to happen when Tom gets older; he says nothing or changes the subject or something"
10. Blames partner for causing illness	"Him accusing me of . . . if I hadn't all those sweets in the house, [child] wouldn't be a diabetic"

Together, they reflect a provocative set of strategies, some of which on the surface appear to be aimed to shore up the target's well-being (e.g., forewarns about imminent stressor; affirmation of coping ability), some to shore up the source's well-being (e.g., spare source from further anxiety-provoking communication; express hope), and some to shore up the relationship between the two parties (e.g., refuses to argue; expresses mutual emotions). But without knowledge of the coping functions that these verbalizations play for the source and without knowledge of their cumulative impact on the target's appraisals and coping, it is impossible to determine their short- and long-term adaptive significance for the parties, their relationship, and ultimately for the child's well-being. The categories mainly expose the variety of verbal statements the spouses level at one another in order to channel, redirect, reinforce, and undermine each other's appraisals and ways of coping with both the stressor and one another's responses to it. These verbal influences are themselves responses to the ongoing and reciprocal interplay that occurs over the course of coping, each party responding to the impact of prior transactions with the partner and initiating new messages conveying needs aroused by their preceding commerce. Over time, the coping process unfolds in relation to the new contingencies that are created by the stress-related interactions between the partners and by the demands of the common stressor they face.

In addition to these verbal influences, we also abstracted 16 types of behavioral influences and 13 indirect influences that the spouses leveled at one another and that further illuminate the constraining and supportive interspousal dynamics in which they were embroiled. For the present purposes, however, we will concentrate on only one additional set of categories that reveal the kinds of *impacts* the spouses reported these influences having on their coping responses. Specifically, Table 2 draws attention to the multiple effects of all three types (verbal, behavioral, and indirect) of spouses' influences on one another's *emotions*. Some had an impact on the expression of emotion such as inhibition, distraction, and confrontive ventilation; some effected dramatic emotional changes, such as the intensification and blunting of emotions; and some even altered the partners' awareness of and attitudes toward their emotions.

In the present study, we did not link particular categories of emotional impact to specific types of interspousal influences. First, the interview schedule was not so highly structured as to require precision from the respondents about the impact of each spousal influence. In fact, we did not aim for such precision given the retrospective nature of the study and the fact that it ranged over many features of the interpersonal context of coping. Our goal was chiefly to generate a preliminary classification of the range and impact of interspousal influences on the support and coping process. Second, and related to this, the respondents often indicated that a combination of behavioral, verbal, and indirect influences was chiefly implicated in shaping their appraisals and coping responses and that the effect was typically cumulative. Our analysis was not capable of addressing this order of complexity. In future research, we plan to draw on the categories generated in this study, using more struc-

Table 2.   Impacts of Spouses' Influences on Emotion-Focused Coping

Class and category	Example
A. *Emotional confrontation*	
1. Expression of anger	"I just yelled, Damn well phone him and tell him my son is sick in hospital, with diabetes"
2. Plea for recognition of own needs	"For God's sake, how much attention do you want me to give the kid? I need a break too!"
3. Confrontive escalation	"He will not react, so I say worse things"
4. Standing ground and fighting for what is needed	"Why should I hide (son) somewhere? He hasn't done anything wrong. You're going to have to accept it. We don't have the problem, you do"
B. *Emotional (self) control*	
1. Emotional inhibition	"I hold it in more than her because a man is not supposed to let it all out"
2. Defiant stoicism	"I go into my martyr syndrome where I just wouldn't say anything and take all the cares and troubles of the world on my shoulders"
3. Avoidance of emotionally arousing information	"You keep a thin shell around you, but still the least tiny little crack can shatter you"
4. Summons up positive emotions	"Sometimes I feel I've got these big shoes to fill. I can never fall down. I always have to be up"
5. Controls emotions by maintaining perspective	"I am not going to blow things out of proportion"
6. Emotional self-preparation	"I can be isolated before I come home. I use that time to prepare my mental state"
7. Emotional recommitment	"I'll get a pep talk from him and then it's: OK, OK, I'll just keep going"
C. *Positive emotional change*	
1. Counts blessing	"Opening your eyes and realizing what you've got to be

(continued)

Table 2.   (*Continued*)

Class and category	Example
	thankful for. And then you do, you see . . . Wow"
2. Finds positive meaning	"It made me realize that maybe this was my destiny. Maybe I was the chosen sibling"
3. Emotional normalization	"You felt like finally you were normal. Like all those nasty feelings was a normal part of bringing up diabetic kids"
4. Emotional amelioration	"By dragging me out of the intensity of the situation I felt better and thanked her"
D. *Other*	
1. Emotional awareness and disclosure	"It was almost impossible, but I had to come up with some real answers for her (about my feelings)"
2. Intensifies stressful emotions	"I get so mad, frustrated, and really hurt because he doesn't want to have anything to do with it"

tured interviews as well as daily diaries, to relate particular interpersonal influences to their impacts. Such analyses would prove very valuable because of the insight afforded into the ameliorative and damaging effects on coping of diverse interpersonal influences.

Having extracted the various categories of verbal influences listed in Table 1, we attempted to discern whether the husbands and wives differed in the extent to which they expressed these influences on one another's appraisals and ways of coping. Due to the exploratory and qualitative nature of this study, we set out to identify tentative patterns or trends rather than undertake an analysis of the frequency with which the husbands and wives expressed these influences. Such a quantitative analyses is planned for a future study with a larger sample of respondents who will be asked to review and rate their own and their spouse's expression of these verbal influences, as well as the 16 behavioral and 13 indirect types of influences. By providing respondents with an opportunity to consider such a comprehensive list of coping influences, more conclusive statements regarding gender and role differences would be warranted.

Among the trends reflected in our interviews with this sample, we found that it was generally the husbands who placed strong pressure on their wives to act more maturely (A4), to spare them from anxiety-provoking communications (A3, F9), to engage less in self-pity (A6) and overdramatizing (E1), and to concentrate on the child's needs and the tasks entailed in managing the caregiving demands (A2, C2, C3) of an illness that must be accepted (A1). Moreover, these influences were voiced in strong, often hostile terms, the majority falling in the two classes labeled "issues directive" and "criticizes/undermines." Interestingly, the types of supportive influences husbands, rather than their wives, exerted on their partners communicated esteem for their ability to withstand the pressures of the stressful ordeal (D1) and for their dedication to the caregiving role (D2).

In sharp contrast, the wives' influences on their husbands reflected countervailing pressures to express greater emotionality (A8) and to assume a larger share of the responsibility for the child's regimen and general welfare (E3). But it is noteworthy that the wives expressed two categories of influences that were emotionally protective of their husbands. One aimed to shelter their husbands from experiencing the full brunt of adverse events associated with the child's illness (F1). Specifically, it was only wives, never husbands, who gave their partners a chance to engage in anticipatory coping by forewarning them about bad news such as a reversal in the child's health status. The second category implied the possibility of permanently insulating the husband from exposure to his wife's own distress (F3); it was only wives who voiced their fear of having to withdraw from the relationship in order to spare their husbands from exposure to their wives' distress. When husbands threatened to leave home permanently and when they actually withdrew into their work and other extradomestic activities, it was typically to protect themselves, not their partners.

DISCUSSION

What interpretation can be placed on these contrasting patterns of influence expressed by husbands and wives? What functions do they play for the partner who exerts the influence, and what is their intended impact on the partner who is the target? Our speculation is that this particular set of interspousal influences stems from repeated clashes in the partners' ways of coping with their shared adversity. The husbands simply do not voice their apprehensions about the child's future, whereas the wives do so frequently and with intense affective displays. The husbands are also largely impassive in the face of the taxing emotional demands that the wives often find insurmountable. From the husbands' perspectives, their wives are emotionally overinvolved, whereas the wives see their husbands as emotionally underinvolved. This fundamental conflict over the amplification and modulation of emotionality thus gives rise to these reciprocal influences; the parties become embroiled in leveling negative sanctions at one another for expressing more or less distress than the other can tolerate.

How does this conflict over the expression of emotionality affect the prospects for supportive exchanges between the partners? If we view social support as coping assistance (Gottlieb, 1985; Thoits, 1984), then these reciprocal influences can be seen as ways of reinforcing coping behaviors each partner approves of, redirecting coping so that it becomes more supportable to the partner, or rechanneling coping so that it poses less threat to the coping behaviors each partner relies on. If support is contingent upon the stance the partner adopts toward the stressful predicament, then the wives will gain support only by shielding their husbands from the tensions of the caregiving role and by concentrating on the instrumental demands of the illness regimen and the routines of caregiving. To maintain their emotional equilibrium, the husbands need their wives' reassurance, expressions of hopefulness, dedication to the caregiving role, and recognition of their main contribution as breadwinners. In turn, the wives' bids for needed emotional support, expressed by venting their anxiety and fearfulness, go unanswered because they disrupt their husbands' reliance on a posture of stoic acceptance, their concentration on the management of the illness, and their denial. Thus, for the most part, the spouses require kinds of support from one another that are antithetical to the ways of coping that each of them relies on. They become involved in a set of transactions, some of which are coercive and some supportive, devoted to persuading one another to abandon coping behaviors that are inimical to their respective coping needs.

We suspect that these mutual influences also play the critical function of redirecting coping so that it becomes more supportable to the partner. By exhorting their emotionally underinvolved spouses to express their sadness, fear, and vulnerability, the wives may not only gain validation of their own emotions but also evoke comfort-seeking behavior from their husbands. That is, their husbands may gain the benefit of the support their wives can offer if they can be moved to express their distress. Similarly, if the husbands can induce their wives to inhibit their emotions, it would effectively maintain the husbands' reliance on a palliative style of coping and free them of unwanted demands for succorance made by their wives. In short, the influences the spouses place on one another can be seen as a set of emotional behavior patterns that have two central purposes: to alter the behaviors of others that undermine one's own coping and to steer their future support-seeking behavior (Greenberg & Safran, 1989).

Our interviews revealed that, over time, the wives adapted to this conflict over the expression of emotionality in two ways. First, they gained compensatory emotional support from interactions with other parents they met through the local chapters of the Cystic Fibrosis and Juvenile Diabetes foundations. Although these interactions were also occasionally upsetting because of the exposure they gave to the problems and suffering of other mothers, on the whole the emotional benefits outweighed the liabilities.

The second adaptation concerned the way the wives managed to gain support from their husbands once they fully recognized that their own emotional expressiveness denied them support in their roles as wives not just as mothers and caregivers. Several of them told us that they simply adopted a more stoic and emotionally impassive posture in their husbands' company, masking their distress and even concealing bad news they had received about their child's illness. In short, they adopted a posture of *public coping*, at least in their husbands' presence, that was at odds with their manner of *private coping*. In the short run, this permitted them to mitigate the strain of marital conflict by not alienating their husbands. However, in the long run, this double emotional life reaped a high cost because it incurred even stronger feelings of resentment and martyrdom and exaggerated their sense of emotional isolation. Besides carrying the bulk of the caregiving burden, this adaptation added another layer of burdens by placing the wives in the unenviable position of having to monitor, censure, and ultimately feign their reactions to caregiving in order to garner their partner's support. Far from being credited by their spouses for these efforts to minimize marital conflict, the wives suffer the extra adverse consequence of losing esteem for themselves by acting in ways that are not faithful to their private feelings. Perversely, they can gain the reward of marital support only by hiding and dissembling their emotions.

What are the factors determining these stressful dynamics that can eventually erode the very fabric of the relationship between marital partners? A growing body of evidence in the stress and coping field suggests that gender and role differences are strongly implicated in creating fertile grounds for the conflict arising from the partners' shared adversity. First, because caregiving is gender-defined in our society, the wives necessarily are far more exposed than their husbands to the harsh realities, the threatening uncertainties, and the taxing pressures surrounding their children's illnesses. The work of adhering to the demanding medical regimen largely falls to them, as do the teacher conferences, the constant consultations with doctors and the trips to clinics, exposure to other children who have the same illness, and the ongoing pressures of family life. In contrast, the lives of men, including those we interviewed, are structured around their jobs, and so they enjoy the luxury the workplace affords of gaining respite, enjoying periods of relative tranquility, and even experiencing positive emotions. Although work carries its own pressures, it can serve as an asylum, sheltering men from reminders of domestic turmoil, and thereby insulating them from feelings of sadness, loss, and defeat. The workplace thus offers a structural resource, aiding the husbands to contain and compartmentalize their emotions and to avoid defining themselves exclusively in terms of their child's illness. The workplace allows men to distance themselves from both the physical and the emotional labor of caregiving.

But the very fact that our culture assigns caregiving according to gender may also account for differences in the *access* that men and women have to extradomestic support for their parenting roles. Cultural norms and stereotypes seem to systematically favor women as the recipients of parenting support, whereas our cultural script largely denies such support to men. Consequently, men have fewer opportunities to acknowledge, much less to explore painful feelings, and they tend to receive less sympathy and recognition as parents than they might need. In their study of parents of children with cancer, Chesler and Barbarin (1984) quote one father who was painfully aware of the discrepancy between the support he and his wife received and of his own responsibility for creating it:

> I think if I knew someone in my position one of the things I'd like to ask him is how are you coping. I did not experience that much, only a couple of people asked me how are you doing. I think my wife experienced that a lot with her friends, but I only had a couple of friends who asked me. If I could wish for anything it would have been more of that. Probably there are things I could have done to make that happen though. (pp. 126–127)

More generally, as McMullen and Gross (1983) conclude on the basis of their review of gender differences in help-seeking: "Our culture has included help-seeking among the behaviors that are designated as more appropriate for females than males" (p. 251). Similarly, Weiss (1985) found that, at least among upper-income men in administrative and business-related occupations, the workplace prohibited and sometimes punished the display of emotions, and these messages often transferred into the home where men concealed their emotional vulnerabilities from both their wives and themselves. The effect of these disparities in men's and women's access to broader network sources of parental support is paradoxical: The husbands are even less prepared to confront painful feelings at home but resent having to struggle alone, denied the comfort and recognition their wives garner.

Perhaps, then, it is the particular combination of circumstances in which men find themselves that accounts for Cummings's (1976) finding that the fathers of chronically ill children have a far more diminished sense of competence as parents than the mothers. On the one hand, they have fewer opportunities to involve themselves directly in the management of the child's illness and thereby to counteract their sense of loss, frustration, and helplessness. On the other hand, men seek and receive relatively little emotional support from their network and from organizations for the parents of children with chronic illnesses. Perhaps it is because they are so rarely the beneficiaries of outside emotional support that they are so rarely the providers of such support on the inside, to their wives, and perhaps that is why they influence their wives not to even seek support from them.

Although role differences in the work and parenting domains differentially expose women and men to the hardships of caregiving (Aneshensel & Pearlin, 1987; Barnett & Baruch, 1987) and give them unequal access to support from the wider network, gender differences may give them different means of psychological coping with the conditions that threaten their well-being. Thoits (1991) notes that there may be gender differences in coping within specific problem contexts such as work, marriage, and parenting, and that generally, individuals will use problem-solving efforts in those domains in which they perceive they have more control, power, and responsibility. So men would tend to rely on problem solving in the occupational arena and women in the domestic (family and marriage) arena. Miller and Kirsch's (1987) review of sex differences in cognitive coping with stress lends only partial support to Thoits's observation; six of seven studies yielding data on significant gender differences in reliance on emotion- versus problem-focused ways of coping revealed that males *are* more likely to use problem-focused coping strategies than females, particularly at work and in situations requiring more information, but also tend to rely on problem-focused coping even in the face of uncontrollable situations.

In the present context, there appears to be at least two major features of the stressful situation that are the objects of perceived controllability for the spouses: the child's illness and the partner's ways of coping with it. Although both parties may appraise the illness as uncontrollable, the husband more than the wife because of his removal from the caregiving role, they may have discrepant views of the controllability of one another's response to it. In this study, the character of the influences the husbands exerted suggest that they were much more aggressive and provocative than their wives in attempting to modify their partners' distressful emotions and threatening communications. Moreover, their supportive influences were largely aimed to reinforce their partners' problem-oriented coping behaviors, namely their involvement in and commitment to the caregiving role. In short, the husbands were much more actively engaged than their wives in modifying the situation to eliminate or reduce the stress-producing *interpersonal processes*. In contrast, the wives adapted by modifying their emotions through feigned emotional self-control in their husband's presence. Gender differences in coping with a shared but uncontrollable stressor may cause men to modify the problematic situation by altering the threatening reactions of others to it. Although the child's illness may be a source of stress intractable to problem-centered coping, the wife's appraisals of it and her emotional reactions to it may be modified to reduce their threatening qualities. However, the long-term impact of this way of coping is to jeopardize the very fabric of the partners' relationship.

CONCLUSION

Some tentative conclusions about both the coping and the support process are suggested by the preceding qualitative study. With respect to the coping process, when two parties in a close relationship are both striving to adjust to the demands of a chronic stressor, the trajectory of coping is determined only in part by their personalities, skills, and perceptual predispositions. In addition, it is highly subject to a varied set of influences that are not exclusively supportive in nature because they are not exclusively directed toward meeting the other's coping needs. These influences arise from each partner's preoccupation with his or her own coping needs. Thus the partners shape and redirect one another's coping responses in order to maintain their own equilibrium. Moreover, these reciprocal influences have the power to modify the course of coping only to the extent that the parties continue to attach importance to their relationship. If clashes in coping persisted, they would rock the foundations of the relationship and eventually sever the union. It appears, then, that coping is at once shaped by the social context and directed toward shaping the social context to maintain both personal equilibrium and valued social relationships.

With respect to the support process, a complex set of situational, behavioral, and relationship contingencies come into play as the two parties strive to manage the instrumental demands of the stressor and particularly the emotions it arouses. Our interviews confirm the impression gained from the studies discussed in the first section of this chapter that the disclosure and intensity of distress play a pivotal role in determining the support conveyed. However, both the open expression of painful emotions and their inhibition are implicated, and a clash along this dimension of the partners' coping is chiefly responsible for limiting the support they exchange. Gender differences in coping and role differences that shelter men from the work of caregiving and place them in a social orbit that is relatively deficient in parental support may underlie this clash in coping. Further study of the contingencies affecting the expression of support in close relationships outside of marriage, in same-sex relationships and in relation to stressful occurrences that are more controllable than the one faced by these couples, may provide a deeper understanding of these gender and role differences. More generally, our understanding of the contingencies affecting the support process is most likely to be advanced by further study of the stress-related transactions that unfold in personal relationships.

REFERENCES

Aneshensel, C. S., & Pearlin, L. I. (1987). Structural contexts of sex differences in stress. In R. C. Barnett, L. Biener, & G. K. Baruch (Eds.), *Gender and stress* (pp. 75–95). New York: The Free Press.

Barnett, R. C., & Baruch, G. K. (1987). Social roles, gender, and psychological distress. In R. C. Barnett, L. Biener, & G. K. Baruch (Eds.), *Gender and stress* (pp. 122–143). New York: The Free Press.

Baxter, L. A., & Wilmot, W. W. (1985). Taboo topics in close relationships. *Journal of Social and Personal Relationships, 2,* 253–270.

Chesler, M. A., & Barbarin, O. A. (1984). Difficulties of providing help in a crisis: Relationships between parents of children with cancer and their friends. *Journal of Social Issues, 40,* 113–134.

Cohen, S., Mermelstein, R., Kamarck, T., & Hoberman, H. M. (1985). Measuring the functional components of social support. In I. G. Sarason & B. R. Sarason (Eds.), *Social support: Theory, research, and applications* (pp. 73–95). Dordrecht, The Netherlands: Martinus Nijhoff.

Coyne, J. C., Wortman, C. B., & Lehmann, D. R. (1988). The other side of support: Emotional overinvolvement and miscarried helping. In B. H. Gottlieb (Ed.), *Marshalling social support: Formats, processes and effects.* Beverly Hills, CA: Sage.

Cummings, S. T. (1976). The impact of the child's deficiency on the father: A study of fathers of mentally retarded and of chronically ill children. *American Journal of Orthopsychiatry, 46,* 246–255.

Featherstone, H. (1981). *A difference in the family.* Markham, Ontario: Penguin Books.

Gottlieb, B. H. (1985). Social support and the study of close relationships. *Journal of Social and Personal Relationships, 2,* 351–375.

Greenberg, L. S., & Safran, J. D. (1989). Emotion in psychotherapy. *American Psychologist,* *44,* 19–29.

Hymovitch, D. P., & Baker, C. D. (1985). The needs, concerns, and coping of parents of children with cystic fibrosis. *Family Relations, 34,* 91–97.

Lazarus, R. S., & Folkman, S. (1984). *Stress, appraisal, and coping.* New York: Springer.

Lehman, D. R., Ellard, J. H., & Wortman, C. B. (1986). Social support for the bereaved: Recipients' and providers' perspectives on what is helpful. *Journal of Consulting and Clinical Psychology, 54,* 438–446.

McMullen, P. A., & Gross, A. E. (1983). Sex differences, sex roles, and health-related help-seeking. In B. DePaulo, A. Nadler, & J. Fisher (Eds.), *New directions in helping* (Vol. 2; pp. 233–263). New York: Academic Press.

Miller, S. M., & Kirsch, N. (1987). Sex differences in cognitive coping with stress. In R. C. Barnett, L. Biener, & G. K. Baruch (Eds.), *Gender and stress* (pp. 278–307). New York: The Free Press.

Notarius, C. I., & Herrick, L. R. (1988). Listener response strategies to a distressed other. *Journal of Social and Personal Relationships, 5,* 97–108.

Pearlin, L. I., & McCall, M. E. (1990). Occupational stress and marital support: A description of microprocesses. In J. Eckenrode & S. Gore (Eds.), *Stress between work and family* (pp. 39–60). New York: Plenum Press.

Procidano, M. E., & Heller, K. (1983). Measures of perceived social support from friends and from family: Three validation studies. *American Journal of Community Psychology, 11,* 1–24.

Rutter, M. (1987). Psychosocial resilience and protective mechanisms. *American Journal of Orthopsychiatry, 57,* 316–331.

Sabbeth, B. (1984). Understanding the impact of chronic childhood illness on families. *Pediatric Clinics of North America, 31,* 47–57.

Sarason, I. G., Levine, H. M., Basham, R. B., & Sarason, B. R. (1983). Assessing social support: The Social Support Questionnaire. *Journal of Personality and Social Psychology, 44,* 127–139.

Thoits, P. A. (1984). Coping, social support, and psychological outcomes. In P. Shaver (Ed.), *Review of Personality and Social Psychology,* Vol. 5 (pp. 219–238). Newbury Park, CA: Sage.

Thoits, P. A. (1991). Gender differences in coping with emotional distress. In J. Eckenrode (Ed.), *The social context of coping* (pp. 107–138). New York: Plenum Press.

Venters, M. (1981). Familial coping with chronic and severe childhood illness: The case of cystic fibrosis. *Social Science and Medicine, 15,* 289–297.

Wagner, F. (1986). *An exploratory study of parental coping in the context of chronic childhood illness.* Unpublished master's thesis. Department of Psychology, University of Guelph, Ontario.

Weiss, R. S. (1985). Men and the family. *Family Process, 24,* 49–58.

9

Effects of Depression on Social Support in a Community Sample of Women

MARY AMANDA DEW and EVELYN J. BROMET

INTRODUCTION

Depression has long been noted by clinicians to have an important impact on their patients' relationships with spouse, family, and friends. Thus a clinical literature dating back at least 40 years has vividly described how depressed persons "make their whole environment feel guilty" (Coyne, 1976, p. 186), provoking others to withdraw support at a time when the depressed individual most needs it (Jacobson, 1954; Kraines, 1957). Similarly, the impact of depression and other psychiatric disorders on social relationships was explicitly recognized in an official position statement of the American Psychological Association, in which Smith and Hobbs (1966) eloquently stated that "mental disorder is not the private misery of an individual; it often grows out of *and usually contributes to* the breakdown of normal sources of social support and understanding, especially the family" (p. 500, italics added).

Early empirical work concerning the social effects of depression

MARY AMANDA DEW • Department of Psychiatry, University of Pittsburgh School of Medicine, Pittsburgh, Pennsylvania 15213.   **EVELYN J. BROMET** • Department of Psychiatry and Behavioral Science, State University of New York at Stony Brook, Stony Brook, New York 11794-8790.

The Social Context of Coping, edited by John Eckenrode. Plenum Press, New York, 1991.

focused on psychiatric patient populations. For example, Weissman and Paykel (1974) presented compelling data showing that depressed women's social relationships were impaired in a variety of domains, including their roles as wife, mother, and worker. Subsequent studies have demonstrated that the more severe an individual's depressive symptoms, the less social support he or she reports to have available, and the worse his or her social functioning in relationships with spouse and friends (e.g., Dohrenwend, Dohrenwend, Link, & Levav, 1983; Sturt, 1981).

Such findings have often been considered to reflect a distortion in the depressed individual's perceptions of social relationships; the actual quality or availability of those relationships has been presumed to be less affected (Ferster, 1973; Henderson, Byrne, & Duncan-Jones, 1981). However, a small but growing body of recent studies shows that spouses' and other family members' *own* perceptions of relationships with an individual are also worsened if the individual is depressed (Coyne, Kessler, Tal, Turnbull, Wortman, & Greden, 1987; Krantz & Moos, 1987).

Unfortunately, the cross-sectional nature of the majority of empirical studies involving depressed patient populations renders the causal interpretation of these studies' findings obscure. Consistent with the dominant theoretical and empirical conceptualization derived from community studies that "much . . . of the causal flow is from social relationships to health rather than vice versa" (House, 1981, p. 51), it may be the case that the depression observed in patient populations does not itself initiate an unraveling of social relationships, so much as that the social relationships began to decline prior to onset of depression and themselves precipitated the depressive episode. It is also possible that declining social relationships may represent an early, prodromal phase of the depressive episode itself.

However, even if we focus on only those studies of patient samples in which causal direction is less ambiguous, that is, studies in which depressive episodes are shown to impair *subsequent* social support levels (e.g., Krantz & Moos, 1987), the generalizability of such findings to psychologically distressed *community residents*—the majority of whom do not seek mental health treatment—is apt to be poor. In particular, the decision to seek help (i.e., to become a patient) is influenced by the nature of preexisting support available from one's social network (e.g., Dew, Dunn, Bromet, & Schulberg, 1988). Thus patient data on the predictive effects of distress on social support are difficult to interpret; factors related to help seeking may bias such studies' results.

Several studies of nonpatient, community-based samples have longitudinally examined the psychological distress–social support relationship. Results suggest that, although distress does have some impact on subsequent support levels (controlling for prior support), the size of the impact may be modest at best (e.g., Aneshensel & Frerichs, 1982; Aneshensel & Huba, 1984; Turner, 1981). These studies focus on subclinical levels of depression and associated psychiatric symptomatology. Effects of clinically significant, diagnosable depression, which would be expected to exert a more profound impact on a variety of relationships with others, have not been longitudinally examined in a community context.

Examination of these effects in community samples is difficult and costly because of low prevalence rates for psychiatric disorders. For example, even though major depression is one of the most prevalent psychiatric disorders (Myers, Weissman, Tischler, Holzer, Leaf, Orvaschel, Anthony, Boyd, Burke, Kramer, & Stoltzman, 1984; Weissman & Myers, 1980), it occurs in only approximately 2% to 3.5% of the general population during a 6-month period (Myers *et al.*, 1984). An additional difficulty in studying the relationship between diagnosable depressive disorder and social support in community residents is that, as for patient samples, even when sufficiently large community samples have been identified, investigators have been unable to collect data on social support and other psychosocial characteristics prior to the onset of clinical impairment (e.g., Bromet, Dunn, Connell, Dew, & Schulberg, 1986; Leaf, Weissman, Myers, Holzer, & Tischler, 1986). These baseline data are essential for distinguishing the effects on social support of recent clinical status from other variables that may antedate recent clinical impairment. Thus, although both Bromet *et al.* (1986) and Leaf *et al.* (1986) found strong cross-sectional associations between marital satisfaction and the presence of diagnosable depressive disorder occurring either at the time of interview or during the prior 6 to 12 months, the causal nature of this association remains to be explored.

In our discussion thus far, we have delineated the issues involved in the two major approaches to study of the depression–social support relationship: what can be referred to as the clinical approach, summarized in the left-hand panel of Figure 1, and the community-based approach, summarized in the right-hand panel of the figure. We had the unusual opportunity to integrate the major features of these two approaches. Specifically, we were able to examine the impact of clinically diagnosable episodes of major depressive illness on perceptions of the nature and availability of social support, utilizing longitudinal data collected from a community sample of women. Our investigation conceptually and methodologically extends previous work not only by examining the effects of clinically significant depression on subsequent social

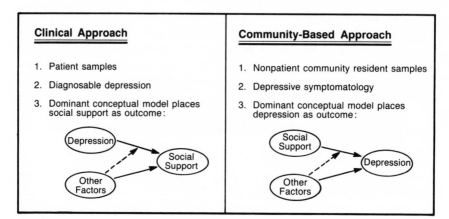

Figure 1. Two major approaches to the study of the relationship between depression and social support. *Note.* Solid lines in models denote direct, or "main" effects. Dashed lines denote interactive, or "buffering" effects.

support in the community but also by (1) utilizing data on social support obtained prior to the onset of depression and (2) considering effects of depression on *multiple* support domains, including that obtained from spouse, friends, and neighbors.

The women in our sample were interviewed on two occasions; some experienced depressive episodes that began during the interim between baseline and follow-up interviews. We focus on three research questions. First, does the nature of social support received at follow-up differ between women who experienced a major depression and those who did not? Second, if such differences exist, do they maintain themselves at a statistically reliable level, and how large are they, after we take baseline support levels prior to the depressive episode into account? Third, if depression affects support at follow-up, even after baseline levels of such support are considered, can we identify specific characteristics of women's depressive episodes that influence their likelihood of experiencing reduced support at follow-up?

METHOD

Subjects

We collected panel data in fall 1981 and fall 1982 from 741 women residing in three semirural, demographically similar regions of Pennsylvania. These women had originally been recruited in a longitudinal investigation of the mental health effects of the 1979 Three Mile Island (TMI) accident (Bromet, Parkinson, Schulberg, Dunn, & Gondek, 1982; Dew, Bromet, & Schulberg, 1987). Each had delivered a child between January 1978 and March 1979. Because Pennsylvania law prohibited access to vital statistics records, women were randomly drawn from area newspaper birth announcements. Hospitals routinely reported birth delivery data to the local newspapers and virtually all local women delivered in a hospital, thus minimizing sample bias. The refusal rate at initial interview was 20%, and the rate of attrition was 6%.

When initially interviewed, the women's median age was 29 (range = 18 to 49); they were predominantly Caucasian (98%), had grown up in the locale where currently living (73%), had at least a high-school education (93%), had total annual family incomes over $20,000 (65%), and had one to three children (91%).

Procedure

Trained interviewers traveled to women's homes to conduct 90-minute interviews with them. Women were initially randomly assigned to interviewers, who were clinicians with an average of 8 years of clinical experience (range: 4–12 years) and with at least a master's degree in a mental health discipline. To reduce attrition, interviewers spoke with the same women at both interviews whenever possible. We conducted comprehensive training programs before both interviews to standardize instrument administration (Bromet et al., 1986).

Measures

Social Supports. We examined variables representing two domains of support: that obtained from the marriage and from neighbors and friends. With one exception noted, we assessed each support measure at both initial and follow-up interviews.

Support from the marital relationship. Three characteristics were considered. First, at each interview we categorized women according to whether they were married (or living with someone as though married) (1 = yes, 0 = no). (Of the 718 women living with a partner, only 3 were not married.) Second, we evaluated their perceptions of the quality of support they received from their marriage at each interview with a questionnaire adapted from Spanier (1976) and Pearlin and Schooler (1978). The questionnaire inquired about such areas as husband showing affection, laughing together, spending time together, and discussing marital problems. Based on results of a principal components analysis, we created a 20-item index of the quality of the marital relationship by averaging the items (1 = poor, 5 = excellent relationship, Cronbach's alpha at initial interview = .89, alpha at follow-up interview = .89). Third, we inquired about women's perceptions of how often they disagreed with their husbands in such areas such as child rearing, leisure activities, and household finances, utilizing items adapted from Spanier (1976). This questionnaire was administered only at follow-up. Principal components analysis indicated that the majority of items loaded on a single underlying factor, and thus we created a 12-item measure reflecting extent of marital disagreements by averaging the items (1 = disagree often, 4 = never disagree, alpha = .83).

Support from friends and neighbors. We assessed support in this domain with three measures. First, support from neighbors was evaluated at each interview with four questions about women's relationship with neighbors, such as how often they entertain neighbors in their homes, how often they do things with neighbors, and how many neighbors they are acquainted with. Principal components analysis indicated that the items could be averaged to form a composite measure (1 = weak relationship with neighbors, 4 = strong relationship, alpha = .65 at baseline, alpha = .64 at follow-up). Second, we measured support from friends with three items modeled after the work of Moos (1975). Based on results of a principal components analysis, we averaged the items to create a measure reflecting the extent to which women felt they expressed personal feelings and obtained practical assistance from friends (1 = none of friends provide support, 4 = all of friends provide support, alpha = .62 at baseline, alpha = .68 at follow-up). Finally, we asked women at each interview about whether they had anyone to turn to in times of emotional or practical need (1 = no one to turn to, 4 = can turn to all of friends; adapted from Moos, 1975).

Major Depression. Interviewers administered the Schedule for Affective Disorder and Schizophrenia–Lifetime Version (SADS-L; Endicott & Spitzer, 1978) at the second interview to determine whether women met Research Diagnostic Criteria (RDC; Spitzer, Endicott, & Robins, 1978) for either definite or probable major depression during the preceding 12 months. Criteria for diagnosis include having (1) a period of at least 1 week characterized by feelings of dysphoria (definite major depression if 2 or more weeks, probable major depression if less than 2 weeks); (2) at least four of eight cardinal symptoms for the worst episode; and (3) evidence of treatment, referral for treatment, or impairment of functioning during the episode.

Clinical characteristics of the depressive episode. For women who experienced a diagnosable depressive episode, length of the episode (in weeks) was ascertained, as well as whether it represented a recurrence of major depression or an incident episode (1 = recurrent depression, 0 = incident depression). We also determined at follow-up how many weeks it had been since the episode had ended. To examine symptom severity during the episode, we modified the SADS-L to assess each symptom on the 6-point severity rating scale from Part I of the instrument (i.e., 1 = symptom absent, 2 = present but not clinically significant, 3–4 = mild to moderate range, 5–6 = severe to extreme range). For analytic purposes, we derived four symptom factors based on a principal components analysis of the eight symptoms: Factor A averaged guilt/worthlessness and suicidal intent ratings; factor B averaged loss of interest, concentration difficulties, and psychomotor agitation/retardation ratings; factor C averaged sleep difficulty and lack of energy ratings; and factor D denoted the rating for appetite/weight change.

Psychosocial characteristics of the depressive episode. Within the Depression Section of the SADS-L, women were asked whether they sought any professional help during the episode (i.e., from mental health professionals, nonpsychiatric physicians, or other professionals such as clergy) (1 = yes, 0 = no). In addition, they were asked whether (1) they sought support from friends or relatives, including their husband, during the episode (1 = yes, 0 = no); and (2) friends or relatives suggested during the episode that they needed professional help (1 = yes, 0 = no).

Psychosocial Background Characteristics. As we described previously, the sample of women was fairly homogeneous. We did, however, include women's age (in years) and education (1 = grammar school, 6 = at least some graduate or professional training beyond college; adapted from Hollingshead & Redlich, 1958) as background variables in the analyses described. In addition, at the first interview we determined lifetime professional help seeking for mental health problems prior to the depressive episode using an expanded section of the SADS-L concerning such behavior (1 = ever sought treatment, 0 = did not).

Analyses

We initially performed descriptive analyses in order to examine the distribution of diagnosable major depression in the sample and to compare the distributions of social support at follow-up among women who did and did not have depressive episodes between interviews. We utilized box plots (Tukey, 1977) to compare these distributions. Box plots are

visual displays of data, based in part on sample percentiles. They highlight major characteristics of a distribution by showing where its middle
lies, how spread out the middle is, and how far the distribution's tails are
from the middle (Fromm, Greenhouse, Holland, & Swindell, 1986;
Tukey, 1977).

Following the descriptive analyses, we considered the size and statistical significance of the relationship between interim depression and
social support at follow-up, controlling for baseline levels of support,
utilizing log-linear analysis.

Finally, focusing specifically on those women who experienced depression, we performed a direct discriminant function analysis to determine whether, controlling for baseline social support and psychosocial
background characteristics, the clinical and psychosocial features of depressed women's episodes could reliably discriminate those women who
had very poor support at follow-up from women whose support levels
were judged to be adequate. Prior to discriminant analyses, we carefully
examined the predictor variables and found them adequately to meet
analytic assumptions (Tabachnick & Fidell, 1983).

RESULTS

Descriptive Data

Ninety-six of the 741 women met the RDC requirements for definite major depression ($n = 56$) or probable major depression ($n = 40$)
during the 12-month interim between interviews. The prevalence rate of
13.0% for major depression (7.6% for definite major depression) among
this cohort during the 12-month study period was at the expected level
applying appropriate normative 6-month rates for women in the Epidemiologic Catchment Area Study (Myers *et al.*, 1984).

We initially examined the distributions of the six support variables
at follow-up among the depressed and nondepressed groups of women.
With respect to marital status, although 4.1% of depressed women had
neither a husband nor live-in partner at follow-up, only 2.5% of nondepressed women were living without a partner. The distributions of the
remaining five support variables at follow-up among depressed and
nondepressed women are depicted by the box plots for each group
shown in Figure 2.

Each box plot (e.g., the plot for depressed women on the marital
relationships quality variable) shows a box that stretches from the first

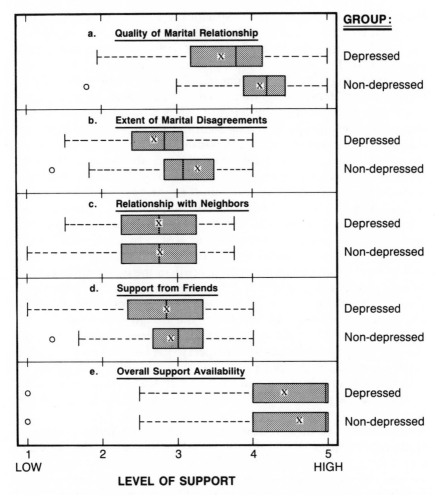

Figure 2. Box plots for support variables at follow-up among women with and without episodes of depression during interim between interviews. *Note.* Variables representing marital relationship quality and overall support availability were measured on 5-point scales; the remaining three variables were measured on 4-point scales.

quartile of a group's distribution to the third quartile (i.e., the middle 50% of the distribution is within the box). The median, a robust measure of the distribution's central location, is depicted by the line inside the box. The *x* represents the location of the group's mean. The dashed lines extending from either side of the box indicate inner "fences." These fences establish regions of observations that have decreasing likelihood relative to a normal distribution. Specifically, if the distribution is Gaussian, then 99.3% of all observations should fall within the inner fences; any values outside the inner fences are outliers (Fromm *et al.,* 1986; Tukey, 1977). The most extreme outliers are indicated by *o*'s.

Considering first the two marital support variables, the plots in Figure 2a and 2b reveal two things. First, distributions for women with depression are shifted to the left compared to nondepressed women: Depressed women have lower median and mean scores on both variables, indicating poorer marital relationship quality and a greater extent of marital disagreements at follow-up. Second, the shape of these distributions differs for depressed versus nondepressed women. Specifically, the middle 50% of the distribution (i.e., the box) for the depressed group is skewed to the *left* toward poor support for both marital variables. In contrast, the middle 50% of the nondepressed group is relatively symmetric on marital quality and is skewed to the *right* toward fewer disagreements. Furthermore, the depressed group shows substantially greater variability on marital quality than the nondepressed group (Inner Quartile Range (IQR) = difference between first and third quartiles, i.e., length of box = .95 for depressed women; IQR = .55 for nondepressed women). Variability on the disagreement variable was more similar (IQR's of .68 and .67 for the depressed and nondepressed groups, respectively). Finally, with respect to the tails of the two variables' distributions, the depressed group has long tails, especially to the left (toward poor support). The nondepressed group has outliers to the left for both marital variables but does not have especially long tails in either direction.

In contrast to these differences on the marital variables, the distributions of depressed and nondepressed women tend to be more similar on the remaining support variables (Figure 2c–e). The two groups' median and mean scores are in similar locations for all three variables, and the lengths of the boxes are identical for neighbor support, as well as for overall support availability (a variable that is extremely skewed for both groups). The distributions' tails also tend to be similar for these two variables. For friend support, however, as for the marital variables, the depressed group shows increased variability, and their distribution has a very long tail to the left (toward poor support).

Relationship of Depression to Follow-Up Support, Controlling for Baseline Support

We have found some evidence at a purely descriptive level that the nature of support received at follow-up differs for depressed and nondepressed women. However, do such differences maintain themselves at a statistically reliable level, and how large are they, after we take baseline support levels prior to the depressive episode into account? To address this question, we dichotomized each support variable into poor support (lower one-third of the distribution of the entire sample of 741 women) and good support (remaining two-thirds) categories. We dichotomized these variables for two reasons: First, our descriptive analyses indicated that these variables were skewed, often extremely so (in the case of overall support availability), and thus not likely to behave well in multivariate linear analyses. Second, from a practical, clinical standpoint, we were interested in a dichotomous research question: Following a diagnosable episode of major depression, what is the likelihood that a women will have quite *poor* support, as opposed to receiving at least an adequate level of support?

Table 1 displays data regarding the relationship of depression to each follow-up support variable: The table presents percentages of depressed and nondepressed groups who have low support in each area at follow-up, stratified according to women's level of *baseline support* in each area. Thus, for example, to examine the relationship between depression and presence of a marital relationship at follow-up, we stratified by whether or not women had a marital relationship at baseline; for quality of marital relationship at follow-up, we stratified by relationship quality at baseline, and so on. The only exception was that in order to examine the depression–marital disagreement association, we had to stratify by baseline marital quality because we did not assess marital disagreements at baseline. (The sample sizes on which the percentages are based— which vary according to the baseline stratification variable under consideration—are also included in the table.)

We performed 3-factor log-linear analyses to evaluate the statistical reliability of the associations of depression with follow-up support, controlling for baseline support. As indicated in the next to last column of Table 1, results indicated that, *even after controlling for baseline levels of support,* experiencing an episode of depression was associated with a significantly increased likelihood of having no marital relationship at follow-up. Among women remaining married at follow-up, depression was associated with a significantly increased likelihood of experiencing a poorer marital relationship at follow-up (controlling for baseline marital support), in terms of both relationship quality and extent of disagreements.

Similarly, with respect to friend and neighbor support, we note that depressed women perceived poorer support at follow-up than nondepressed women. However, depression did not exert a significant effect on these areas once baseline support levels were taken into account.

Finally, concerning the size of the depression–follow-up support

Table 1. Relationship of Depression to Follow-Up Support, Stratified by Support Level at Baseline

| | Support at baseline | | | | | | Associations with follow-up support: Z^a | |
| | Poor | | | Good | | | | |
Support at follow-up	Depression present	Depression absent	ϕ^b	Depression present	Depression absent	ϕ	Baseline support	Depression
From the marriage								
Marital status, % unmarried	$100.0(4)^c$	70.6(17)	.271	6.6(92)	0.6(628)	.168	7.44**	2.90*
Quality of relationship, % poor	81.3(48)	62.8(191)	.156	26.3(38)	12.7(433)	.126	8.81**	3.27*
Marital disagreements, % many	71.4(48)	54.5(191)	.150	34.2(38)	20.4(433)	.092	6.27**	2.99*
From friends and neighbors								
Overall availability, % poor	61.0(41)	54.2(155)	.056	27.3(50)	22.1(489)	.037	8.63**	1.45
Support from friends, % poor	34.1(41)	42.2(230)	.058	22.0(55)	12.6(404)	.085	4.33**	0.64
Relation with neighbors, % poor	39.0(39)	58.3(235)	.041	17.5(57)	11.3(408)	.063	5.93**	1.16

^{a}Z statistic from log-linear analysis tests the partial relationship of a predictor to follow-up support, controlling for the second predictor.
^{b}Correlation between depression and follow-up support within each level of baseline support.
^{c}Figures in parentheses indicate cell sample sizes for each combination of support and depression.
*$p < .01$; **$p < .001$.

associations, we observed that the sizes of these correlations, indicated by the values of ϕ in Table 1, were somewhat weaker among women with good baseline support than among women with poor baseline support, suggesting a buffering effect of baseline support. However, the interaction terms in the log-linear analyses that (in part) test these effects were not significant for any of the support variables examined.

Relationship of Characteristics of Depressive Episode to Follow-Up Support

Given evidence that depression had an independent effect on follow-up marital support, even after we took baseline levels of such support into account, we sought to determine whether specific characteristics of women's depressive episodes were related to experiencing low support. We categorized the 96 women who had experienced major depression into three groups in the analyses in this section: those with good marital support at follow-up, those with poor marital support at follow-up, and those with no marital relationship at follow-up. Because the measures of follow-up marital quality and disagreements were correlated ($r = .60$), we created a single measure of overall marital support by averaging the two measures. Again, because the distribution of this composite marital support measure was skewed, we dichotomized the distribution into poor support and good support groups. In Table 2 we present descriptive data on women according to their membership in the three outcome groups.

Univariate analyses show that baseline as well as clinical and psychosocial features of depressive episodes differ across the three outcome groups in several respects (see fourth column of Table 2). The descriptive data indicate that with regard to baseline characteristics, women with no marital support at follow-up were less educated at baseline, and women with poor or no follow-up support were also likely to have had less support at baseline. With regard to characteristics of the depressive episode, women with subsequently poor or no relationship at follow-up had longer episodes, and their episodes continued until closer to the time of follow-up interview. They were marginally more likely to have sought professional help during (as well as prior to) their episode and to have had more severe symptoms involving appetite and weight change.

The univariate tests reveal group differences but do not directly evaluate whether women experiencing poor support, or no support, can be distinguished from those experiencing good support at follow-up. We therefore performed a direct discriminant function analysis.

We found that a single discriminant function accounted for the bulk of the discriminating power of the 14 variables (76% of the between-

Table 2. Relationship of Baseline and Episode-Related Characteristics to Marital Support at Follow-Up among Depressed Women

Characteristic	Follow-up marital support			Analysis	
	Good (N=33)	Poor (N=53)	None (N=10)	3-group comparison[a]	Discriminant coefficient
Baseline					
Age (years)	28.0	29.2	25.9	2.28	.07
Education (1=grammar school, 6=college+)	3.4	3.5	2.6	3.77*	.28
Marital support (1=low, 2=none, 3=high)	2.5	1.5	1.4	16.55***	-.77
Prior professional help (% yes)	48.5	73.6	70.0	5.74@	.19
Depressive episode: clinical features					
Recurrent depression (% yes)	42.4	56.6	60.0	1.92	.06
Length (weeks)[b]	6.5	9.5	12.0	6.50**	.30

Weeks since episode ended[b]	20.1	12.4	8.3	4.32*	−.30
Mean symptom severity (1–6 points)					
Factor A: guilt, suicidal ideation	2.0	2.2	2.2	0.48	.13
Factor B: interest, concentration, psychomotor change	3.1	3.1	3.2	0.06	.01
Factor C: sleep, energy	3.7	3.6	3.9	0.29	.23
Factor D: appetite, weight change	3.4	3.2	4.3	2.88@	.16
Depressive episode: psychosocial features					
Sought professional help (% yes)	24.2	49.1	50.0	5.60@	.36
Sought family/friend support (% yes)	33.3	34.0	40.0	0.16	.19
Family/friends suggested help (% yes)	12.1	28.3	40.0	4.50	.36
Canonical correlation coefficient					.65

[a] $F_{(2, 92)}$ for continuous variables, χ^2 $(2, n = 96)$ for discrete variables.
[b] Transformed to reduced skewness, as follows. Episode length: $0 = 1$ week $(n = 31)$, $1 = 2$–8 weeks $(n = 42)$, $2 = 9+$ weeks $(n = 23)$. Weeks since episode ended: $0 = 0$ weeks [i.e., still depressed at follow-up] $(n = 27)$, $1 = 1$–8 weeks $(n = 27)$, $2 = 9+$ weeks prior to follow-up $(n = 53)$. Group means for both variables are presented in original, untransformed units.
@$p < .07$; *$p < .05$; **$p < .01$; ***$p < .001$.

group variability in follow-up support). After removal of this function, insignificant discriminating power remained (prior to removal: $\chi^2(28,n = 96) = 66.96, p < .001$; after removal: $\chi^2(13,n = 96) = 18.50, p = .140$). The function maximally discriminated those who had good marital support at follow-up (group centroid of 1.18) from those who had either poor support or no marital relationship at follow-up (centroids of -0.62 and $-.59$, respectively). Indeed, additional results indicated that the group with good marital support at follow-up differed significantly from the two other groups ($F(14,80) = 4.13, p < .001; F(14,80) = 2.36, p = .008$ for comparison to the poor support and the no relationship groups, respectively), whereas the latter two groups did not reliably differ from each other ($F(14,80) = 1.36, p = .191$).

The variables' standardized discriminant function coefficients are shown in the last column of Table 2. These indicate which variables contribute most heavily to discrimination among groups, after adjusting for remaining variables. They show that, in addition to the strong contribution of prior marital support, the best episode-related predictors of poor or no support at follow-up—as opposed to good support—were having a longer episode that occurred closer to the time of follow-up interview, having more severe symptoms in the sleep and energy domain (symptom factor C), seeking professional help during the episode, actively seeking support from family and/or friends, and family/friends recommending that the person needed professional help (coefficients ranging from .23 to .36). More severe appetite and weight change symptoms (symptom factor D) and seeking professional help for previous episodes were more marginally associated with experiencing poor or no marital support at follow-up.

The variables classified 76% of the women correctly. Classification accuracy was best for women with good support (78.8%) and those with poor support (83.0%). Although classification for women with no support was worst (30.0%), an additional 50% of these latter women were classified into the poor support group—the group they were found to resemble in the analysis. Although the overall classification rate of 76% indicates that the discriminant function does not fully explain the nature of group differences, the canonical correlation of .65 indicates that these particular variables, as a set, are quite important predictors of follow-up support.

DISCUSSION

Researchers studying the association between social support and psychological distress have repeatedly acknowledged the difficult issues involved in determining whether levels of support reflect outcomes or antecedents of individuals' distress (e.g., see Turner, 1983, and Kasl & Wells, 1985, for reviews). In community studies, where conceptual interest has long centered on the *predictive* contribution of social support, researchers have designed increasingly rigorous studies to assess the role of prior support levels in the pathogenesis of and vulnerability to psychological distress (e.g., Alloway & Bebbington, 1987; Thoits, 1982; Turner, 1981). Although the possibility that distress itself may influence subsequent social support is faithfully raised as an important caveat when interpreting data from such community studies, there has been little systematic attention directed to this causal link in nonpatient populations, especially with regard to the impact of clinically significant levels of distress. Our study, then, substantially extends previous work by (1) examining the predictive effects of diagnosable depression on social support in a community sample of women and (2) incorporating data on levels of social support obtained prior to the onset of women's depressive episodes.

We considered the effects of depression on a variety of domains of social support, including that obtained from husband, friends, and neighbors. Its effects on the marital relationship were by far the most profound, a finding consistent with a large body of clinical studies that have shown the marital relationship to be a sensitive barometer of both partners' psychological well-being (e.g., Briscoe & Smith, 1973; Bullock, Siegel, Weissman, & Paykel, 1972; Ilfeld, 1977). Thus we found that, even after taking women's level of marital support at baseline into account, depression in the interim between interviews remained a significant predictor of a poorer marital relationship at follow-up, defined in terms of both overall relationship quality and extent of disagreements with husband. Our descriptive analyses further revealed that depressed women—as a group—showed greater variability in their perceptions of their marriages than did remaining women, who, with few exceptions, perceived their marriages in a uniformly more positive way.

Not only did depressed women's *perceptions* of their marriages differ from remaining women at follow-up, but their marital status was more likely to be affected as well. Overall, women who experienced depressive episodes were 1.5 times more likely than other women to have no husband or live-in partner at follow-up. When we took marital status at baseline into account, considering only women who were initially living with a partner, we found that women who became depressed in the interim between interviews were *almost 11 times more likely* to have ended their relationship by follow-up (see Table 1). We raised the possibility earlier that women's depressions may color their perceptions of their social supports, whereas the actual nature or availability of such supports might be less affected. However, the magnitude of the association between depression and follow-up marital status itself suggests that more is involved than biased perceptions.

Even though we controlled for baseline levels of marital support, it is conceivable that depressed women's marriages worsened between baseline assessment and depression onset. Thus the associations between interim depression and marital support variables at follow-up might instead reflect an earlier change in support that actually precipitated the depression. Additional data that we have available about our sample are not consistent with such an interpretation, however. Specifically, we reviewed information obtained from the 13 women who reported that marital problems precipitated their depressions. Ten of these women had already reported low marital support—defined in terms of both of our marital perception variables—at the baseline interview. (Our analyses, then, had already taken their low support levels at baseline into account.) Only one woman reported high support at baseline but low support at follow-up. The remaining two women reported high support at both baseline and follow-up interviews.

Turning to our analyses of friend and neighbor support, we found remarkably little relationship between depression and follow-up support from these sources, once we considered initial support levels. These results, again, are inconsistent with the hypothesis that depression acts only to distort women's perceptions because this hypothesis would have led us to anticipate that depressed women would perceive reduced support in these areas by the follow-up interview. Instead, our data suggest that, for the majority of these women, nonfamily relationships may have suffered few ill effects because friends and neighbors may have been unaware either that they were experiencing significant mental health problems, or exactly how severe their distress was. Support for this possibility comes from the fact that, of the already small group of 23 women who reported that someone suggested that they seek help, only 7 stated that the suggestion came from nonfamily friends, and none reported that the suggestion was made by other neighborhood acquaintances.

Perhaps the depressed women we studied were fortunate that their relationships with friends and neighbors did not appear to have been affected by their recent bouts of depression. On the other hand, however, we note that the presence of initially strong friend or neighbor relationships at baseline also failed to confer much protection against the experience of depression in our sample: The associations of these baseline support variables with interim depression were extremely small (r's of .03 and .06 for friend support with subsequent depression and for neighbor support with depression, respectively). In sum, nonfamily social supports were neither important predictors nor outcomes of depression in our sample.

Our final analyses, then, returned to consideration of the marital relationship and identified characteristics of depressed women's episodes that predicted follow-up level of support from the marriage, controlling for baseline support level. These analyses revealed that by far the most critical distinction among depressed women pertained not to whether they *had* a marital relationship at follow-up, but to whether they had a *good* one. Women with good marital support at follow-up systematically differed in a variety of features of their depressions from both those women with poor follow-up support and those with no relationship at all. Although data regarding the women with no relationship at follow-up must be viewed with caution appropriate to the small sample size in this group, we note that the similarity of these women to those with poor marital support emerged on clinical as well as psychosocial features associated with the depressive episode.

Our data suggest that the profile of the depressed woman who went on to experience poor or no marital support includes more extensive impairments, with those impairments falling in areas likely to have been visible to her husband. Thus, compared to depressives with good support at follow-up, the former individuals experienced episodes of longer duration that were likely to have continued until close to the time of the follow-up interview; had more observable, behavioral symptoms (i.e., problems in the sleep, energy, and appetite and weight change areas); were more likely to have sought professional help and/or support during the depression from family and friends; and more often were recommended to seek professional help.

This profile is exemplified by Mrs. B:

> Mrs. B. was a 23-year-old mother of one child, aged 3 at the time of the initial interview. She had a high-school education and, at baseline, was a part-time department supervisor for a food service company. She had been married for 4 years to a cable handler with a local coal mining company and described her marriage as a happy one. She reported that she and her husband frequently laughed together and did things together outside the home, she rarely thought about marital problems, and she and her husband had rarely ever considered ending their marriage. Her depression began 1 month prior to the follow-up interview, due (she felt) to her employer's refusal to give her a full-time position. She was depressed for 3 weeks; she reported that it had begun to lift at the time of the follow-up. During her depression, she had had a severe decrease in her appetite and lost approximately 10 pounds. She had thought seriously about sui-

cide, reporting that she had made "no preparations, but did rehearse in my mind a plan." She had discussed her feelings only with her mother, who suggested that she seek counseling. At follow-up, she reported a much poorer relationship with her husband than she had described at baseline: She now described her marriage as "neither happy nor unhappy," she found herself frequently thinking over marital problems, she and her husband did not laugh together or do things together very frequently, and they had discussed whether their relationship should be ended.

In contrast, Mrs. F. who—like Mrs. B.—had reported a good marital relationship at baseline. However, despite an interim episode of depression, Mrs. F.'s relationship remained at a good level at the follow-up interview:

> Mrs. F. was a 26-year-old housewife and mother of four children who had been married for 9 years to an engineer for a local steel manufacturer. At baseline, she reported that her marriage was an "extremely happy" one. Three months prior to follow-up, she became depressed for a period of 2 weeks after losing a contest in a magazine. Her depression was substantially less severe than Mrs. B.'s and was characterized primarily by difficulty in making decisions and feelings of little energy or interest in things. At follow-up, her description of her relationship with her husband was virtually identical to what it had been at the initial interview.

Conclusions

We would be greatly oversimplifying the lives of the women in our two case examples, as well as the other women in our sample, if we concluded that the nature and severity of their depressions were the only factors influencing their marital relationships during our 1-year study period. Clearly, a variety of features of these women's lives combined to produce the substrate in which their social relationships were embedded (Gore & Colten, this volume). Nevertheless, both our empirical analyses and anecdotal descriptions suggest that depressive disorder is a critical factor to consider when evaluating the supports community residents derive from their social relationships, especially from intimate relationships such as the marriage. In this regard, our findings parallel the relatively extensive literature documenting such effects in psychiatric patient populations.

As such, our data have several important implications. First, from an intervention standpoint, in spite of the availability of efficacious treatments for many depressive conditions (Regier, Hirschfeld, Goodwin, Burke, Lazar, & Judd, 1988), less than half (40.6%) of the women in our sample who became clinically depressed actually sought professional help for their depressive episode. It would be useful to design and evaluate whether an early intervention effort by mental health professionals—that is, an intervention begun before the depression comes to have a permanent effect on close relationships with others—can successfully weaken any such effects.

Second, in terms of future research on the depression–social support relationship, our findings suggest that studies in this area must not only acknowledge but more often explicitly evaluate both directions of effects. Contrary to the view that much of the causal flow is from social supports to psychological distress (House, 1981; Turner, 1983), our data indicate profound effects in the reverse direction as well. Designing studies that are capable of disentangling the reciprocal effects of social supports and clinically significant disorder appears to be an eminent—and very difficult—task facing researchers in this domain.

Finally, our data have important implications for predicting and understanding individuals' mental health, from either clinical or research perspectives. Specifically, to the extent that depression damages social relationships, the disorder acts to create a population of community residents with a special vulnerability: As for seriously ill psychiatric patient populations (Heller, 1979; Henderson, 1977; Tolsdorf, 1976), a loss of support subsequent to the onset of psychological distress may place the affected community resident in a more precarious position should he or she experience recurrent mental health problems in the future.

ACKNOWLEDGMENTS

This research was supported in part by grant MH35425 from the National Institute of Mental Health, Rockville, MD. We wish to thank Leslie O. Dunn, M. P. H., and David K. Parkinson, M.D., for their help in implementing the study and the Psychiatric Epidemiology Training Program Data Analysis Seminar for suggestions regarding the analyses.

REFERENCES

Alloway, R., & Beggington, P. (1987). The buffer theory of social support: A review of the literature. *Psychological Medicine, 17*, 91–108.
Aneshensel, C. S., & Frerichs, R. R. (1982). Stress, support, and depression: A longitudinal causal model. *Journal of Community Psychology, 10*, 363–376.
Aneshensel, C. S., & Huba, G. J. (1984). An integrative causal model of the antecedents

and consequences of depression over one year. *Research in Community and Mental Health, 4,* 1–56.

Briscoe, C. W., & Smith, J. B. (1973). Depression and marital turmoil. *Archives of General Psychiatry, 29,* 811–817.

Bromet, E. J., Parkinson, D. K., Schulberg, H. C., Dunn, L. O., & Gondek, P. C. (1982). Mental health of residents near the Three Mile Island reactor: A comparative study of selected groups. *Journal of Preventive Psychiatry, 1,* 225–276.

Bromet, E. J., Dunn, L. O., Connell, M. M., Dew, M. A., & Schulberg, H. C. (1986). Long-term reliability of lifetime major depression in a community sample. *Archives of General Psychiatry, 43,* 435–440.

Bullock, R. C., Siegel, R., Weissman, M., & Paykel, E. S. (1972). The weeping wife: Marital relations of depressed women. *Journal of Marriage and the Family, 8,* 488–495.

Coyne, J. C. (1976). Depression and the response of others. *Journal of Abnormal Psychology, 85,* 186–193.

Coyne, J. C., Kessler, R. C., Tal, M., Turnbull, J., Wortman, C. B., & Greden, J. F. (1987). Living with a depressed person. *Journal of Consulting and Clinical Psychology, 55,* 347–352.

Dew, M. A., Bromet, E. J., & Schulberg, H. C. (1987). A comparative analysis of two community stressors' long-term mental health effects. *American Journal of Community Psychology, 15,* 167–184.

Dew, M. A., Dunn, L. O., Bromet, E. J., & Schulberg, H. C. (1988). Factors affecting help-seeking during depression in a community sample. *Journal of Affective Disorders, 14,* 223–234.

Dohrenwend, B. S., Dohrenwend, B. P., Link, B., & Levav, I. (1983). Social functioning of psychiatric patients in contrast with community cases in the general population. *Archives of General Psychiatry, 40,* 1174–1182.

Endicott, J., & Spitzer, R. L. (1978). A diagnostic interview: The Schedule for Affective Disorders and Schizophrenia. *Archives of General Psychiatry, 35,* 837–844.

Ferster, C. B. (1973). A functional analysis of depression. *American Psychologist, 28,* 857–870.

Fromm, D., Greenhouse, J. B., Holland, A. L., & Swindell, C. S. (1986). An application of exploratory statistical methods to language pathology: Analysis of the Western Aphasia Battery's Cortical Quotient in acute stroke patients. *Journal of Speech and Hearing Research, 29,* 135–142.

Heller, K. (1979). The effects of social support: Prevention and treatment implications. In A. Goldstein, F. Kanfer (Eds.), *Maximizing treatment gains: Transfer enhancement in psychotherapy* (pp. 353–382). New York: Academic Press.

Henderson, S. (1977). The social network, support and neurosis: The function of attachment in adult life. *British Journal of Psychiatry, 131,* 185–191.

Henderson, S., Byrne, D. G., & Duncan-Jones, P. (1981). *Neurosis and the social environment.* New York: Academic Press.

Hollingshead, A., & Redlich, F. (1958). *Social class and mental illness.* New York: Wiley.

House, J. S. (1981). *Work stress and social support.* Reading, MA: Addison-Wesley.

Ilfeld, F. W. (1977). Current social stressors and symptoms of depression. *American Journal of Psychiatry, 134,* 161–166.

Jacobson, E. (1954). Transference problems in the psychoanalytic treatment of severely depressive patients. *Journal of the American Psychoanalytic Association, 2,* 595–606.

Kasl, S. V., & Wells, J. A. (1985). Social support and health in the middle years: Work and the family. In S. Cohen & S. L. Syme (Eds.), *Social support and health* (pp. 175–198). Orlando, FL: Academic Press.

Kraines, S. H. (1957). *Mental depressions and their treatment.* New York: Macmillan.

Krantz, S. E., & Moos, R. H. (1987). Functioning and life context among spouses of remitted and nonremitted depressed patients. *Journal of Consulting and Clinical Psychology, 55,* 353–360.

Leaf, P. J., Weissman, M. M., Myers, J. K., Holzer, III, C. E., & Tischler, G. L. (1986). Psychosocial risks and correlates of major depression in one United States urban community. In J. E. Barrett & R. M. Rose (Eds.) *Mental disorders in the community: Progress and challenge* (pp. 47–73). New York: Guilford Press.

Moos, R. (1975). *Evaluating correctional and community settings.* New York: Wiley.

Myers, J. K., Weissman, M. M., Tischler, G. L., Holzer, III, C. E., Leaf, P. J., Orvaschel, H., Anthony, J. C., Boyd, J. H., Burke, J. D., Kramer, M., & Stoltzman, R. (1984). Six-month prevalence of psychiatric disorders in three communities. *Archives of General Psychiatry, 41,* 959–967.

Pearlin, L., & Schooler, C. (1978). The structure of coping. *Journal of Health and Social Behavior, 19,* 2–21.

Regier, G., Hirschfeld, R., Goodwin, F., Burke, J. D., Lazar, J. B., & Judd, L. L. (1988). The NIMH Depression Awareness, Recognition, and Treatment Program: Structure, aims, and scientific basis. *American Journal of Psychiatry, 145,* 1351–1357.

Smith, M. B., & Hobbs, N. (1966). The community and the community mental health center. *American Psychologist, 21,* 499–509.

Spanier, G. (1976). Measuring dyadic adjustment: New scales for assessing the quality of marriage and similar dyads. *Journal of Marriage and the Family, 38,* 15–30.

Spitzer, R., Endicott, J., & Robins, E. (1978). Research Diagnostic Criteria: Rationale and reliability. *Archives of General Psychiatry, 35,* 773–782.

Sturt, E. (1981). Hierarchical patterns in the distribution of psychiatric symptoms. *Psychological Medicine, 11,* 783–794.

Tabachnick, B. G., & Fidell, L. S. (1983). *Using multivariate statistics.* New York: Harper & Row.

Thoits, P. A. (1982). Conceptual, methodological, and theoretical problems in studying social support as a buffer against life stress. *Journal of Health and Social Behavior, 23,* 145–159.

Tolsdorf, C. C. (1976). Social networks, support and coping: An exploratory study. *Family Process, 15,* 407–417.

Tukey, J. W. (1977). *Exploratory data analysis.* Reading: Addison-Wesley.

Turner, R. J. (1981). Social support as a contingency in psychological well-being. *Journal of Health and Social Behavior, 22,* 357–367.

Turner, R. J. (1983). Direct, indirect, and moderating effects of social support and psychological distress and associated conditions. In H. Kaplan (Ed.), *Psychosocial stress: Trends in theory and research* (pp. 105–155). New York: Academic Press.

Weissman, M. M., & Myers, J. K. (1980). Psychiatric disorders in a U.S. community. The application of Research Diagnostic Criteria to a resurveyed community sample. *Acta Psychiatrica Scandinavica, 62,* 99–111.

Weissman, M. M., & Paykel, E. S. (1974). *The depressed woman: A study of social relationships.* Chicago: University of Chicago Press.

10

Marital Engagement/Disengagement, Social Networks, and Mental Health

NAN LIN and JEANNE WESTCOTT

INTRODUCTION

The general relationship between marital status and health is well documented in the research literature. Married individuals tend to exhibit less psychological distress than the unmarried (Bloom, Asher, & White, 1978; Ensel, 1986a; Menaghan & Lieberman, 1986; Pearlin & Johnson, 1977). The married are also shown to be less physically vulnerable. For example, disease morbidity and disability data show the nonmarried to be at higher risk (Bloom, Asher, & White, 1978; Verbrugge, 1979). For both blacks and whites, the married enjoy lower mortality rates than those who are nonmarried (Berkman & Syme, 1979; Bloom, Asher, & White, 1978). The married also have lower rates of utilization of health care facilities such as contact with physicians, admission to general and psychiatric hospitals and the use of clinics (Riessman & Gerstel, 1985; Spanier & Thompson, 1984). Further, marital disengagement, through

NAN LIN • Department of Sociology, Duke University, Durham, North Carolina 27706.   JEANNE WESTCOTT • Department of Sociology, State University of New York at Albany, Albany, New York 12222.

The Social Context of Coping, edited by John Eckenrode. Plenum Press, New York, 1991.

separation, divorce, or death of the spouse, is detrimental to one's mental health (Henderson & Argyle, 1985; Leslie & Grady, 1985; Wilcox, 1981).

The prevailing explanation for this positive correlation between married status and health consists of two components, both of which involve the partners themselves. One view argues that marriage affords an opportunity for confiding and intimate interactions, which provide the partners steady psychic comfort and support (Kessler & Essex, 1982). It may also involve an identity-building process. Marriage redefines the focus of interpersonal conversation to the specific partner rather than a more general social circle. Self-identity as well as personal biography are now associated with the spouse (Berger & Kellner, 1964).

A second component focuses on the resources of the partners. Marriage allows the pooling of personal resources of the two partners. Thus the expanded resource repertoire allows better coping with social problems and stressors. These two components identify the expressive and instrumental support each partner provides for the other.

When this relationship is threatened or severed, the loss triggers both an identity crisis because of the absence of confiding and intimate conversation opportunities as well as a loss of resources for coping. Thus it exerts psychological and physical stress that cannot be compensated through other social relationships.

This explanation seems reasonable, for research evidence clearly shows that married individuals overwhelmingly name their spouses as confidants (Lin, Woelfel, & Dumin, 1986, pp. 283–306) and seek their support in time of a major life crisis (Lin, Woelfel, & Light, 1986, pp. 307–332). Further, when the spouse is named as the confidant or source of support, potential stress evoked by undesirable life events tends to be reduced to a greater extent than when others are used as confidant or source of support (Lin, Woelfel, & Dumin, 1986; Lin, Woelfel, & Light, 1986).

However, this explanation cannot be considered as the only viable theory regarding the relationship between marital status and well-being, for there are variations in both the married and nonmarried contexts that deviate from the expectation of this explanation. For example, not all married individuals show better mental health than nonmarried individuals. Nor does every married individual name his or her spouse as confidant or source of support.

In the panel study we conducted in upstate New York during 1979, 1980, and 1982, we found (Lin, Woelfel, & Dumin, 1986, p. 297) up to 90% of the married males named females (the great majority being spouses) as confidant, whereas less than 80% of the married females named males as confidant. When confronted with a major life event, between 50% to 60% of the married respondents sought support from their spouses (p. 323). In other words, up to half of them used others for support. These variations suggest that merely being married does not necessarily imply confiding relationships and that such a confiding relationship is no guarantee of a source of support in time of stress.

Further, there is some evidence that not necessarily all maritally disengaging (e.g., separating or divorcing) individuals suffer psychological or physical distress or that they all suffer the same degree of distress (Brown, Feldberg, Fox, & Kohen, 1976; Riessman & Gerstel, 1985; Gerstel, Riessman, & Rosenfield, 1985; Wallerstein, 1986; Wheaton, 1989). These findings suggest that other factors either contribute along with marital interactions to induce distress or mediate between marital status and distress.

The present chapter proposes a network theory to supplement the marital interaction theory in explaining the relationship between marital status and distress. We will argue that this network perspective allows explanations of (1) variation in distress among married individuals, (2) differential effects of marital disengagement on distress, and (3) a cyclical rather than linear view of the marital engagement/disengagement process.[1]

Also, attention is focused on mental health and psychological well-being rather than physical health. This is simply due to the fact that more research evidence can be brought to bear in this area. The theory, however, should be meaningful in implications for physical health as well.

THE THEORY

The theory begins with the assumption that social support is critical in maintaining and promoting one's well-being. *Social support* is here defined as *the process (e.g., perception or reception) by which resources in the*

---

[1] When appropriate, we will refer to data gathered in a three-wave panel study conducted in 1979, 1980, and 1982 in the Albany–Schenectady–Troy metropolitan area of New York (Lin, Dean, & Ensel, 1986; Lin & Ensel, 1989). From a representative sample of the adults in the community, data were obtained about life events experienced in the past 6 to 12 months, social support, and psychological distress (CESD–D scores). By separating the respondents into various marital status categories (single, married over the study period, married during past 12 to 24 months, separated in past 6, 12, or 24 months, divorced during past 6, 12, or 24 months, widowed during past 6, 12, or 24 months, and remarried), we analyzed data relevant to the present discussion. Due to design limitations and subsample sizes, findings are presented here for heuristic purposes only.

social networks are brought to bear to meet the functional needs (e.g., instrumental and expressive) in routine and crisis situations. Thus social support is seen as the process of evoking resources embedded in social ties to meet instrumental and expressive needs.

This definition clarifies the mechanism by which social support operates to render an effect on health and mental health. Previous theoretical statements on social support tend to argue that social support, especially expressive support, affects health or mental health (Cobb, 1976; Cohen & Syme, 1985; Lin, 1986; Dean & Lin, 1977); yet, how such support is transmitted has remained unclear. The definition offered here proposed that social network and social ties are the media by which such supports are transmitted. Attention, therefore, must be given to the specification as to how social network and ties transmit such support.

Recent network theory (Granovetter, 1973, 1974) suggests that social ties can be characterized along a continuum of strength as measured by such indicators as intimacy, intensity, frequency of interactions and reciprocity of services. As Granovetter points out, strong ties are characterized by relations in a close social circle. For information outside the social circle, it is necessary to use bridges. Bridges tend to be formed by weaker rather than stronger ties.

Lin (1982, 1986) extended this notion to analyze how different social ties can provide different social resources to the individual. Social resources are defined as resources associated with social ties and usually involve some aspects of status, wealth, and power of the ties. This view sees social ties not only in terms of closeness to ego but also in terms of their positioning in the hierarchical structure of society. It was hypothesized that strong ties tend to be ties closer to ego in the hierarchical structure and share resources similar in characteristics to those personal resources possessed by ego. On the other hand, weaker ties tend to be ties farther away from ego in the hierarchical structure and offer social resources dissimilar to personal resources possessed by ego. If these hypotheses are valid and the research evidence so far seems to support them (e.g., Lin, Ensel, & Vaughn, 1981; Campbell, Marsden, & Hurlbert, 1986; Linn & Dumin, 1986; Marsden & Hurlbert, 1988; De-Graaf & Flap, 1988), then social support would be differentially effective as represented by these ties and their social resources.

Social support is meaningful in terms of expressive and instrumental needs. In the case of expressive needs, ego wishes to access someone who can share, understand, and empathize with his/her feelings. Strong and homophilous ties, which are characterized by shared socioeconomic characteristics, lifestyles, attitudes, and behaviors, may provide support for expressive and psychic needs and the opportunity for understanding life experiences and crises. It is argued, therefore, that expressive needs are better served by strong ties because these ties tend to be homophilous, sharing similar statuses, characteristics, and lifestyles.

Weaker ties, on the other hand, serve as important links for accessing resources not readily available among the strong and homophilous ties. In the case of instrumental needs, ego wishes to access someone who can help in carrying out specific tasks. Depending on the task at hand, the resources required may be either similar or different from ego's own personal resources. Chances are such that resources are not readily available among ties in the close social circle. Thus, we argue instrumental needs are better met by diverse ties (a mix of strong and weak ties), depending on the specific need. Some of these needs (e.g., child care) may best be met by strong ties; and other needs may require bridges or weaker ties (e.g., finding a better job). That is, instrumental needs would be best met if one has a more diverse and heterogenous set of ties.

In general, then, an individual can be expected to benefit from a resource-rich network that contains heterogenous social ties. It is proposed that two criteria determine the richness of resources in a social network: range (or diversity) and composition. Range indicates the extent of different types of tie characteristics in a network. It reflects the diversity of resources in the network. The hypothesis is that the greater the range or diversity of ties, the greater the choice and, therefore, the opportunity one has in accessing a tie that can provide the necessary resources for expressive or instrumental needs (Campbell, Marsden, & Hulbert, 1986; Lin, 1982; Lin & Dumin, 1986).

There are at least two indicators of range, *heterophily* and *vertical extensity.* Heterophily describes the variation of all values on a characteristic or attribute among the ties, usually reflected by statistical variance. For example, a person seeking employment who has access to ties with varied job titles is presumed to have an advantage over another person with ties who have similar job titles in that the former may access more information and influence regarding availability of and access to a variety of jobs.

Range can further be analyzed in terms of extensity. Extensity describes variation of a characteristic or attribute among the ties in terms of the extreme values (for example, the difference between the highest value and the lowest value). If the values of a characteristic or attribute can be rank-ordered, such as occupational or economic positions, then vertical extensity becomes meaningful and important. Vertical extensity measures the extent to which a person's social ties reach the upper and lower positions in this hierarchical system. A more diverse network is usually related to greater vertical extensity. Such extensity offers the opportunity to reach up toward the top of the social structure and the higher the position reached the greater information and influence one is likely to obtain (Lin, 1982). Thus diversity of a network is seen as a function of the network's heterophily and vertical extensity. A more heterophilous and greater vertically extensive network tends to offer more diverse social resources.

Composition indicates the size and principal features of the social network. The general hypothesis is that the larger the network size and the "better" the characteristics of the average tie, the better off the person is. This hypothesis is deducible from the general homophily principle (Homans, 1950; Lazarsfeld & Merton, 1954), that postulates a relationship between status similarity and likelihood of association and interaction. A person is more likely to interact with others with similar or slightly higher status than with those of lower status. Thus the characteristics of one's network suggest the status level of the person and the assumption is that the higher the status the more likely the person can access better resources to meet his/her expressive and, especially, instrumental needs (Lin, 1982). A person having a larger network and ties with higher averages of education and income, for example, is presumed to have an advantage over another person with a smaller network and ties of lower socioeconomic characteristics in that the former may acquire better resources.

Range and composition are complementary but independent characteristics of a social network. A diverse network does not imply a larger network, even though it may correspond to a network with higher statuses. In general, we argue range is a more critical criterion than composition in identifying a resource-rich network.

Thus social support is said to be more effective when one can access and use a more diverse and a more vertically extended network to reach more and better social resources. A network with these characteristics is hypothesized to be more effective in providing resources to meet various instrumental and expressive needs.

In the following, this theory will be used to analyze the relationship between marital engagement/disengagement and mental health.

MARRIAGE AND INTEGRATION OF SOCIAL NETWORKS

Marriage brings two persons into a relationship that promotes the opportunity for companionship and help, fulfilling, to a certain extent, expressive as well as instrumental needs of the partners. The marital relationship compels frequency of interactions and assistance between the two persons constituting the basic components of a family. To uphold the vitality of the family, mutual understanding and help are necessary. Many aspects of family life, economic, social, sexual, child rearing as well as companionship, can be fulfilled with a coordinated and close relationship between a husband and a wife. It is not surprising, therefore, that the overwhelming evidence shows the married, especially the newly wed, are psychologically happy and healthy.

The Albany data show that married respondents have the lowest scores on depressive symptomatology as measured with the CES-D among all marital status groups.[2] As shown in Table 1, the married experience the least psychological distress, followed by the never married (single). Those in the process of being maritally disengaged showed significantly higher distress, in comparison. Also, the married show the lowest number of life events or undesirable life events. This suggests that marriage provides a social context in which many instrumental and expressive needs are adequately met.

The marital union, however, has the added social significance in that two distinct social networks are now being merged. As shown in Figure 1, we can represent the social network of each person by a circle and the relationships between the two networks for the two persons by the relationship between the circles.

Before marriage, each person draws expressive and instrumental support from social ties in his/her respective network, represented in diagram 1 in Figure 1 for ego and alter. When the two persons become acquaintances and later friends, the two networks become overlapped (diagram 2 in Figure 1). The liaison between the two partners forges a bridge linking the two persons' networks. As the relationship intensifies, the distance of the bridge, by definition, decreases.

The distance of the bridge is further reduced upon marriage, as linkage increases between the two kinship networks. Also, partners are

[2]Table 1 presents the mean scores on the depressive symptom scale, CESD, for the various marital statuses. We introduce 14 statuses: (1) single (never married), (2) married in the last 12 months, (3) married in the last 24 months, (4) married (stably married with no status change within the study period), (5) separated within the past 6 months, (6) separated within the past 12 months, (7) separated within the past 24 months, (8) divorced within the past 6 months, (9) divorced within the past 12 months, (10) divorced within the past 24 months, (11) widowed within the past 6 months, (12) widowed within the past 12 months, (13) widowed within the past 24 months, and (14) remarried. Whenever appropriate, each respondent is assigned a status at each time period of the study. So when considering those married in the past 12 months, the single status is reported at T1, the newly married status 12 months later at T2. Similarly, being married in the last 24 months is reported as single at T2, then newly married 24 months later at T3. The same type of status change is reported for those who become separated, divorced, or widowed. Those remarried are reported as being in marital disruption (separated, divorced, or widowed) at T1, then remarried at T2 and remarried at T3).

Table 1. Life Events and CESD by Marital Status

Marital status	Mean CESD			Total life events			Undesirable life events		
	T1	T2	T3	T1	T2	T3	T1	T2	T3
Single (N=79)	9.7	8.2	9.3	5.8	4.9	4.5	1.6	1.4	1.7
Married									
(12 MO, N=5)	10.2	11	—	8.8	7.8	—	2.4	2.6	—
(24 MO, N=14)	—	7.5	6.7	—	6	6.5	—	2.1	1.7
Married									
(N=368)	7	7.5	7.5	3.7	3.6	3.3	1	1.1	0.9
Separated									
(6 MO, N=14)	8	21.6	14.7	8.8	8.2	8.7	1.8	3.7	2.5
(12 MO, N=11)	7.5	23.3	—	6.8	7.9	—	2.5	4.2	—
(24 MO, N=11)	—	9.7	14.9	—	4.3	5.7	—	1	1.3
Divorced									
(6 MO, N=1,9)	11	8.8	11.5	6	9.3	8.3	3	1.3	2.7
(12 MO, N=6)	8	6.6	—	7.6	5.5	—	2.1	0.6	—
(24 MO, N=10)	—	19.3	12.3	—	8	6.3	—	3.8	1.8
Widowed									
(6 MO, N=2,4)	1.6	15	13.2	2.3	3.5	4	2.3	1.3	2.5
(12 MO, N=4)	13	12.6	—	1	2.6	—	0.3	0.3	—
(24 MO, N=9)	—	5.8	11.4	—	3.1	2.6	—	1.1	1.6
Remarried									
(12 MO, N=5)	7	3.2	—	6.6	9.6	—	1.6	1	—

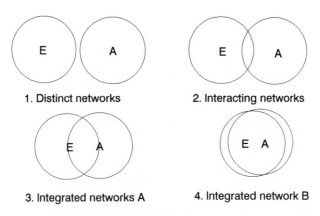

Figure 1. Relationships of two networks.

obligated to socialize together, thereby integrating some of their friendship networks as well. Even though division of labor and differential employment status may not allow complete integration of work-related ties, each partner is at least indirectly accessible to such ties.

Marriage strengthens the bridge integrating the two previous separate networks. A social process proceeds in which the partners selectively maintain, intensify, or disengage previous ties to consolidate the integrated network (Berger & Kellner, 1964; Daniels-Mohring & Berger, 1984). In general, marriage brings each partner into contact, both directly and indirectly, with a more diverse network than each had access to before the marriage. Thus, they collectively enjoy access to more diverse social resources enabling them to better meet their expressive and instrumental needs.

Some evidence for this hypothesis is provided by the Albany data. Each respondent was asked to name the person who helped him or her during a most important life event. As seen in Table 2, for the married, spouse/lover constitutes the largest percentage of helpers in case of encountering a most important life event (44%–75%). However, this group also shows the greatest use of other types of relationships as helper including parents and siblings (6%–13%), inlaws (2%–4%), close friends (11%–12%) and others (13%–31%). The use of extended networks as a result of marriage is best seen when considering the case of those who became married in the past 24 months. At T2 these persons were single. Table 2 shows that when single at T2, the helper with the most important life event was shared between the spouse/lover and others (37.5% each) and parent/siblings (25%). After the marriage, at T3, the spouse/lover becomes the helper of choice (75%) with parent/sibling and others still

Table 2. Helper with Most Important Life Event

Marital status	Spouse/lover		Parent/sibling		In-laws		Close friends		Others	
	T2	T3	T2	T3	T2	T3	T2	T3	T2	T3
Single (N=79)	20.7	15.4	13.8	30.8	0	0	24	19	41	27
Married										
(12 MO, N=5)	75	—	0	—	0	—	0	—	25	—
(24 MO, N=14)	37.5	75	25	12.5	0	0	0	0	37.5	12.5
Married (N=368)	47	44	6.3	10.1	3.9	2	11	12	31.4	26.8
Separated										
(6 MO, N=6,14)	0	0	11	33	0	0	66.6	33	22	33
(12 MO, N=11)	0	—	14.2	—	0	—	57.1	—	28.5	—
(24 MO, N=11)	25	0	0	20	0	0	25	40	50	40
Divorced										
(6 MO, N=1, 9)	0	0	40	12.5	0	0	0	37.5	60	50
(12 MO, N=6)	0	—	50	—	0	—	0	—	50	—
(24 MO, N=10)	20	0	10	9	0	0	40	27	30	63.6
Widowed										
(6 MO, N=2,4)	0	0	0	0	0	33	0	0	100	66.6
(12 MO, N=3)	0	—	0	—	0	—	0	—	100	—
(24 MO, N=9)	33	0	0	0	0	20	0	0	66	80
Remarried										
(12 MO, N=5)	75	—	0	—	25	—	0	—	0	—

being named but by a smaller number (12.5%). These data suggest that marriage provides a bridge to a more diverse network that becomes useful as a support resource.

Each respondent in the Albany study was also asked to name a most important confidant with whom he or she could talk about their personal problems. The presence of a confidant has been found to be associated with better psychological well-being (Lin, Woelfel, & Dumin, 1986). As seen in Table 3, those persons who are married for the duration of the study or have recently become married, show the greatest use of spouses as confidants. Among those who are married for the duration of the study, the spouse is the overwhelming choice of confidant (61% to 71%). The trend toward use of the spouse as confidant can also be seen among those becoming married at T2. Initially, while they are still single at T1, the confidant role is shared by the lover (20%), parent/siblings (60%), and close friends (20%). Once the marriage takes place, the spouse becomes the most utilized confidant (75% compared to 25% for the parent/sibling and no close friends being named). The same trend is seen among those who have become married in the past two years. At T2 when they are still single, the confidant role is shared by the lover (58%), parent/sibling (17%), and close friends (25%). Once married at T3, the spouse becomes the most frequently named confidant (82%) with the parent/siblings (18%) and no close friends being named. For those becoming remarried after a period of marital disruption, the same trend is evident. While still in marital disruption at T1, the lover (20%), parent/sibling (20%), and close friends (60%) all share the confidant role. However, after the marriage at T2, the confidant role is exclusively that of the spouse (100%). As presented in Table 3, spouse/lover is the overwhelming choice of confidant among the married. Thus there is evidence that expressive support is essentially provided by one's spouse.

Although a married couple is expected to forge toward an integrated social network for both partners, such a network may, nevertheless, exhibit different structural characteristics. We may identify two ideal types of integrated networks in a marriage partnership. In both types of networks, we assume that there is a full cognitive map of the networks on the part of both partners. That is, each partner is fully aware of the elements (ties) of both partners' networks, even though they may not be in direct contact with all the other partner's elements. In the case of a lack of such a cognitive map, there is obviously a lack of communication and/or concealment between the partners. This would be symptomatic of, or lead to, an unstable marriage. On the other hand, having a full cognitive map does not necessarily indicate both partners must be in direct contact with all the ties.

In fact, in one integrated network, to be called Type A network (see

Table 3. Relationship of Confidant

Marital status	Spouse/lover			Parent/sibling			In-laws			Close friends			Others		
	T1	T2	T3	T1	T2	T3	T1	T2	T3	T1	T2	T3	T1	T2	T3
Single ($N=79$)	5.3	32.7	19.6	36	27.2	37.2	4	1.8	0	40	32.7	35	14.6	5	8
Married															
(12 MO, $N=5$)	20	75	—	60	25	—	0	0	—	20	0	0	0	0	—
(24 MO, $N=14$)	—	58	81.8	—	16.6	18	—	0	0	—	25	0	—	0	0
Married ($N=368$)	63	70.6	60.7	8.8	5.3	8.9	2.3	1.5	2.7	21.6	17	17	3.9	5	10.2
Separated															
(6 MO, $N=6, 14$)	17	0	0	17	20	22	0	10	0	66.6	50	66.6	0	20	11
(12 MO, $N=11$)	63.6	0	—	0	12.5	—	9.1	12.5	0	18.2	50	—	9.1	25	—
(24 MO, $N=11$)	—	57.1	11.1	—	14.3	11.1	—	0	0	—	14.3	78	—	14.3	0
Divorced															
(6 MO, $N=1, 9$)	0	0	12.5	100	75	0	0	0	0	0	25	75	0	0	12.5
(12 MO, $N=6$)	17	0	—	50	100	—	0	0	—	33	0	—	0	0	—
(24 MO, $N=10$)	—	16.6	0	—	16.6	0	—	8.3	8.3	—	41.6	85.7	—	16.6	7
Widowed															
(6 MO, $N=2, 4$)	0	0	0	67	0	0	0	0	0	33	50	0	0	50	0
(12 MO, $N=3$)	50	0	—	0	0	—	0	0	—	0	0	—	50	100	—
(24 MO, $N=9$)	—	44	0	—	0	0	—	0	0	—	22	11	—	33	89
Remarried															
(12 MO, $N=5$)	20	100	—	0	—	0	0	—	60	0	—	0	0	—	

diagram 3 in Figure 1), the two partners maintain significant non-overlapping portions of their respective networks. That is, each partner engages in direct interactions with certain ties from the other partner's network while maintaining interactions with some other ties in their respective network.

On the other hand, the Type B network (diagram 4 in Figure 1) represents a situation where both partners are almost in direct contact with all ties in each other's networks. In this case, there is little non-overlapping between the two networks.

We hypothesize that a Type A network is superior to a Type B network for support purposes. This argument is derived from the two criteria of the network as support resources that was stated previously. The Type A network, because of the extensity of nonoverlapping between the two networks, tends to be larger in size and more diverse in resources. If we hold the network sizes as constants, then the less overlapping of the two networks, the more distinctive elements there will be (compare diagrams 3 and 4 in Figure 1) and the larger the overall size of the two networks—for example, if each network consists of 100 nodes or ties. If there is substantial overlap, say 50 of the 100 ties are shared or overlapped, then the total number of ties is 150. If there is less overlap, say 25 of the ties are shared or overlapped, then the total number of ties becomes 175. Further, the more distinctive elements there are in the networks, the greater the likelihood for more heterophilous elements, if we hold other factors constant. Thus the Type A network should be a resource-rich network from which support can be drawn to satisfy a wider variety of support needs.

It is not clear what factors determine the formation of a particular type of integrated network following marriage. We suspect a number of factors help determine the effect of each type of network on the couple and the family. Among these factors are socialization, solidarity of each's kinship network, economic dependence, and expectations of each other's roles. This remains an important area for further research.

As the marital engagement proceeds, the initial euphoric dyadic relationship is more and more substituted by shared responsibility to meet the demands of carrying on a family life. Life demands (children, employment, economic, daily chores, etc.) not only increase further investment in the dyadic interactions but also call for additional mobilization of social resources through social ties.

However, this dual responsibility, maintaining the intense and intimate dyadic relationship and mobilizing diverse social resources, carries intrinsic tension. On the one hand, the intensive relationship between the partners demands not only strengthening the tie between the partners but also sharing of resources in the network. The merging of individual social circles into one heavily overlapped circle is expected. On the other hand, there is a general and increasing awareness that differential expressive and instrumental needs of each partner may require accessibility to different types of ties. Thus the more diverse and vertically extensive network would be more efficient. The competing loyalties of forging a strong dyadic relationship and sharing of social ties and social resources, while maintaining a more diverse and, thus, more supportive personal network, can become problematic. Some couples seem adaptive enough to recognize the need for nonoverlapping ties for each partner while maintaining a strong relationship between the partners. Others are less adaptive, either creating a close social circle without a diverse network or establishing a diverse network while weakening the strong (dyadic, marital) partnership.

GENDER ROLE DIFFERENCES IN THE NETWORKS

It is not our purpose to explore further the causal forces leading to network variation, but rather we wish to point out the existence and significance of these variations. We suspect, however, that in general this tension is more strongly felt by married women than by married men. In American society, men generally are allowed to take on more social roles than women (Gore & Mangione, 1983). Men have acquired greater accessibility to a variety of ties through work, family, and other social circles. Women, on the other hand, have until recently been more restricted in work as well as other roles. Even today, there is evidence that men and women tend to have unequal access to social resources in the labor market due to differential placement within that market. Women tend to be located in job positions in the less central segments, with less extensive opportunity for mobility, and with more homophilous ties (especially in positions with high concentration of women). Thus even in work-related networks, women are involved in more dense, homophilous, and less vertically extensive networks.

When confronted with the tension between strong commitment to the partnership of the marriage and a more diverse network, women are more likely to be pulled into an integrated network that is oriented toward catering to the needs of the male as opposed to their own needs. Even when both the man and the woman make "equal" sacrifice in reducing the tension, the woman would be disadvantaged because of the initial and continued unequal status and position in the social network.

In terms of the diagrams in Figure 1, we would argue that married women are more likely to be involved in a Type B network than married men. Note that, whereas in Figure 1, each network is represented by an equal-sized circle, this gender differentiation would be better expressed with two unequal circles. The smaller circle, representing a married woman's network, would be substantially overlapped or even encircled by the larger network circle of her husband.

In sum, marriage affords and commands an extended network in which each partner serves as a node in an important bridge. Such a network fulfills many expressive and instrumental functions for the married and their family that, in turn, lead to better psychological well-being. Thus marriage promotes psychological well-being indirectly through the integration of the social networks. Nevertheless, the sense of well-being varies depending on the balance between dyadic relationships and access to diverse network and social resources.

MARITAL DISENGAGEMENT AND BREAKUP OF NETWORK AND SUPPORT

When the marriage breaks down,[3] it has immediate and direct consequences, among other things, on each partner's well-being. There are a variety of reasons offered to explain this effect. One source of the effect concerns losses suffered in all aspects of one's life—intimate relationship, social role, household composition, sometimes residence and contact with one's children (Menaghan & Lieberman, 1986). These losses severely challenge one's self-identity and self-worth. Further, resources previously available for coping are also truncated. One's expected and actual ability to manage both routine and crisis-centered stressors is immediately threatened and often crippled. These problems will have a negative impact on one's psychological and physical well-being.

The degree of such a direct impact is in part conditioned by the expectation of the event and by anticipation of establishing an alternative identity and resources. For example, it is expected that an elderly person who suffers the death of a spouse, a person whose spouse dies after a long illness, a person who has suffered an unhappy relationship with a spouse, or a person who expects to establish an intimate relationship with another person, is less likely to be affected psychologically than another who did not have such an expectation or anticipation (Daniels-Mohring & Berger, 1984; Renne, 1971; Wallerstein, 1986).

In the Albany study (see Table 1), those in the process of separation and divorce register substantially higher CES-D scores than the married

---

[3]It is beyond the scope of the present chapter to discuss causes of marital disengagement. The process involves separation, divorce, and/or death of the spouse (for potential causes, see Cherlin, 1981; Goetting, 1982).

or the single. They also experience the most life events or undesirable life events.

Just as important is the impact of the marital disengagement on the previously forged social network. *As the bridge is broken, so are many of the ties accessed through the bridge.* For example, Rands (1981) found the loss of 42% of the shared friendship network after separation.[4] Wilcox (1981) also found such losses. Functions served by prior ties now must be fulfilled by ego or other ties. Realigning social ties for expressive and instrumental functions may either be impossible or, if possible, require time. When these functions, either expressive or instrumental, cannot be fulfilled, even temporarily, they exert strain on the person's psychological well-being. Wilcox (1981) reported that the degree of overlap between the spouses' network prior to the separation was a factor contributing to poor adjustment. Similarly, Daniels-Mohring and Berger (1984) found the postdivorce stability among their respondents to be related to the stability of networks after the divorce.

Thus, it is hypothesized that marital disengagement tends to bring about the truncation of a social network, which had served many support functions for the well-being of the individual as well as the family, leading to psychological distress. What is proposed, therefore, is that marital disengagement is expected to have direct and indirect consequences on a person's psychological well-being. The indirect consequence follows from the loss of functional supports provided by ties in the social network in which the married partners served as the bridge.

According to this theoretical formulation, the extent to which a person suffers psychologically from marital disengagement is determined by the extent of her/his dependence on the functional support provided by that portion of the social network to which the spouse served as the bridge (Daniels-Mohring & Berger, 1984; Gerstel, Riessman, & Rosenfield, 1985; Henderson & Argyle, 1985; Wallerstein, 1986). The more such reliance, the more likely ego would suffer psychologically.

Thus the degree of impact on the individual of the marital disengagement is in part dependent upon the characteristics of the truncated network. If the truncated network remains to a large extent more diverse and more vertically extensive, we would argue, the impact would be relatively less severe. The hypothesis is that the various instrumental and expressive needs will be met through a search of this diverse network for appropriate support sources. On the other hand, if the trun-

---

[4]Only recently some states have recognized the legal right of grandparents to maintain contact with grandchildren following divorce. Such legal status may allow linkage between members of the separated/divorced family, but the linkage will continue to be limited.

cated network becomes less diverse and less vertically extensive, then we argue that replacements of social ties to meet the instrumental and expressive needs are less likely to be successful.

If we return to Figure 1 and examine diagrams 3 and 4 for the Type A and Type B networks, we can also speculate that Type A partners might suffer less than partners in a Type B network when the overlapping networks are broken up. Because of the substantial overlapping of the two networks in a Type B network, the overlapped ties are suspect as support providers because of their linkage to both partners. In addition, the remaining nonoverlapping portions of the networks are too small and dense to provide adequate support in the crisis. The Type A network, on the other hand, has a larger remaining nonoverlapping portion of the personal network from which each partner may draw relatively greater support in times of crisis.

Further, because of gender differentiation and the hypothesis stated earlier about married women's increased likelihood of having a Type B network, it follows that marital disengagement brings about a greater support crisis for women than for men. Further, we would predict that during a marital disengagement, a woman who has forged a segmented network of her own during marriage for a variety of support functions would suffer less psychologically than a woman who had not created such a supportive network, holding everything else (e.g., expectations and anticipations) constant. Some (Gerstel *et al.*, 1985; Price-Bonham & Balswick, 1980) have noted gender differences in stress following a dissolution of marriage suggesting that women suffer more economically, whereas men feel the loss of a supportive network. We argue, however, that the loss of network support should apply to both men and women. Women, in the more traditional role, feel the additional loss of economic support. In fact, we suspect that because of the traditionally restricted role set, women tend to rely more on the bridge between themselves and their husbands to access social ties to meet various instrumental and expressive needs during marriage than do men. When the bridge is broken, the truncated network of the woman should show less diversity in general than that of men. Women would find it much more difficult to find ties to meet their needs, as previously accessed through the bridge formed with the husband.

REFORMULATION OF SOCIAL NETWORK AND SUPPORT

Although prior conditions dictate, to some extent, the severity of the loss suffered by a person in marital disengagement in terms of access to social ties and resources, some loss is inevitable. How does one recover from such losses? We propose two hypotheses here.

The first hypothesis is that strong ties, especially kinship (family of origin) ties, serve an important but temporary social safety net from which the maritally disengaged can draw support and decrease the severity of psychological distress (e.g., Spicer & Hampe, 1975; Rosenman, Shulman, & Penman, 1981; Baker, 1984; Henderson & Argyle, 1985; Daniels-Mohring & Berger, 1984; McLanahan, Wedemeyer, & Adelberg, 1981; Ahrons & Bowman, 1982; Leslie & Grady, 1985). These strong ties are the most readily available and responsive ties, even through they may not be the most effective ties to meet certain support needs.

During the initial phase of marital disengagement, the bonds between two family lines are broken (Goode, 1956) as well as those to friends and acquaintances through the spouse. Gerstel, Riessman, and Rosenfield (1985) found that the separated/divorced had smaller networks, an average of four members less than the network for the married. Meeting expressive and instrumental needs previously provided by these ties constitutes the primary support concern (Coletta, 1979). For these reasons, it is expected that, during a marital crisis, kinship ties (i.e., parents, especially mother, siblings, and children) are most likely to be called upon to form a safety net. In particular, women with economic constraints are forced to rely on kin ties, the most economic and convenient sources of support. Spanier and Thompson (1984) found that 68% of the divorced and separated women in their sample named a member of the family as an intimate, as compared to 55% of the separated and divorced men who did. Family ties were used for both financial and moral support. However, there is evidence that kin ties are more often used for financial and practical support than for expressive support (Gerstel, 1988; Leslie & Grady, 1985).

For these reasons, it is incumbent upon ego to seek out new ties or renew old ties to fulfill those needs that previously were met by that portion of the network to which the spouse served as a bridge and from which ego is now truncated (Wilcox, 1981). Therefore, we further hypothesize that after a transitional period, psychological well-being will be associated with the extent to which the maritally disengaged individual is successful in reconstructing a more diverse network.[5]

[5]Not all literature agrees on this hypothesis. McLanahan, Wedemeyer, and Adelbert (1981), for example, suggest that the relationship between network types and adjustment for single mothers is determined on the type of women involved. For the "changers" who attempted to establish new identities, they hypothesized that loose networks with large

Again, the evidence is that men seem to be able to amend and diversify their network faster than women following separation and divorce (Gerstel, 1988; Gerstel, Riessman, & Rosenfield, 1985; Spanier & Thompson, 1984). This, we suspect, is due largely to the initially more diverse ties through multiple roles played by men, especially ties through the work and employment environments.

For example, the Albany data show that among those recently divorced, kin ties (especially mother and siblings) become confidants for a significant number of these individuals, and they report better mental health (less depressive symptoms) than others who did not have such ties as confidants. However, after a period of 1 year or more, a portion of the maritally disengaged again found opposite-sex and, to a greater extent among women, same-sex confidants beyond their kin ties. When this occurs, this group reports better mental health than those who continually rely on their kin ties as confidants (Lin, Woelfel, & Dumin, 1986).

These new and reconstructed ties again fulfill the expressive and instrumental needs and provide meaningful bridges to additional ties who can fulfill other support needs. Thus the relationships among marital status, social network and support, and psychological well-being come full cycle. The maritally engaged has become unmarried, and his or her network may eventually resemble that of the single person. Such newly constructed networks provide the structure within which meaningful relationships may develop. These relationships increase the likelihood that another maritally engaging process may commence.

Remarriage does not necessarily resemble first marriage, due to the likely presence of children (Roberts & Price, 1985) and sustained economic burden (payment to previous spouse and child support; Goetting, 1982). Likewise, the reintegration of the two partners' networks involves more complications, as a sorting process concerning previous ties relative to their relationships to the new spouse must take place. Nevertheless, the integration of the networks and resources accessible through the newly established bridge alleviate many instrumental and expressive needs and present an opportunity for improving well-being.

---

ties, less density and uniplex, are more support. For the "stabilizers" who wished to maintain the predivorce role, they argue, the close networks are more support. Leslie and Grady (1985) also suggested that in adjustment to single parenting, new experiences and flexibility may not be realistic. These studies, however, focused on the short-term activities following divorce (within a year). Long-term adjustments should require more diverse networks to meet support needs.

THE CYCLIC PROCESS OF MARITAL
ENGAGEMENT/DISENGAGEMENT

What this analysis suggests is a cyclical rather than linear view of martial engagement and disengagement (Lin, Woelfel, & Light, 1986, p. 327). In this conceptualization, two dimensions of marital status are taken into account: (1) the current marital status and (2) the stability of recent changes in marital status. These two are conceptualized as a cyclic process of marital engagement and disengagement. The cyclical nature is appropriate in two separate perspectives. First, the engaging and disengaging are reciprocal, in the sense that one can enter from one status to the other. For example, when a person is being married, he/she enters into the married status from the unmarried status. When a person is separated, divorced, or widowed, he/she enters into the unmarried status from the married status. All occupants of the unmarried status have some probability of entering or reentering the married status.

Second, because of the relationship between the married status and psychological well-being and of the mediating effect of different types of integrated social network and social support, married status reflects a stable condition, whereas the unmarried status constitutes a relatively unstable condition. Furthermore, the maritally engaged and disengaged statuses can be divided into more and less stable states. The process is depicted in Figure 2.

We begin describing this process with the single status. This is a

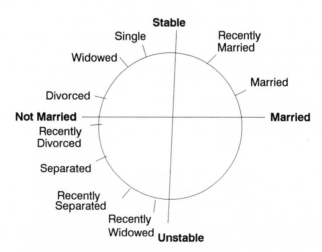

Figure 2. The marital engagement/disengagement process.

status that shows a social network with relatively homogenous characteristics (e.g., age, gender, education, occupation, etc.) with mixed elements of kin and nonkin. This is followed by becoming married, bringing two somewhat disconnected networks together. Integration of the network and its resources occurs. We also anticipate that psychological well-being peaks when such integration first takes place (e.g., for the recently married).

Marital disengagement takes one of two routes: separation and/or divorce or death of a spouse. Regardless of the route taken, the marital disengagement not only involves the parting of the couple but also the severance of the integrated social network. At this time, the individual is in the most vulnerable position for psychological distress. Temporary support is sought from the kin-related network. Subsequent recovery from the psychological distress is aided by once again extending one's own social ties and reestablishing a network of mixed kin and nonkin, somewhat similar, though not identical, to those who are single. For some, the marital disengagement signals the beginning of a new marital engagement process.

SUMMARY

We can now summarize the proposed theory concerning the relationships among marital status, social network and support, and mental health. The propositions can be restated as follows:

1. Married status promotes an integrated social network offering access to diverse ties to fulfill various expressive and instrumental needs of the partners serving as the bridge. Fulfilling these needs promotes psychological well-being for the married.
2. Different types of integrated networks emerge between partners in marriage. In a Type A network, each partner maintains a significant part of his or her independent network, whereas in the Type B network, much of the integrated network is shared by both partners. It is argued that the Type A network is a resource-richer network in providing support because of its relatively large size and diversity of resources.
3. In general, married men tend to maintain a Type A network, and married women tend to have a Type B network. Thus we expect different effects on their psychological well-being.
4. Marital disengagement leads to inaccessibility of a portion of the network previously linked through the spouse as the bridge. Loss

of support provided by such ties exacerbates the marital crisis
and negative effect on psychological well-being.

5. Partners in a Type A network tend to experience less psychological stress during disengagement crisis because there is a significant independent portion of the integrated network capable of
providing some degree of support during the crisis. Partners in
the Type B network, on the other hand, tend to suffer more
psychologically because of the lack of such independent network
elements.

6. In general, women in marital disengagement suffer more psychologically than men because the tendency for married women
to be involved in a Type B network is greater than that for
married men.

7. During the marital crisis period, kin ties serve as surrogate ties
because of their responsiveness in providing expressive support.
These ties serve as a safety net during a transitional period.

8. The maritally disengaged need to reconstruct social ties to meet
the expressive and instrumental needs provided by the former
marital partner and other ties bridged by him/her. The eventual
psychological well-being of this individual depends to a large
extent upon success in reconstructing such nonfamilial ties, especially with opposite-sex confidants.

9. When a reconstructed network becomes diverse and, therefore,
effective, the maritally disengaged becomes similar to the unmarried or single in status. He or she will benefit from the experience of nonkin supports psychologically and may move toward
another maritally engaging process.

If the current trends in marital disengagement continues, we may
expect that one-half to two-thirds of all marriages in the United States
will eventually dissolve. The impact on family members, friends, co-
workers is pervasive throughout the society. It is hoped that the proposed network perspective and the processual view of marital engage-
ment/disengagement expand our theoretical analysis of marital status
and well-being as well as our appreciation of the social and structural
implications of this process.

ACKNOWLEDGMENTS

The work is supported in part by research grants from the National
Institute of Mental Health (#4254902) and the National Institute of
Alcohol Abuse and Alcoholism (#07060001). An earlier version was

presented at the Family Structure and Health Conference August 8–9, 1989, at the University of California, San Francisco.

REFERENCES

Ahrons, C. R., & Bowman, M. E. (1982). Changes in family relationships following divorce of adult child: Grandmothers' perceptions. *Journal of Divorce, 5*(1–2), 49–68.

Anspach, D. F., (1976). Kinship and divorce. *Journal of Marriage and the Family, 38*(May), 323–330.

Baker, M., (1984). Women helping women: The transition from separation to divorce. *Conciliation Courts Review, 22*(1): 53–63.

Berger, P., & Kellner, H., (1964). Marriage and the construction of reality. *Diogenes, 46,* 1–24.

Berkman, L. F., & Syme, S. L., (1979). Social networks, host resistance and mortality: A nine-year follow-up study of Alameda county residents. *American Journal of Epidemiology, 109*(2), 186–204.

Bloom, B. L., Asher, S. J., White, S. W., (1978). Marital disruption as a stressor: A review and analysis. *Psychological Bulletin, 85*(4), 867–894.

Brown, C. A., Feldberg, R., Fox, E. M., & Kohen, J. (1976). Divorce: Chance of a new lifetime. *Journal of Social Issues, 32*(1): 119–133.

Campbell, K. E., Marsden, P. V., & Hurlbert, J S., (1986). Social resources and socioeconomic status. *Social Network, 8,* 97–117.

Cherlin, A. J., (1981). *Marriage, divorce, remarriage.* Cambridge, MA: Harvard University Press.

Cobb, S., (1976). Social support as a moderator of life stress. *Psychosomatic Medicine, 38,* 300–314.

Cohen, S. & Syme, S. L., (1985). Issues in the study and application of social support. In S. Cohen & S. L. Syme (Eds), *Social support and health* (pp. 3–22). New York: Academic Press.

Coletta, N. D., (1979). Support systems after divorce: Incidence and impact. *Journal of Marriage and the Family, 41*(Nov.): 837–846.

Daniels-Mohring, D., & Berger, M., (1984). Social network changes and the adjustment to divorce. *Journal of Divorce, 8*(1), 17–32.

Dean, A., & Lin, N., (1977). The stress-buffering role of social support. *Journal of Nervous and Mental Diseases, 165*(2), 403–413.

DeGraaf, N. D., & Flap, H. D., (1988). With a Little Help from My Friends: Social Capital as an Explanation of Occupational Status and Income in The Netherlands, the United States, and West Germany. *Social Forces, 67*(2): 452–472.

Ensel, W. M., (1986a). Sex, marital status, and depression: The role of life events and social support. In N. Lin, A. Dean & W. M. Ensel (Eds.), *Social support, life events and depression* (pp. 231–247). New York: Academic Press.

Ensel, W. M. (1986b). Study design and data. In N. Lin, A. Dean, & W. M. Edsel (Eds.), *Social support, life events and depression* (pp. 31–48). New York: Academic Press.

Gerstel, N., (1988). Divorce and kin ties: The importance of gender. *Journal of Marriage and the Family, 50*(Feb), 209–219.

Gerstel, N., Riessman, C. K., & Rosenfield, S., (1985). Explaining the symptomatology of separated and divorced women and men: The role of material conditions and social networks. *Social Forces, 64*(1), 84–101.

Goode, W. J., (1956). *After divorce.* New York: Free Press.

Goetting, A. (1982). The six stations of remarriage: Developmental tasks of remarriage after divorce. *Family Relations, 31,* 213–222.

Gore, S., & Mangione, T. W. (1973). Social roles, sex roles, and psychological distress: Additive and interactive effects. *Journal of Health and Social Behavior, 24,* 300–313.

Granovetter, M. (1983). The strength of weak ties. *American Journal of Sociology, 78,* 1360–1380.

Granovetter, M., (1974). *Getting a job.* Cambridge, MA: Harvard University Press.

Henderson, M., & Argyle, M. (1985). Source and nature of social support given to women at divorce/separation. *British Journal of Social Work, 15,* 57–65.

Homans, G. C., (1950). *The human group.* New York: Harcourt, Brace.

Kessler, R. C., & Essex, M. (1982). Marital status and depression: The importance of coping resources. *Social Forces, 61*(2), 484–507.

Lazarsfeld, P. F., & Merton, R. K. (1954). Friendship as social process: A substantive and methodological analysis. In P. L. Kendall (Ed.), *The varied sociology of Lazarsfeld* (pp. 298–348). New York: Columbia University Press.

Leslie, L. A., & Grady, K. (1985). Changes in mother's social networks and social support following divorce. *Journal of Marriage and the Family, 47*(3), 663–673.

Lin, N., Ensel, W. M., & Vaughn, J. C. (1981). Social resources and strength of ties: Structural factors in occupational status attainment. *American Sociological Review, 46,* 393–405.

Lin, N. (1982). Social resources and instrumental action. In P. Marsden & N. Lin (Eds.), *Social structure and network analysis* (pp. 131–145). Beverly Hills, CA: Sage.

Lin, N. (1986). Conceptualizing social support. In N. Lin, A. Dean, & W. M. Ensel (Eds.), *Social support, life events and depression* (pp. 17–30). New York: Academic Press.

Lin, N., & Dumin, M. (1986). Access to occupations through social ties. *Social Networks, 8,* 365–385.

Lin, N., & Ensel, W. M. (1989). Life stress and health: Stressors and resources. *American Sociological Review, 54,* 382–399.

Lin, N., Dean, A., & Ensel, W. M. (1986). *Social support, life events and depression.* New York: Academic Press.

Lin, N., Woelfel, M., & Dumin, M. Y. (1986). Gender of the confidant and depression. In N. Lin, A. Dean, & W. M. Ensel (Eds.), *Social Support, Life Events and Depression* (pp. 283–306). New York: Academic Press.

Lin, N., Woelfel, M., & Light, S. G. (1986). Buffering the impact of the most important life event. In N. Lin, A. Dean, & W. M. Ensel (Eds.), *Social support, life events and depression* (pp. 307–332). New York: Academic Press.

Marsden, P. V., & Hurlbert, J. S. (1988). Social resources and mobility outcomes: A replication and extension. *Social Forces, 66*(4), 1038–1059.

McLanahan, S. S., Wedemeyer, N. V., & Adelberg, T. (1981). Network structure, social support, and psychological well-being in the single-parent family. *Journal of Marriage and the Family, 43*(Aug.), 601–612.

Menaghan, E. G., & Lieberman, M. A. (1986). Changes in depression following divorce: A panel study. *Journal of Marriage and the Family, 48*(May), 319–328.

Mott, F. L., & Moore, S. F. (1983). The tempo of remarriage among young American women. *Journal of Marriage and the Family, 45*(May), 427–436.

Pearlin, L. I., & Johnson, J. S. (1977). Marital status, life-strains and depression. *American Sociological Review, 42,* 704–715.

Price-Bonham, S., & Balswick, J. O. (1980). The noninstitutions: Divorce, desertion and remarriage. *Journal of Marriage and the Family, 42*(Nov.), 959–972.

Rands, M. (1981). Social networks before and after marital separation: A study of recently divorced persons. Unpublished dissertation. *Dissertation Abstracts International, 41*(07), 2828.

Renne, K. S. (1971). Health and marital experience in an urban population. *Journal of Marriage and the Family, 34,* 338–350.

Riessman, C. K., & Gerstel, N. (1985). Marital dissolution and health: Do males or females have greater risk? *Social Science and Medicine, 20*(6), 627–635.

Roberts, T. W., & Price, S. J. (1985). A systems analysis of the remarriage process: Implications for the clinician. *Journal of Divorce, 9*(2), 1–25.

Rosenman, L., Shulman, A. D., & Penman, R. (1981). Support systems of widowed women in Australia. *Australian Journal of Social Issues, 16*(1), 18–31.

Spanier, G. B., & Thompson, L. (1984). *Parting: The aftermath of separation and divorce.* Beverly Hills: Sage Publications.

Spicer, J. W., & Hampe, G. D. (1975). Kinship interaction after divorce. *Journal of Marriage and the Family, 37*(Feb.), 113–119.

Verbrugge, L. M. (1979). Marital status and health. *Journal of Marriage and the Family, 39* (May), 267–285.

Walker, K. N., MacBride, A., & Vachon, M. L. S. (1977). Social support networks and the crisis of bereavement. *Social Science in Medicine, 11,* 35–41.

Wallerstein, J. S. (1986). Women after divorce: Preliminary report from a ten-year follow-up. *American Journal of Orthopsychiatry, 56*(1), 65–77.

Wheaton, B. (1989). Where work and family meet. In J. Eckenrode & S. Gore (Eds.). (1990). *Stress between work and family* (pp. 153–174). New York: Plenum Press.

Wilcox, B. L. (1981). Social support in adjusting to marital disruption. In B. H. Gottlieb (Ed.), *Social networks and social support* (pp. 97–115). Beverly Hills: Sage Publications.

11

Translating Coping Theory into an Intervention

SUSAN FOLKMAN, MARGARET CHESNEY, LEON
MCKUSICK, GAIL IRONSON, DAVID S. JOHNSON, and
THOMAS J. COATES

During the 1980s, the Berkeley Stress and Coping Project conducted a number of studies about the coping process based on a cognitive theory of stress and coping (Lazarus, 1966; Lazarus & Folkman, 1984). These studies furthered understanding of the coping process, including its multidimensionality, the contextual person and environmental factors that influence it, and its relationship to emotions, psychological well-being, and physical health (e.g., Folkman & Lazarus, 1980, 1985, 1986; Folkman, Lazarus, Dunkel-Schetter, DeLongis, & Gruen, 1986).

In this chapter we describe a brief coping intervention in which we translate coping theory and research into practice by integrating findings of the Berkeley Stress and Coping Project with leading stress management techniques. The purpose of the intervention is to increase individuals' effectiveness in appraising and coping with the demands of daily life.

SUSAN FOLKMAN, MARGARET CHESNEY, LEON MCKUSICK, and THOMAS J. COATES • Center for AIDS Prevention Studies, University of California, San Francisco, California 94143.   GAIL IRONSON • Department of Psychology, University of Miami, Coral Gables, Florida 33124.   DAVID S. JOHNSON • Pacific Graduate School of Psychology, Palo Alto, California 94117-1030.

The Social Context of Coping, edited by John Eckenrode. Plenum Press, New York, 1991.

BACKGROUND

The coping intervention is based on a cognitive–relational definition of stress in which stress is viewed as a relationship between the
person and the environment that is cognitively appraised by the individual as personally significant and as taxing or exceeding resources
(Lazarus, 1966; Lazarus & Folkman, 1984). The relationship between
the person and the environment is influenced by two processes: *cognitive
appraisal,* which determines the meaning of the person–environment
relationship and the person's emotional response, and *coping,* through
which the person alters or manages the person–environment relationship. The person–environment relationship is always in flux and
constantly being reappraised. Reappraisals generate new emotions and
coping behaviors that in turn change the relationship.

Most programs to help people cope with stress are based on one of
two definitions of stress—the response definition or the stimulus definition. The response definition was articulated by Hans Selye, who used it
to refer to an orchestrated set of bodily defenses against any form of
noxious stimulus (Selye, 1950). He called this response the General Adaptation Syndrome. Programs based on the response definition discuss
stress reactions such as distress, anxiety, irritability, or physical ills and
teach methods such as relaxation, meditation, biofeedback, and exercise
to control reactivity. Bernstein and Borkovec's program for Progressive
Muscle Relaxation (Bernstein & Borkovec, 1973) is perhaps the most
widely known of the scientifically based stress management programs
based on the response definition of stress.

The response and stimulus definitions have specific limitations
when applied to intervention. The response model does not help resolve
the problems that are causing undesirable psychophysiological states.
Moreover, research evidence does not support the notion that relaxa-
tion-based strategies reduce reactivity to stressors (Jacob & Chesney,
1986). The stimulus model tends to imply that the individual can control
environmental conditions. This implication, which derives from a belief
in the efficacy of personal control that is deeply embedded in our Western tradition, is often wrong. Many conditions are not within individuals'
power to change.

The cognitive–relational definition of stress as applied to intervention differs from programs based on the response and stimulus definitions in that it takes into account characteristics of both the person and
the situation in defining sources of stress, and it highlights processes,
namely appraisal and coping, that can ameliorate the stressful person–
situation relationship.

The intervention program focuses on the concepts of effective appraisal and coping. We summarize what is meant by these concepts in the following sections. For more complete descriptions, see Lazarus and Folkman (1984) and Folkman and Lazarus (1988a).

Cognitive Appraisal

Appraisal is the process through which the individual evaluates a given person–environment relationship with respect to its significance (primary appraisal) and resources and options for changing the relationship (secondary appraisal). Primary appraisal and secondary appraisal converge to shape the meaning and emotional quality of every encounter.

Stressful appraisals include appraisals of harm/loss, threat, and challenge. Harm/loss refers to injury or damage already done, as in harm to or loss of a job, a friendship, or self-esteem. Threat refers to a potential for harm or loss, as when there is uncertainty about the outcome of a test or an unresolved problem between parent and child, and challenge refers to an opportunity for growth, mastery, or gain, as in a promotion at work, a new friendship, or the birth of a child. The intensity of an appraisal of harm/loss, threat, or challenge depends on the relationship between the personal significance of the goal, commitment, or value that has been harmed, threatened, or challenged and the adequacy of the person's resources for managing the harm/loss, threat, or challenge.

Theoretically, harm/loss, threat, and challenge appraisals are distinct. However, in reality people have complex appraisals. Harm/loss and threat, for example, are often mingled, as when a divorce (loss of marriage) threatens future financial security. Similarly, challenge is usually mingled with threat because the possibility for mastery or gain that characterizes challenge also contains the possibility for harm or loss. Without this threat, a challenge appraisal would not be stressful.

The appraisal process is suffused with emotion. Harm/loss appraisals, for example, can generate feelings of sadness, anger, guilt, and relief, depending on the meaning of the harm or loss to the individual. Threat appraisals can generate feelings of worry, fear, or anxiety. Challenge can generate feelings of eagerness, hopefulness, and excitement. When appraisals are complex, as when harm/loss and threat or threat and challenge are appraised simultaneously in a given situation, people are likely to report conflicting emotions. Fear and hopelessness, for example, might both be reported by a student anticipating an entrance exam or a person entering a marriage.

Appraisals, whether harm/loss, threat, or challenge, are influenced by psychological, sociological, health, and contextual variables. Relevant psychological variables include dispositions, beliefs, values, and goals; sociological variables include ethnicity and cultural background, socioeconomic status, and gender; health variables include medical history and present general health; contextual variables include work conditions, family conditions, and sociopolitical conditions.

For any given situation, these variables help explain individual differences in appraisals of harm/loss, threat, and challenge. For example, students who differ in their commitment to academic achievement will differ in their appraisals of a grade of B on a midterm exam. A black person and a white person are likely to differ in their appraisals of the same racial slur. A woman with a family history of breast cancer and a woman with a family history free of breast cancer will differ in their appraisals of a breast lump.

Coping

Coping refers to changing cognitive and behavioral efforts to manage specific demands that are appraised as taxing or exceeding the resources of the person (Lazarus & Folkman, 1984). This definition contains three important features:

First, it is *process-oriented.* Coping refers to what the person actually thinks or does and changes in these thoughts and actions as a situation unfolds. This approach contrasts with structural, trait-oriented approaches, which refer to what the person usually does, would do, or should do.

Second, the definition is contextual; it refers to what the person actually thinks or does *within a specific context.* Thus, coping is not determined solely by personal dispositions but by the person's appraisal of the demands of a particular situation. The contextual approach highlights specific stressful situations as opposed to general stressful conditions. General stressful conditions are simultaneously complex and ambiguous, which makes it difficult to identify what the person is coping with. For example, it is much more difficult to respond to the question, "How do you cope with your stressful marriage?", which refers to a general condition, than to the question, "What did you do to cope when your spouse forgot to deposit a paycheck last week?", which refers to a specific stressful situation that is also an example of the general condition.

Third, coping is defined *without reference to its outcome;* it refers to efforts to manage, not the success of these efforts. In some systems of coping, especially in animal models, coping is equated with successfully altering the outcome (cf. Miller, 1980; Ursin, 1980). However, to equate coping with successfully altering the outcome is to confound coping with its outcome such that coping cannot be used to predict outcomes. To equate coping with successful outcomes also implies that all effective coping results in mastery. However, people are often confronted with situations or conditions that are recurrent or that cannot be mastered. In such cases, effective coping involves coming to terms with undesirable outcomes rather than mastering them.

This approach to coping has important implications for interventions. Coping processes, which by definition are changeable, lend themselves to modification through education, counseling, and brief psychotherapy. In contrast, coping traits and dispositions, which by definition are relatively stable and enduring properties of the person, are not easily changed, especially through brief interventions.

Coping has two major functions: to manage or alter the problem that is causing distress and to regulate emotional responses to the problem. The former is called "problem-focused coping" and the latter is called "emotion-focused coping" (Folkman & Lazarus, 1980). These two major functions of coping have been noted by others, including Billings and Moos (1981), George (1974), Kahn et al. (1964), Leventhal and Nerenz (1983), Mechanic (1962), and Murphy (1974), and are implicit in the models suggested by Pearlin and Schooler (1978) and White (1974). In general, problem-focused forms of coping are relied upon more when situations are appraised as amenable to change, whereas emotion-focused forms of coping are relied upon more when situations are apprised as not amenable to change.

Problem-focused forms of coping include cognitive problem solving and decision making, interpersonal conflict resolution, information gathering, advice seeking, time management, and goal setting as well as problem-oriented behaviors such as joining a weight control program, following a prescribed medical therapy, fixing a broken part, or allowing more time to travel from one place to another. Emotion-focused forms of coping include cognitive efforts that change the meaning of a situation, without changing the environment, through the use of techniques such as cognitive reframing, social comparisons (e.g., Taylor & Lobel, 1990), minimization, or looking on the bright side of things; behavioral efforts to make oneself feel better, as through the use of exercise, relaxation, meditation, support groups, religion, humor, or talking to someone who cares and understands; and efforts to escape through the use of drugs or alcohol.

Problem-focused forms of coping and emotion-focused forms of coping can be mutually facilitative. For example, a person who is anxious about making public presentations needs to use emotion-focused coping to reduce anxiety in order to cope with the instrumental demands of the presentation. If the person's anxiety remains high, the presentation will be ineffective. In this case, emotion-focused coping facilitates problem-focused coping. Conversely, a person who is anxious about completing a job by a deadline may find that the problem-focused act of tackling the job also has an anxiety-reducing, emotion-focused effect, in which case problem-focused coping facilitates emotion-focused coping. Emotion-focused forms of coping can also impede problem-focused coping, as when a woman denies or minimizes the significance of a breast lump and fails to seek prompt medical attention.

Coping processes are influenced by available resources for coping, which include skills and abilities (e.g., analytic skills, mechanical ability), social resources (people from whom one can obtain tangible, emotional, and informational support), physical resources (health and stamina), tangible resources (e.g., money with which to purchase goods and services), psychological resources (e.g., self-efficacy beliefs, morale, and control expectancies), and institutional, cultural, and political resources (e.g., agencies, social groups, and procedures for changing policies and laws).

Some resources affect the *options* for coping in a given situation. Money, for example, which is rarely mentioned in discussions of coping (see also Antonovsky, 1979), greatly increases the coping options in many stressful situations by providing more effective access to legal, medical, financial, and other professional assistance. Knowledge, such as of a bureaucratic process, can also increase options for coping. Other resources, such as energy and morale, primarily affect coping *persistence*. People who believe in their self-efficacy, for example, are more persistent in their coping efforts than are people who doubt their self-efficacy (Bandura, 1982).

Even though resources may be adequate, people might not use them to their fullest because to do so might create additional conflict and distress (see Gottlieb & Wagner, this volume). Factors that can constrain the use of coping resources include internalized cultural values and beliefs that proscribe certain types of actions or feelings, and psychological deficits and vulnerabilities that are unique to each individual. For example, although people might have access to appropriate social support, they may be reluctant to seek support because to do so implies they are inadequate or needy.

Coping processes are also influenced by situational factors, most notably the changeability of the demands that are causing distress. In general, situations in which the demands are appraised as amenable to resolution or change call for problem-focused forms of coping, whereas demands that are appraised as not changeable call for emotion-focused forms of coping. The typical pattern is that both forms of coping are used during the course of a stressful encounter, with the proportion of problem-focused versus emotion-focused coping varying depending on the changeability of the outcome (Folkman & Lazarus, 1980, 1985; Thoits, this volume).

Reappraisal

The individual constantly evaluates changes in the person–environment relationship. Changes may occur because of new information, fortuitous occurrences in the environment, or the person's own coping efforts. Regardless of the source of change, reappraisal is likely to change how the person–environment relationship is construed, the emotions that are experienced, and subsequent coping efforts. Situations that were initially appraised as changeable, for example, may be reappraised as unchangeable, or vice versa. Threatening situations may be reappraised as challenging or benign; benign situations may be reappraised as threatening. Coping efforts may shift from efforts to change the environment to efforts to modify emotional responses to a difficult situation. Or coping efforts may shift from an avoidant mode to an active mode. The model is summarized in Figure 1.

Effective Coping

The judgment as to what constitutes effective coping is debated in the coping literature (for review, see Lazarus & Folkman, 1984; Menaghan, 1983). Definitions of effective coping are influenced by the choice of underlying theoretical model. For example, when the underlying theoretical model is ego-psychological (e.g., Haan, 1977; Vaillant, 1977), the criteria used to evaluate coping have to do with adherence to reality. If the underlying theoretical model is based on the animal model, effective coping is equivalent to performing adaptive tasks successfully (Miller, 1980; Ursin, 1980). (See Folkman, 1991 and Lazarus & Folkman, 1984 for discussion of major theoretical models.)

The contextual model, with its emphasis on the relationship between the person and the environment in a specific context, leads to a contextual definition of coping effectiveness. This definition centers on two types of fit: the fit between reality and appraisal and the fit between appraisal and coping (Folkman, Schaefer, & Lazarus, 1979; Folkman, 1984, 1991; Lazarus & Folkman, 1984; Menaghan, 1983).

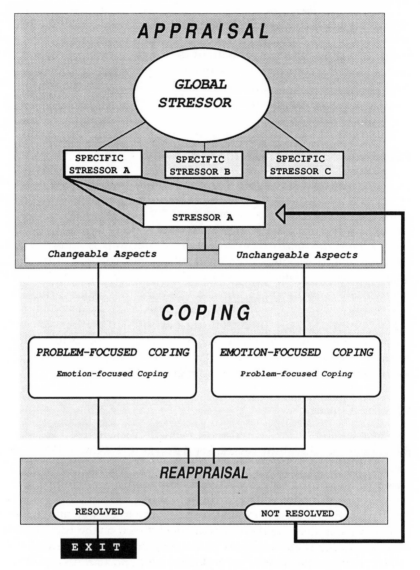

Figure 1. Appraisal and coping model.

The fit between reality and appraisal refers to the match between what is actually going on in the person–environment transaction and the person's appraisal of that transaction. Serious deviation from veridical appraisals can lead to maladaptive coping. For example, failure to appraise a situation as potentially harmful means that necessary anticipatory coping will not take place, and appraising a situation as threatening when in fact it is benign can lead to unnecessary coping that deflects attention and resources from other more pressing tasks. Alternatively, a person may realistically appraise what is happening but be unrealistic in his or her appraisal of resources or personal skills for coping with the demands. An overly pessimistic appraisal of coping resources or skills could result in restricted coping efforts, whereas an overly optimistic appraisal of resources could lead to excessive disappointment and self-blame for an unsatisfactory outcome. (For further discussion, see Folkman, 1984.)

The fit between appraisal and coping refers to the fit between situational appraisals of changeability (secondary appraisal) and actual coping processes. People use both problem- and emotion-focused forms of coping in virtually every stressful encounter (Folkman & Lazarus, 1980). However, as noted earlier, in general it is appropriate to rely more on problem-focused coping in situations in which there is a potential for changing the outcome, whereas it is appropriate to rely more on emotion-focused coping in situations where there is little the individual can do to change the outcome.

A poor fit between situational appraisals of changeability and actual coping processes should decrease the possibility for the management or reduction of distress, and indeed, could even lead to increased distress. By persevering in problem-focused coping in situations that are not controllable, for example, a person remains engaged in a frustrating situation that is likely to result in increased distress as well as fatigue (Cohen, Evans, Stokols, & Krantz, 1986). And by failing to engage in problem-focused coping in situations that are changeable, a person is not likely to bring about the desired change (e.g., Katz, Weiner, Gallagher, & Hellman, 1970).

It is important to recognize that people who decide there is nothing that can be done to change the outcome of a situation are likely to reappraise the situation in terms of what *can* be changed, namely, their emotional response. "I can't change what's happening; but I can change how I feel about it." In this case emotion-focused coping is used to *change*, to *control*, to *manage*, the emotional response. Thus, we should not assume that an individual who relies on emotion-focused coping in a situation where he or she has little apparent control necessarily feels helpless and bereft of control.

Although good fits between reality and appraisal and appraisal and coping are a necessary condition of effective coping, they are not sufficient; the individual must also be effective in his or her coping skills to achieve the desired outcome. Within the realm of problem-focused coping, as noted earlier, relevant skills include problem-solving skills, decision-making skills, communications skills, social skills, and skills specific to particular tasks such as job-related skills. Relevant emotion-focused skills include skills for achieving desired physical states such as relaxation or meditation, and skills for cognitive restructuring and distancing.

Social Aspects of Coping

The coping literature has developed largely within the tradition of psychology and psychiatry. As a result, it emphasizes the individual and his or her cognitive and emotional processes. However, coping rarely takes place in a social vacuum; most stressful events of daily living involve other persons. Coping must therefore be viewed within a social context and as part of a dynamic social process. Curiously, only recently have the links between coping and social processes begun to be considered (cf. Gottlieb, 1988).

In a seminal paper that links coping and social support, Thoits (1986) discusses social support as coping assistance. She points out that coping and social support have several functions in common. These include instrumental functions, emotional functions, and perceptional functions. Instrumental functions in social support include tangible assistance and aid, and in coping they include problem-focused coping. Emotional functions in social support include emotional support, and in coping they include emotion-focused coping. Perceptional support in social support includes informational support that alters perceptions of meaningful aspects of stressful situations, and in coping it includes cognitive reappraisal or restructuring. Thoits hypothesizes that the same coping methods used by individuals in response to their own stressors are also the methods that they apply to others as assistance (see also Thoits, 1984).

Thoits's purpose in linking coping and social support is to explicate how and when support is effective. Until now, research investigating the buffering effects of social support has focused primarily on establishing that there is a buffering effect. By looking at social support as coping assistance, Thoits provides a model for testing hypotheses about the conditions under which various types of support are used and the conditions under which they may or may not be effective in reducing distress and solving problems.

A second approach, which has come primarily from the coping literature, emphasizes social support as part of contextual coping processes. Pearlin and Schooler (1978), for example, assessed advice seeking as an aspect of the coping process in their community study. The Ways of Coping (Folkman & Lazarus, 1980, 1985, 1988b), a self-report measure of coping thoughts and behaviors that has now been used by a number of investigators, assesses the extent to which an individual seeks emotional and informational support during specific stressful situations. Viewing social support contextually, as part of the coping process leads to questions about the personal and environmental conditions under which social support is offered and received (e.g, Dunkel-Schetter, Folkman, & Lazarus, 1987) and the timing of social support (Jacobson, 1986; Eckenrode & Wethington, 1990). Such questions are not likely to arise when social support is assessed as a stable feature of the social environment.

Like effectiveness in coping, the effectiveness of social support as coping assistance depends on a fit between the need of the social support seeker and the resources of the social support provider and skill. For example, Cohen and his colleagues (Cohen & McKay, 1984; Cohen & Wills, 1985; Cohen, Lichtenstein, Mermelstein, Kingsolver, Baer, & Kamarck, 1988) state that social support is most effective when there is a match between the needs elicited by the stressful event and the functions of support that are perceived to be available. Accordingly, to increase the probability of receiving effective social support, the support seeker should know the preferred styles of his or her support providers and, whenever possible, seek support from those persons whose preferred style matches his or her needs.

A mismatch between the support seeker's needs and the support provider's strengths not only will fail to produce beneficial effects, it might even make things worse. For example, consider a woman who turns to her husband for comfort and understanding following a difficult day at work. It happens that the husband is more comfortable providing advice and solutions to his wife's problems than he is providing comfort and understanding. Upon offering advice and solutions (with the best of intentions), he is surprised to find that his wife becomes irritated and impatient. She needed emotional support but received informational support. She would have fared better turning to someone, such as a friend, who may not have been as close to her as her husband but who might be more comfortable at providing emotional support. See Gottlieb and Wagner (this volume) for an excellent discussion of this subject.

Whether or not social support is obtained successfully depends in part on the fit between the type of support needed and the type of relationship that exists between the support seeker and support provider. Some forms of support are appropriately sought only from people with whom one has a close relationship. For example, a request for tangible assistance in the form of $5,000 is likely to be refused by a person with whom one is not close, even if the person has the resources to provide such assistance. The same person, however, may be entirely appropriate as a source of advice or information.

Whether or not social support is helpful depends also in part on the psychosocial attributes of the person who is seeking the support as well as the psychosocial attributes of the person who is providing it. With respect to the person seeking social support, for example, effectiveness involves the support seeker's social skills (Cohen, Sherrod, & Clark, 1986), other coping strategies that the support seeker uses (Dunkel-Schetter *et al.*, 1987), and personal outlook (Vinokur, Schul, & Caplan, 1987). Overall the more socially skillful a person is, the more problem-focused the person is, and the more positive his or her outlook, the more effective he or she is in obtaining social support (Dunkel-Schetter *et al.*, 1987).

With respect to the person providing support, Lehman, Ellard, and Wortman (1986) suggest that support is most successfully provided when the provider is comfortable and not anxious. Overinvolvement on the part of the support provider is particularly troublesome. Coyne, Wortman, and Lehman (1988) note emotional overinvolvement may interfere with their problem solving or performance of instrumental tasks, or it may create additional issues about the relationship having to do, for example, with intrusiveness. Thoits (1986) suggests that sociocultural and situational similarity enhance effective support because they increase the likelihood of perceiving and receiving empathic understanding.

COPING EFFECTIVENESS TRAINING: A BRIEF INTERVENTION

In this section we describe a pilot intervention program, Coping Effectiveness Training, that we have conducted for persons affected by the AIDS epidemic. This intervention is based on the theoretical model described and uses cognitive–behavioral principles to improve people's skills in appraising, coping, and obtaining social support in stressful situations. It differs from other established cognitive–behavioral coping interventions (e.g., Meichenbaum & Cameron, 1983) in its emphasis on (1) appraisal, (2) the fit between appraisal and coping, and (3) social aspects of coping.

The program is conducted in groups with leaders knowledgeable in the underlying theoretical model as well as the goals of each of the intervention sessions. The group size with which we have experience is between 8 and 10 people. Instruction is provided through brief didactic lectures, modeling by the group leaders, and behavioral rehearsal by the participants in dyads or the full group. The participants are provided with a workbook that includes summaries of the major points of each session and paper-and-pencil exercises for the participant to complete during the week. To keep the workbook from being too serious, material that is used to illustrate points made in the sessions tends to be humorous, and cartoons are used throughout. The humor may be more effective if it is tailored to issues that are relevant to the group, as we did with the workbook we developed for use with gay men.

Appraisal Training

Appraisal training is based on the contextual approach to stress and coping described. Appraisal training consists of teaching people to distinguish between *global* stressful conditions and *specific* stressful situations and to distinguish between their *unchangeable* and *changeable* aspects.

Effective coping depends in part on defining the problem with which the person must cope. Often people think about the stress in their lives in global terms. They will report that they "are stressed" because of their job, their marriage, their children, having cancer, or in the case of our pilot program, being infected with Human Immunodeficiency Virus (HIV). As we noted earlier, these global conditions tend to be simultaneously ambiguous and highly complex, which makes them very difficult to cope with. How does one cope with "my family," "my job," or "my cancer"?

The first step in appraisal training is therefore to teach people to disaggregate global stressors into specific stressful situations. The disaggregation involves successive refinements of the definition of the source of stress. Thus the global stressor of "my job" might be disaggregated into having inadequate staff support to complete assignments on time, receiving conflicting directions, not having adequate information with which to complete assignments, or having equipment that constantly breaks down. The global stressor of "being infected with HIV" might be disaggregated into not having enough energy to put in a full workday, informing close friends and family about being infected, or difficulties adhering to disruptive treatment schedules. Each of these sources of stress represents a specific stressful context.

For the effective application of coping strategies, each of these stressful contexts in turn needs to be narrowed further to specific stressful situations. Thus, having inadequate staff support might be narrowed to a specific incident: for example, yesterday an employee was not able to finish a report by deadline because no one was available to compile needed data. Not having enough energy due to HIV infection to put in a full workday might be narrowed to the specific incident of requesting a transfer to a less taxing job.

Once a global stressor is disaggregated into specific stressful situations, specific demands can be identified and goals for coping can be established. The more precise the specification of the specific stressful context is, the easier it is to establish goals for coping and to apply coping strategies that best fit the stressor. At first, this process of narrowing may seem laborious, but with time it is accomplished with ease.

To help people narrow the focus from global stressful conditions to specific stressful situations we suggest that they ask questions that begin with Who, What, Where, and When, namely "Who is involved?", "What kinds of situations cause stress?", "Where is this kind of situation likely to occur?", and "When did it last occur?" "Why" questions are purposely not recommended in this process. Asking why a situation has come about invites conjecture, speculation, and theorizing that diverts attention from the specific tasks at hand.

Coping Training

Coping training begins by familiarizing participants with the distinction between problem-focused and emotion-focused coping, using paper-and-pencil exercises with hypothetical situations and examples from real life. The concept of "fit" between appraisals of changeability and coping is introduced so that participants become aware that in certain situations they will rely more heavily on problem-focused coping whereas in other situations they will rely more heavily on emotion-focused coping.

Problem-focused training involves identifying the possibilities for changing the situation, estimating the probable outcomes of various strategies for accomplishing change, and ranking the strategies in order of preference. These basic decision-making skills are shown to be fundamental to making choices in many daily activities including managing time and resolving conflicts. Participants are encouraged to be wide ranging in considering their options for changing the situation, to envision humorous as well as serious or realistic outcomes, and to order the options according to what is important to them. These skills are practiced in dyads, reviewed by the group leaders, and reinforced through workbook assignments that are completed at home during the week. Throughout this training, participants are encouraged to apply their skills to specific stressful situations in their lives.

Emotion-focused training involves cognitive and behavioral strategies for reducing distress. The cognitive strategies include, but are not limited to, selective attention, use of humor, reframing the situation, and using spiritual or religious resources. Behavioral strategies include exercise, relaxation, and pursuit of pleasant activities such as going to the movies, shopping, or listening to music. Humor is emphasized throughout the program. Participants are encouraged to bring cartoons or other humorous material to the meetings and to see the humor in their own stressful life situations. Hypothetical examples of unchangeable situations are presented, and participants are urged to brainstorm emotion-focused strategies. Real life examples are shared in dyads. Participants are helped to become familiar with their own repertoire of emotion-focused coping to identify possible maladaptive forms such as overeating, smoking, drinking, or drug use, and to learn more adaptive alternatives. The skills are taught didactically, modeled (where appropriate) by the group leaders, and rehearsed by the participants.

Communications skills training is an integral part of the entire program. Participants are taught how to listen well, empathize, communicate their own points of view, and negotiate. These skills become especially important when the program shifts to training in the use and provision of social supports.

Social Support Training

Social support training is presented as a social or interpersonal aspect of coping. The training involves learning the distinctions among informational, emotional, and tangible social support, how to identify what kind of support is needed, from whom to seek it, how to seek it, and how to maintain it. These skills are taught in three parts: "Choosing It," "Obtaining It," and "Keeping It."

Choosing social support involves two steps. The first concerns identifying the type of social support that is needed in a particular situation—emotional support, informational/advice support, and tangible assistance. The second concerns identifying key people in the social support network who can provide the various types of support. Thus, for example, a person at work may be a good source of informational support but not emotional support, whereas a spouse or partner at home may be a good source of emotional support but not informational support. Or a spouse may be a good source of advice support but when it comes to emotional support, a friend may be a better provider. *Obtaining* social support involves letting the support provider know what type of support is needed, giving the support provider permission to say no to the request, and setting boundaries to the request. *Keeping* social support focuses on social support providers as resources that can be exhausted if not cared for properly. Participants are provided skills for acknowledging support, providing feedback about how things turned out, and giving the support provider permission to ask for support.

EMPIRICAL SUPPORT FOR THE INTERVENTION MODEL

Several studies provide support for various components of the appraisal–coping goodness-of-fit model. For example, Forsythe and Compas (1987) found that level of psychological symptoms varied as a function of the match between appraisals of control and coping in life events. The use of relatively more problem-focused than emotion-focused coping in events that were appraised as controllable was associated with an adaptive outcome, and conversely the use of relatively more emotion-focused than problem-focused coping was associated with an adaptive outcome for events that were appraised as uncontrollable.

Collins, Baum, and Singer (1983) evaluated the use of problem-focused and emotion-focused coping in residents of Three Mile Island following the nuclear accident there and found that problem-focused coping in dealing with the aftermath of the event (which was uncontrollable) was positively associated with psychological symptoms. Vitaliano, DeWolfe, Maiuro, Russo, and Katon (1990) studied three groups: people with physical health problems, spouse caregivers of Alzheimer's patients, and camp counselors. They report a robust interaction among the appraisal of change and coping and depression: An appropriate fit between the appraised changeability of a situation and coping modified depression, whereas an inappropriate fit did not.

Support for providing training in problem- and emotion-focused coping is found in studies by Auerbach and his colleagues, who evaluated interventions based on the concept of problem- and emotion-focused coping in experimental studies with surgical patients (Martelli, Auerbach, Alexander, & Mercuri, 1987) and airplane employees undergoing the extreme stress of a simulated hijacking attempt (Strentz & Auerbach, 1988). The simulated hijacking attempt emphasized training in (1) problem-focused coping, (2) emotion-focused coping, and (3) combined problem- and emotion-focused coping. In evaluating the efficacy of the program, Strentz and Auerbach conjecture that the combined problem-focused and emotion-focused training provided subjects with the mix of coping devices that were congruent with the demands they experienced in the hijacking situation, which varied with respect to their controllability.

Although these studies provide support for various components of the intervention model we presented in this chapter, no one study provides support for the total model. We have begun a series of studies to determine the feasibility and effectiveness of the model as a clinical intervention. As a preliminary step in this research, we conducted a small pilot study to determine whether we could teach the model to group leaders and whether group leaders in turn could teach the model to subjects. In addition, even though the sample was small, we were interested in seeing whether or not the intervention would affect coping and depressive symptoms.

Subjects

Forty mildly depressed homosexual males living in San Francisco participated in the 8-week intervention program. Subjects were recruited through public notices and two advertisements in the San Francisco gay press. Of the 139 people who requested information within the first 3 weeks of the notices, after learning more about the study, 123 indicated they were interested in participating. Of those who were interested, the first 40 who met the study criteria were enrolled. Inclusion criteria were self-identified homosexual male, knowledge of HIV status, fewer than two symptoms of HIV infection, absence of AIDS diagnosis, absence of hospitalization within the last 3 years, not currently under psychiatric care, and CES-D score at screening between 11 and 22.

Methods

The pilot study used a 2 × 2 design: Group (treatment vs. waitlist control), and Serostatus (HIV− vs. HIV+). Subjects were stratified on the basis of their serostatus and randomly assigned to treatment and control groups so that there were 10 subjects in each of the four groups.

Assessments of depressive symptoms and coping were made prior to the intervention program (Time 1), at its completion (Time 2), and 6 weeks following completion (Time 3). Depression was assessed with the Center for Epidemiological Studies Depression measure (CES-D; Radloff, 1977). Coping was assessed with the Ways of Coping (Folkman & Lazarus, 1988b), a self-report measure that assesses eight types of coping including confrontive coping, distancing, self-control, accepting responsibility, escape–avoidance, planful problem solving, and positive reappraisal. During an initial screening interview, subjects described an ongoing source of stress. To hold the source of stress as constant as possible over occasions, on each of the assessment occasions subjects completed the Ways of Coping with respect to a specific situation that was representative of the ongoing source of stress described in the screening interview.

Results

Multivariate analyses of variance (MANOVA) indicated that HIV+ subjects and HIV− subjects did not differ on the coping measures ($F_{8,35}$ = 1.07, p = .41) or the depression and morale measures ($F_{2,38}$ = .18, p = .84) prior to the program, nor were there differences following the program. We therefore pooled HIV+ and HIV− subjects for analysis. Following the program the treatment groups differed from the control groups on coping (multivariate $F_{8,22}$ = 2.0, p <.10); the effect was primarily to the reduction of self-blame coping in the treatment groups (F = 6.2, p <.02). The effects remained evident at the 6-week follow-up. Analysis of 6-week follow-up scores for depression and positive morale showed that the treatment groups also differed on depression and positive morale (multivariate $F_{2,26}$ = 3.42, p <.05), with the treatment accounting for 15% of the variance. Univariate tests showed the effects were due both to reductions in depression (F = 3.65, p <.07) and increases in positive morale (F = 6.66, p <.02).

Evaluations of audiotapes made during the sessions indicated that the group leaders had learned the model and were teaching it appropriately. Feedback from the subjects indicated that the model was comprehensible. At debriefing, the subjects indicated that they would have benefited from more time to integrate and practice the attained skills.

POTENTIAL APPLICATIONS OF THE INTERVENTION MODEL

Coping Effectiveness Training may provide healthier alternatives to risk behaviors, including smoking, eating, self-medication, alcohol use, and unsafe sexual activity, that many people report engaging in to help them cope with stress. For example, Chesney (1988) points out that smoking cessation programs traditionally place an emphasis on breaking the smoking "habit" without recognizing that smoking may be serving a coping function. She suggests that environmental stress provokes negative mood states such as depression, anxiety, and anger in the person undergoing the stress, which in turn elicit coping responses, including maladaptive ones such as smoking. A coping effectiveness training program would have the double aim of reducing distress by increasing the individual's effectiveness at coping with environmental stress, thereby reducing the need to turn to cigarettes for coping assistance, and increasing the repertoire of nonharmful coping strategies to use on those occasions when distress remains high.

Coping Effectiveness Training may also help people who tend to respond to stressful situations with anger and hostility. Effective coping patterns can be substituted for maladaptive ones, thereby reducing the frequency and intensity of negative outcomes and hostile responses. Over and above the interpersonal value that is inherent in reducing hostile responses, evidence that hostility is a predictor of mortality from all causes (Krantz, Contrada, Hill, & Friedler, 1988; Taylor, Ironson, & Burnett, 1990) has increased interest in programs designed to track individuals' alternative approaches for anger management (Chesney & Ward, 1985).

We developed the Coping Effectiveness Training program within the context of the AIDS epidemic to help people who are infected with HIV and their loved ones and care providers cope with their extraordinary day-to-day stress (e.g., Coates, Stall, Kegeles, Lo, Morin, & McKusick, 1988; Martin, 1988; Pearlin, Semple, & Turner, 1988). Although we developed CET within the context of the AIDS epidemic, it should also be appropriate for use by health care professionals, educators, and community service providers with other constituencies. Although the effectiveness and generalizability of the program await further evaluation through controlled clinical trials, we believe CET, grounded in theory and selectively incorporating recognized stress management techniques, holds a promise as a brief intervention to help people in diverse settings manage the stressful demands of daily living.

ACKNOWLEDGMENTS

We want to thank Bobby Hilliard for his assistance with data analysis and Anne Christopher for creating the graphic representation of our model.

REFERENCES

Antonovsky, A. (1979). *Health, stress, and coping*. San Francisco, Jossey-Bass.

Auerbach, S. M. (1989). Stress management and coping research in the health care setting: An overview and methodological commentary. *Journal of Consulting and Clinical Psychology, 57*, 388–395.

Auerbach, S. M., Martelli, M. F., & Mercuri, L. G. (1983). Anxiety, information, interpersonal impacts, and adjustment of a stressful health care situation. *Journal of Personality and Social Psychology, 44*, 1284–1296.

Bandura, A. (1982). Self efficacy mechanism in human agency. *American Psychologist, 37,* 122–147.

Bernstein, D. A., & Borkovec, T. D. (1973). *Progressive relaxation training.* Champaign, IL: Research Press.

Billings, A. G., & Moos, R. H. (1981). The role of coping responses and social resources in attenuating the impact of stressful life events. *Journal of Behavioral Medicine, 4,* 139–157.

Coates, T., Stall, R. D., Kegeles, S. M., Lo, B., Morin, S. F., & McKusick, L. (1988). AIDS antibody testing: Will it stop the AIDS epidemic? Will it help people infected with HIV? *American Psychologist, 43,* 859–864.

Chesney, M. A. (1988). *Women, work-related stress and smoking.* Paper presented at the Wen-ner-Gren Center Foundation and MacArthur Foundation Women, Work and Health Symposium, Stockholm, October 12–15, 1988.

Chesney, M. A., & Ward, N. M. (1985). Biobehavioral treatment approaches for car-diovascular disorders. *Journal of Cardiopulmonary Rehabilitation, 5,* 226–232.

Cohen, S., & McKay, G. (1984). Social support, stress and the buffering hypothesis; A theoretical analysis. In A. Baum, S. E. Taylor, & J. E. Singer (Eds.), *Handbook of psychology and health* (pp. 253–267). Hillsdale, NJ: Lawrence Erlbaum Associates, Inc.

Cohen, S., & Wills, T. A. (1985). Stress, social support, and the buffering hypothesis. *Psychological Bulletin, 98,* 310–357.

Cohen, S., Evans, G. W., Stokols, D., & Krantz, D. S. (1986). *Behavior, health, and environmen-tal stress.* New York: Plenum Press.

Cohen, S., Lichtenstein, E., Mermelstein, R., Kingsolver, K., Baer, J. S., & Kamarck, T. W. (1988). Partner and team support for health habit change. In B. Gottlieb (Ed.), *Marshaling social support* (pp. 211–240), Newbury Park, CA: Sage.

Cohen, S., Sherrod, D. R., & Clark, M. S. (1986). Social skills and the stress-protective role of social support. *Journal of Personality and Social Psychology, 50,* 963–973.

Collins, D. L., Baum, A., & Singer, J. E. (1983). Coping with chronic stress at Three Mile Island: Psychological and biochemical evidence. *Health Psychology, 2,* 149–166.

Coyne, J. C., Wortman, C. B., & Lehman, D. R. (1988). The other side of support: Emo-tional overinvolvement and miscarried helping. In B. Gottlieb (Ed.), *Marshaling social support* (pp. 305–330). Newbury Park, CA: Sage Publications.

Dunkel-Schetter, C., Folkman, S., & Lazarus, R. S. (1987). Correlates of social support receipt. *Journal of Personality and Social Psychology, 53,* 71–80.

Eckenrode, J. (1990). The process and outcome of mobilizing support. In S. Duckwirth and R. C. Silver (Eds.), *Personal relationships and social support* (pp. 83–103). Newbury Park, CA: Sage.

Folkman, S. (1984). Personal control and stress and coping processes: A theoretical analy-sis. *Journal of Personality and Social Psychology, 46,* 839–852.

Folkman, S. (1991). Coping over the life-span: Theoretical issues. In M. Cummings, A. L. Greene, & K. H. Karraker (Eds.). *Life-span perspectives on stress and coping* (pp. 3–19). Hillsdale, NJ: Erlbaum.

Folkman, S., & Lazarus, R. S. (1980). An analysis of coping in a middle-aged community sample. *Journal of Health and Social Behavior, 21,* 219–239.

Folkman, S., & Lazarus, R. S. (1985). If it changes it must be a process: Study of emotion and coping during three stages of a college examination. *Journal of Personality and Social Psychology, 48,* 150–170.

Folkman, S., & Lazarus, R. S. (1986). Stress processes and depressive symptomatology. *Journal of Abnormal Psychology, 95,* 107–113.

Folkman, S., & Lazarus, R. S. (1988a). The relationship between coping and emotion: Implications for theory and research. *Social Science and Medicine, 26,* 309–317.

Folkman, S., & Lazarus, R. S. (1988b). *The ways of coping questionnaire.* Palo Alto, CA: Consulting Psychologists Press.

Folkman, S., Schaefer, C., & Lazarus, R. S. (1979). Cognitive processes as mediators of stress and coping. In V. Hamilton & D. M. Warburton (Eds.), *Human stress and cognition; An information-processing approach* (pp. 265–298). London: Wiley.

Folkman, S., Lazarus, R. S., Dunkel-Schetter, C., DeLongis, A., & Gruen, R. (1986). The dynamics of a stressful encounter: Cognitive appraisal, coping, and encounter outcomes. *Journal of Personality and Social Psychology, 50,* 992–1003.

Forsythe, C. J., & Compas, B. (1987). Interaction of cognitive appraisals of stressful events and coping. *Cognitive Behavior Therapy, 11,* 473–485.

George, A. L. (1974). Adaptation to stress in political decision making: The individual, small group, and organizational contexts. In G. V. Coelho, D. A. Hamburg, & J. E. Adams. *Coping and adaptation* (pp. 176–245). New York: Basic Books.

Gottlieb, B. (1988). Marshaling social support: The state of the art in research and practice. In B. Gottlieb (Ed.), *Marshaling social support* (pp. 11–51). Newbury Park, CA: Sage.

Haan, N. (1977). *Coping and defending: processes of self-environment organization.* New York: Academic Press.

Jacob, R. G., & Chesney, M. A. (1986). Psychological and behavioral methods to reduce cardiovascular reactivity. In K. A. Matthews, S. M. Weiss, T. Detre, T. Dembroski, B. Falkner, S. B. Manuck, & R. Williams (Eds.), *Handbook of stress, reactivity and cardiovascular disease* (pp. 417–457). New York: Wiley.

Jacobson, D. E. (1986). Types and timing of social support. *Journal of Health and Social Behavior, 27,* 250–264.

Kahn, R. L., Wolfe, D. M., Quinn, R. P., Snoek, J. D., & Rosenthal, R. A. (1964). *Organizational stress; Studies in role conflict and ambiguity.* New York: Wiley.

Katz, J. J., Weiner, H., Gallagher, T. G., & Hellman, L. (1970). Stress, distress, and ego defenses. *Archives of General Psychiatry, 23,* 131–142.

Krantz, D. S., Cotrada, R. J., Hill, D. R., & Friedler, E. (1988). Environmental stress and biobehavioral antecedents of coronary heart disease. *Journal of Consulting and Clinical Psychology, 56,* 333–341.

Lazarus, R. S., (1966). *Psychological stress and the coping process.* New York: McGraw-Hill.

Lazarus, R. S., & Folkman, S. (1984). *Stress, appraisal, and coping.* New York: Springer.

Lehman, D. R., Ellard, J. H., & Wortman, C. B. (1986). Social support for the bereaved; Recipients' and providers' perspectives on what is helpful. *Journal of Consulting and Clinical Psychology, 54,* 438–446.

Leventhal, H., & Nerenz, D. R. (1983). A model for stress research with some implications for the control of stress disorders. In D. Meichenbaum & M. E. Jaremko (Eds.), *Stress reduction and prevention* (pp. 5–38). New York: Plenum Press.

Martelli, M. F., Auerbach, S. M., Alexander, J., & Mercuri, L. C. (1987). Stress management in the health care setting: Matching intervention to patient coping type. *Journal of Consulting and Clinical Psychology, 55,* 201–207.

Martin, J. L. (1988). Psychological consequences of AIDS-related bereavement among men. *Journal of Consulting and Clinical Psychology, 56,* 856–862.

McKusick, L., Folkman, S., Chesney, M. A., Ironson, G., & Johnson D. (1989). *Coping Effectiveness Training Workbook.* Unpublished manuscript. San Francisco: Center for AIDS Prevention Studies, University of California.

Mechanic, D. (1962). *Students under stress; A study in the social psychology of adaptation.* New York: The Free Press. (Reprinted in 1978 by the University of Wisconsin Press.)

Meichenbaum, D., & Cameron, R. (1983). Stress inoculation training: Toward a general paradigm for training coping skills. In D. Meichenbaum & M. E. Jaremko (Eds.), *Stress reduction and prevention* (pp. 115–154). New York: Plenum Press.

Menaghan, E. G. (1983). Individual coping efforts and family studies: Conceptual and methodological issues. In H. I. McCubbin, M. B. Sussman, & J. M. Patterson (Eds.), *Social stress and the family* (pp. 113–135). New York: The Haworth Press.

Miller, N. E. (1980). A perspective on the effects of stress and coping on disease and health. In S. Levine & H. Ursin (Eds.), *Coping and health* (NATO Conference Series III: *Human factors* (pp. 323–353). New York: Plenum Press.

Murphy, L. B. (1974). Coping, vulnerability, and resilience in childhood. In G. V. Coelho, D. A. Hamburg, & J. E. Adams (Eds.), *Coping and adaptation* (pp. 69–100). New York: Basic Books.

Pearlin, L. I., & Schooler, C. (1978). The structure of coping. *Journal of Health and Social Behavior, 19,* 2–21.

Pearlin, L. I., Semple, S., & Turner, H. (1988). The stress of AIDS caregiving. *Death Studies, 12,* 501–517.

Radloff, L. S. (1977). The CES-D Scale: A self-report depression scale for research in the general population. *Applied Psychological Measurement, 1,* 385–401.

Selye, H. (1950). *The physiology and pathology of exposure to stress.* Montreal: Acta.

Strentz, T., & Auerbach, S. M. (1988). Adjustment of the stress of simulated captivity: Effects of emotion-focused versus problem-focused preparation of hostages differing in locus of control. *Journal of Personality and Social Psychology, 55,* 652–660.

Taylor, C. B., Ironson, G. H., & Burnett, K. (1990). Adult medical disorders. In A. S. Bellack, M. Hersen, & A. Kazdin (Eds.), *International handbook of behavior modification and therapy* (2nd ed., pp. 371–397). New York: Plenum Press.

Taylor, S. E., & Lobel, M. (1990). Social comparison activity under threat: Downward evaluation and upward contacts. *Psychological Review, 96,* 569–575.

Thoits, P. A. (1984). Coping, social support, and psychological outcomes: The central role of emotion. In P. Shaver (Ed.), *Review of personality and social psychology, 5* (pp. 219–238). Beverly Hills, CA: Sage.

Thoits, P. A. (1986). Social support as coping assistance. *Journal of Consulting and Clinical Psychology, 54,* 416–423.

Ursin, H. (1980). Personality, activation and somatic health. In S. Levine & H. Ursin (Eds.), *Coping and health* (NATO Conference Series III: *Human factors*) (pp. 259–279). New York: Plenum Press.

Vaillant, G. E. (1977). *Adaptation to life.* Boston: Little, Brown.

Vinokur, A., Schul, Y., & Caplan, R. D. (1987). Determinants of perceived social support: Interpersonal transactions, personal outlook, and transient affective states. *Journal of Personality and Social Psychology, 53,* 1137–1145.

Vitaliano, P. P., DeWolfe, D., Maiuro, R. D., Russo, R. D., & Katon, W. (1990). Appraised changeability of a stressor as a modifier of the relationship between coping and depression. *Journal of Personality and Social Psychology, 59,* 582–592.

White, R. W. (1974). Strategies of adaptation: An attempt at systematic description. In V. B. Coelho, D. A. Hamburg, & J. E. Adams (Eds.) *Coping and adaptation* (pp. 47–68). New York: Basic Books.

12

The Study of Coping

An Overview of Problems and Directions

LEONARD I. PEARLIN

INTRODUCTION

A primary focus of this volume centers on a pivotal domain of the stress process; namely, those conditions having the capacity to blunt what would otherwise be the severe stressful impact of difficult life experiences. Generically, these conditions are referred to as mediators (or moderators). In addition to coping, they include social support, mastery or sense of control, self-esteem, and, potentially, various personality dispositions. Although my attention in this chapter is largely confined to coping, much of my discussion is equally applicable to other mediators. Regardless of the particular mediator that is under study, there is usually a single question that draws the interest of the researcher to it: Does it help to account for the fact that people experiencing the same stressors are differentially affected by them?

The importance of this question is best recognized in the context of the more general stress process framework. The notion of a stress process is specified in various ways in the literature, but it essentially encompasses the emergence of hardships in people's lives, their social and experiential sources, and their consequences for well-being.

LEONARD I. PEARLIN • Human Development and Aging Program, Center for Social and Behavioral Sciences, University of California, San Francisco, California 94143-0848.

The Social Context of Coping, edited by John Eckenrode. Plenum Press, New York, 1991.

Past research has revealed an array of hardships—or stressors—that have the capability of adversely affecting people. However, even in the case of stressors that are manifestly deleterious, we typically find that some individuals seem to escape their harm or to be minimally affected by them. There is, in other words, considerable *outcome variability* that is usually observed in tracing the consequences of stressors. Coping and the other mediators to a large extent owe their prominence in stress research to their utility in accounting for this outcome variability.

The ability of coping to explain outcome variability is best demonstrated when this variability is related to the ways people cope with identical stressors. For example, we might observe that divorce is a stressor related to depression. We would probably also observe that despite this overall relationship, some people seem to be less depressed than others by divorce. It might then be reasoned that people who experience this stressor are differentially harmed by it because they cope with it in different ways. Were this supposition put to empirical test, we could expect to find that coping does make some difference to whether or not people are depressed. But it is also very likely that we would discover that a substantial part of the variation in depression would remain unexplained by coping. Although this is a hypothetical scenario, it is consistent with much research into coping and the assessment of its ability to reduce the impact of stressors.

I submit, therefore, that if we were to search the rather vast coping literature for indications of its capacity to explain outcome variability, we would find ample evidence that some kinds of coping in response to some kinds of exigencies do make a difference. Yet, we would also be somewhat disappointed in the magnitude of the difference coping makes. There are two possible reasons for the limited success research has had in explaining outcome variability by coping. One is that we have not yet learned how best to study coping, to recognize and deal with its many conceptual and methodological problems. The second possible reason is that coping, along with other mediators, is inherently not equal to the burden being placed on it as an explanatory construct. Specifically, there may be conditions other than the mediators that also need to be reckoned with if we are to account for outcome variability more fully. Before taking up some of the conceptual and methodological problems in research into coping, I shall address this issue. In particular, I shall argue that some of the variability in outcomes may be the result of unobserved stressors that are contributing to the outcomes.

UNOBSERVED STRESSORS AND THE
ASSESSMENT OF COPING

Traditionally, stressors have been treated in only three ways: as an ambient state of being—such as being disabled or a member of a dispriviledged social or economic group; as an event or group of events; or as a chronic or recurrent strain within the context of an institutionalized role, such as job, marriage, or parenthood. Stress research is usually designed to target but one of these types of stressors. As I indicated, when one or another of these stressors is related to an outcome measure, it is likely that the relationship will be in the statistically modest range. I believe that these modest relationships do not result solely from differences in coping or other mediators but also from the ways we evaluate the nature and extent of the stressors that are present in people's lives. By targeting only certain ambient stressors, disruptive events, or role strains, we may fail to capture significant variations in the range and clustering of stressors that are simultaneously impinging on people who experience the targeted stressor. We should not assume, as we often do, that because people share one stressful circumstance that we happen to be observing that they are therefore alike with regard to their total exposure to stressors.

We have some pretty good, albeit incomplete, evidence that over time one stressor tends to generate other stressors (Pearlin & Lieberman, 1978; Pearlin et al., 1981). The original or primary stressor, as I refer to it (Pearlin, 1989), may be in the form of an event, a role strain, or an ambient condition (e.g., living in a dangerous neighborhood). This stressor then may eventually give rise to other, secondary events or strains that then exert their own stress. To use divorce as an example once again, this disruptive event may result in heightened conflict with children, in being fired because of deteriorated job performance, in the loss of network (as hypothesized by Lin in this volume), and in having to move to a neighborhood that is less safe, and so on. Once established, each one of these secondary conditions may act as an independent source of stress.

Because stressors beget stressors, people who are similar with regard to a primary stressor—divorce in this example—may nevertheless vary widely in the configuration of secondary stressors existing in their lives. One reason, therefore, that relationships between a given stressor and an outcome may be modest is because for some the stressor may be the sole stressor they are experiencing, and for others a host of secondary stressors may have come to be organized around the primary stressor. The variability in outcome may thus partly reflect variability in the scope and intensity of other stressors that are impinging on individuals but that are not being observed or assessed. To the extent that this is so, it has obvious implications for coping and our evaluation of it. Some people may have to cope, for example, only with the loss of the marriage, and others with much more in the form of secondary stressors. In such a case, demands for coping with unobserved secondary stressors are likely to be entirely overlooked by the researcher (or practitioner).

Given the potential for these kinds of hidden differences, it is notable that analyses of coping and its effects yield as much paydirt as they do. If the yield is to be increased, it would seem necessary to broaden the scope of stressors that are assessed, such that a configuration of primary and secondary stressors is taken into account. It is not a simple task to know what configurations can be reasonably expected to exist; and even if they were known, their measurement might be problematic. Nevertheless, unless efforts are bent in this direction, we will remain at least partly in the dark about the spectrum of appreciable stressors with which people are coping at a given time. If we are comparing people who not only are simultaneously using different coping responses but also grappling with different stressors, we cannot then determine whether outcome variations are a result of the coping differences, the differences in stressors, or both. Knowing what people are coping with is a requirement of evaluating coping effectiveness.

EQUIVALENT STRESSORS, NONEQUIVALENT MEANINGS

One of the problems in assessing the role of coping in the stress process, therefore, results from ignoring differences in the nature and range of appreciable stressors people may be facing at any moment of their lives. Another problem concerns the meaning of stressors. In addition to the possibility that outcome variability results from the presence of unrecognized stressors and not from differences in coping, there is also the possibility that the same life circumstances may act as a powerful stressor on some people and less so or not at all on other people. Not all circumstances, by any means, can be judged as being stressors because of their inherent nature. Perhaps direct threats to one's own life or those of loved ones are universal stressors. However, in many—if not most—instances, the same circumstances are not necessarily equivalently experienced as stressors.

The intensity and quality with which the same circumstances are experienced as stressors will vary with the meanings attached to the circumstances. This has a direct bearing on coping, of course. Specifically, it can lead us to erroneous conclusions about the capacity of coping to explain outcome variability. Even ignoring the development of secondary stressors, we may be misleading ourselves if we assume that an equivalent circumstance, such as divorce, is an equivalent stressor in people's experience. Consequently, coping behavior that we assume to be in response to the same stressor may, in fact, not be. Coping with divorce may represent for some an attempt to deal with severe threat, loss, or failure, whereas others in the same circumstance may experience relief and freedom from an onerous relationship. Because meaning can determine the extent to which a given circumstance is a stressor and because meaning varies among people and with time, those in the same circumstances may be coping with qualitatively different stressors. Small wonder, then, we do not often find that coping provides a powerful explanation of outcome variability. Instead of comparing different ways of coping with the same stressor, too often, I believe, we are comparing different ways of coping with stressors of different meaning and valence. We cannot be sure, therefore, whether the results of our comparisons bespeak the power of coping or the quality and power of the stressors.

What influences the meaning of life circumstances and, consequently, their diversities as stressors? A detailed answer to this query would take this chapter far afield and, therefore, I shall briefly consider but two meaning-shaping factors. One pertains to values and the other to the contexts of experience.

Values refer to the hierarchies of importance people attach to different activities, relationships, possessions, goals, and aspirations (Williams, 1960). Typically there is great variability in the values held by collectivities and groups. An important, though not exclusive, source of this variability can be traced to people's locations in stratified systems, such as social class and gender. The experiences structured by these locations can shape what comes to be regarded as necessary and important or trivial and ignorable (Hyman, 1953; Pearlin, 1988). Problematic circumstances that emerge within highly valued areas of people's lives, or areas in which they stake their personal identities (Thoits, 1986a) will generally constitute severe stressors; when these areas are less valued, the same circumstances will constitute less severe stressors. The more central the area is to one's value system and identity, the more stressed one will be when threats arise within that area. Indeed, a mode of coping that has been identified involves the devaluation of those areas of life that are problematic (Pearlin & Schooler, 1978). Problems on the job, for example, can lead individuals to define occupation as being of lesser importance in the scheme of their lives. Devaluation does not necessarily reduce the problem, but it does reduce its standing as a stressor.

Obviously, the influence of values on stressful experience should be part of the agenda of research into stress and coping, something earlier recognized by Lazarus and Folkman (1984). For example, a study of divorce might ask if the impact of this event on distress varies with religious beliefs about the sanctity of marriage. Knowledge of how values shape the meaning of events and strains and thus condition their effects would help us, in turn, to make a more reasonable assessment of the capacity of coping to account for outcome variation.

In addition to broadly held values, the extent to which a condition or event constitutes a stressor can vary with past, current, and anticipated experience. Again taking divorce as an example, the impact of this event is known to vary with the perceived quality of the marriage that preceded it (Wheaton, 1990). For some, divorce is a fall from heaven, for others a rescue from hell. Moreover, being newly single might initially be experienced in one way but end up in quite a different way. Thus, we can speculate that the meaning originally attached to divorce may be modified or displaced by subsequent secondary stressors, such as economic deprivation, or by subsequent transitions, such as remarriage. The meaning of an event and its significance as a stressor, therefore, might change as the natural history of the stress process unfolds.

An issue that has been underscored in this chapter is that seemingly equivalent stressors often lead to different outcomes. In some instances, this is because there may be unobserved stressors present; in other instances, it is because the meanings of the same circumstance may differ. In either case, we should not rely on coping to explain outcome variance that is more appropriately explained by other factors. Differences in coping, social support, or other mediators certainly can influence differences in outcomes. Outcome differences, however, may also be a reflection of unobserved differences in the configurations, meanings, and power of stressors that on the surface appear to be commonly shared. We would be in a much more favorable position to observe the workings of the mediators, I submit, if we do more to identify relevant underlying differences in stressful circumstances that appear to be uniformly experienced but, in fact, are not. The constellations of primary and secondary stressors and the meanings attached to them are among the conditions that need to be more systematically brought into our studies. In order to understand whether coping makes a difference to outcomes, we need a clearer understanding of the forces producing the outcomes.

CONCEPTUAL AND METHODOLOGICAL ISSUES
IN THE STUDY OF COPING

I would argue, then, that the study of coping is inseparable from the study of the origins of stress; coping is best understood when viewed within the larger context of the stress process. This will enable us to avoid imposing on coping and other mediators an explanatory burden better borne by other constructs elsewhere in the process. At the same time, it is equally important that the explanatory burden that does belong to the mediators be pursued in the most effective manner. In this section, I shall explore some of the conceptual and methodological issues surrounding the construct of coping itself that seem to impede this pursuit.

As a preamble, I would like to emphasize that coping is not a snake-oil that can cure whatever ails us. Coping can be seen as having three functions: (1) the modification of the circumstances giving rise to stress; (2) the cognitive and perceptual management of the meaning of the circumstances in a way that minimizes their potency as stressors; and (3) the control and relief of symptoms of distress that result from the stressors (Pearlin & Aneshensel, 1986). The first of these—the modification or elimination of the noxious situation—is often beyond the reach of individual coping. *Certain kinds of life exigencies seem to be particularly resistant to individual coping efforts.* Thus, our earlier work suggests that when stressors are embedded in formal organization, such as a bureaucratized workplace, it may be beyond the ability of the individual to change or alleviate the difficult situation (Pearlin & Schooler, 1978). By contrast, coping seems to be more effective when it involves problems or conflicts within informal role sets, such as those found in the family. At any rate, stressors and the contexts in which they arise are differentially responsive to individual coping efforts. This means that there are situations in which "problem solving" is not a realistic option; instead one must rely more on the management of meaning or on the control of distress itself. The nature and magnitude of certain life problems impose limits on the mediating capabilities of coping.

One of the issues threaded through much research concerns the *specificity or generality* of our measures of coping. The type of measure we select for use fundamentally reflects whether we regard coping as entailing a particular set of responses to a particular exigency or as involving a characteristic repertoire of responses that is independent of the nature of the exigency. In general, it seems entirely reasonable to suppose that coping responses are geared to the situations with which people are coping (Pearlin *et al.*, 1989). Thus, one would not cope with a difficult marriage in the same way that one would cope with divorce.

Nevertheless, the specificity of coping might be observed to vary with coping functions. I believe that specificity is most apparent in problem solving—that is, where individuals are attempting to change situations giving rise to stressors. Coping aimed at eliminating interpersonal conflicts, by way of example, is likely to vary with whether the conflict is with an employer, parent, spouse, child, friend, or neighbor. However, coping that functions for the management of the meaning of these conflicts may be a somewhat different story. The modes of perceiving and thinking about the conflicts in ways that reduces their threat may cut across the particular relationship involved. For instance, regardless of the particular relationship in which conflict occurs, we may use positive comparison or selective ignoring or some other device that makes the conflict less ominous. Finally, the control of symptoms of distress, like the management of meaning, may also call forth basic coping dispositions. Thus, it is unlikely that we get high on drugs to relieve the effects of one problem but meditate to manage those of another problem. These kinds of coping responses may be more easily interchanged with different kinds of stressor situations.

I would tentatively propose, therefore, that to whatever extent there is a basic set of coping dispositions, it is least in evidence as we attempt to deal directly with the noxious situation and comes increasingly into view around functions involving the subjective appraisal of the situation and the management of distress produced by the situation. However, although the generality or specificity of coping may vary with coping functions, it is nevertheless advisable to construct specific measures geared to the situation being studied. This is a requirement in investigating coping as it functions for the management of the problematic situation and is a desideratum as it functions at other levels. It is not easy to construct new measures of coping for each life problem or stressor we study, but it may be necessary if we are to get a clear fix on the effects of coping. Standard measures of coping, when applied to unstandard vicissitudes, may be of limited utility.

Another issue concerns *time and timing*. It is evident that stressors differ with regard to the immediacy or lag of their impact. The death of a parent or divorce, for example, probably have their maximum effects closely following the occurrence of the event or, perhaps, even in the anticipation of it. By contrast, the involuntary loss of a job might not exert its full impact until a time considerably after the event, possibly after the emergence of secondary stressors. The time of maximum effects might also vary with the different coping functions. Specifically, I suspect that the effects of coping that primarily function for the alleviation of symptoms can be detected soon after the coping response is initiated. Drinking, meditation, and other mechanisms to assist escape from awareness of tensions are responses of this sort. By contrast, the effects of certain perceptual adjustments may take much longer to come into view. Let's say that a person who is demoted copes by coming to view his or her job as being of less importance than spending more time with his or her family. The effects of this kind of perceptual fine tuning may become evident only with the passage of considerable time.

Research into coping has given little consideration to these kinds of timing issues surrounding coping. Obviously, we need to be more alert to the optimal time interval for observing any buffering action that might be produced by coping with different types of stressors. At the present stage of our knowledge, there is little to guide us in judging what these optimal intervals might be or how these intervals might vary with different coping functions. Nevertheless, we can be quite sure that whether or not coping effects are detected may depend on when we search for different kinds of effects.

There is a somewhat different aspect of time that also needs attention. This one concerns differences in *short-term and long-term effects* of the same coping response. There is some evidence that the same coping acts may produce different effects at different intervals. This is particularly suggested in the case of drinking (Aneshensel & Huba, 1983; Pearlin & Radabaugh, 1976). Short-run relief can apparently be gained from using alcohol, but what may be successfully used as a quick fix can also eventually produce long-range boomerang effects.

Still another issue pertains to the distinction between direct and indirect effects of coping. In most research into coping or other mediators, we look at the dependent variable for indications of effects. If we were doing a study of divorce and depression, we would see if divorced people who coped in one way were more or less depressed than those who coped in another way. Whether we are looking for main or buffering effects, this is a reasonable way to assess coping effects. But it is not the only way. Whereas in the preceding example we would be searching for direct effects on depression, other effects may be exercised indirectly. Only Turner (1983), in his studies of social support, has considered these indirect effects.

My interest in indirect effects is basically anchored in the distinction between primary and secondary stressors discussed earlier. One way that coping can reduce the impact of a stressor is by minimizing the number and intensity of secondary stressors that might otherwise emerge from the primary circumstances. In the case of my now-familiar example of divorce, one may have to cope not only with the loss of an important relationship but also with the difficult life conditions that can follow it: reduced economic resources, disrupted social relations, responsibility for young children as a single parent, and so on. To the extent that coping, or any of the mediators, succeeds in constraining the development of secondary stressors, it is exercising an important indirect effect on depression. By confining our attention only to the direct effects, we may be failing to appreciate the total efficacy of the coping behavior. Just as it is possible to exaggerate the capacity of coping in accounting for outcome variability, it is possible to underestimate its capacity if we fail to take into consideration its indirect effects.

I move now to a different issue, this one involving *the interactive aspects of coping*. Because coping pertains to the ways individuals act in their own behalf, it is treated as being exclusively in the realm of individual behavior. In a limited sense, this is a reasonable view; thus, one can support another but one cannot cope for another. However, because coping resides in the actions of individuals, this does not mean that these actions take place in a social vacuum. Though, by definition, coping is a construct ultimately anchored in individual actions, it is often in response to stressors that arise in social situations where other people are also involved with the stressor, either because they have helped to create it or because they, too, are attempting to cope with it. In both instances, the coping actions of one person will be constrained, encouraged, or channeled by the expectations and actions of the others.

As a result, the success of one's coping response will be determined not only by the nature of that response but also by the actions and reactions of others who are involved with the stressor. Consequently, if, in our research, we seek to identify good and bad coping, our quest may be only partially rewarded, at most. The reason is that a given set of coping responses may be efficacious in the context of one role set and less than that in another having a different set of actors imposing a different set of constraints or reinforcements.

There is, of course, a structural foundation to these observations. Many potent stressors arise within major institutional roles, and such roles always involve role sets, people who interact with each other within the boundaries of the roles (Merton, 1957). Whether in the form of events or more enduring strains, these stressors usually affect all parties of the role set though not necessarily in the same ways. Even stressors that an individual may experience in one role may come to be expressed as problems experienced by the multiple members of another role set. One person's job problems, for example, may easily be transformed into the problems of a family (Pearlin & Turner, 1987; Pearlin & McCall, 1990).

In circumstances such as these, it would be desirable to treat the entire stress process as essentially interactive in character: Multiple individuals within a role set may be experiencing, directly or indirectly, the same stressor circumstances; these stressors may unify the actors, or they may be the cause of conflict among them; they attempt to deal with the stressors similarly or differently; one's coping efforts may be supported, deflected, or opposed by others; and each may experience similar or different outcomes. This is a promising, albeit difficult, direction toward which studies of stress and coping should move. Indeed, in their chapter in this volume, Gottlieb and Wagner provide a rich and excellent example of interactional influences in the stimulation or inhibition of support and on its effectiveness.

Virtually all of the preceding discussions assume that research into coping always includes an assessment of the effects of coping. This assumption, however, is not consistent with actual practice, for much of coping research either examines coping for its own sake or takes for granted that what is called coping does, in fact, have coping functions. Eventually, however, we are faced with the necessity of determining whether the acts and dispositions we label as coping really make any difference along the stress process, and, if they matter, with what kinds of stressors and for what kinds of people they matter. Furthermore, as discussed earlier, we need also to know whether effects are direct or indirect and when in the stress process they can be discerned and for how long they remain.

It is fair to state, I believe, that the evaluation of coping effects has not been at the level of attention given to other aspects of coping. Considering that it is potentially one of the most important naturalistic interventions that can occur to blunt the consequences of the stress process, it is necessary that we have a clearer understanding of whether and how coping makes a difference to the lives of people.

NATURALISTIC AND PLANNED INTERVENTIONS

Research into stress by social and behavioral scientists is driven by many intellectual agendas. Nevertheless, stress researchers who have very diverse interests are bound by a common concern: the health and well-being of individuals and groups. Regardless of how their work might be fueled by a desire for basic knowledge, researchers usually harbor the hope that the knowledge will be used for the welfare of people. This desire is sometimes clearly manifest, as in the chapter in this volume by Folkman and her associates, and sometimes latent. Unfortunately, acquiring knowledge and applying knowledge as a tool of intervention are very different things and probably less easily joined than is immediately apparent. In this chapter, which is an overview of problems and directions for future work, it is fitting to compare coping with other types of intervention and to examine their interrelationships.

Coping can be seen as a naturalistic intervention undertaken by individuals into the problematic circumstances of their own lives. It is a spontaneous intervention whose activation is not necessarily at a level of the individual's awareness. Moreover, coping can be aroused in response to virtually any problematic situation. Because it is a readily available repertoire of the individual, quickly activated, and adjustable to a variety of threatening conditions, it is potentially the most utilitarian and flexible form of intervention available to people. *Social support is also an intervention,* one that shares some of the features of coping. It, too, is typically informal and unplanned and, for most people, easily available. Similarly, support may be mobilized in response to a host of threats. Although they are conceptually and phenomenologically distinct, there can be close connections between social support and coping. In particular, Thoits (1986b) has convincingly posited that support systems may act as the contexts in which coping behavior is both learned and assisted.

Beyond these informal, spontaneous, and easily accessed interventions are *those that are more formal, often contractual, and typically designed not for the whole person but for particular life exigencies* that circumscribed groups confront. This type of intervention is often in the form of community programs aimed at people with specialized needs. Programs aimed at helping people to stop smoking, to practice safe sex, or to deal with the death of a loved one are but a few examples of an endless array. Programs built around shared exigencies would seem to be a reasonable vehicle for sharing and teaching effective ways to help people cope with these exigencies. Such programs, however, often assume that people's coping repertoires are built on information and knowledge; once these are provided, we expect coping behavior to change in a rational and effective direction. The faith we place on information and education in giving substance and direction to individual coping may be unwarranted. I suspect that the change of coping repertoires in the face of life problems is influenced by many factors more powerfully motivating than knowledge alone. One must also bear in mind that not everyone is necessarily able to adopt the same coping response to the same problem, nor will the same response necessarily be equally effective for all. Both the learning of the response and its efficacy may vary with the social and economic characteristics of people and the extent and severity of secondary stressors that develop over time. Thus, if a way of coping with a problem is effective with some people, it may be less so for others.

Because people bring different social and economic characteristics to coping and because of differences in the broader problematic landscape of their respective lives, the same coping responses cannot be assumed to be either equally attractive or equally effective for all people. This should not be taken to mean that specialized programs and services are not or cannot be useful in teaching people how to cope with specialized problems. It can be asserted, however, that knowledge is not simply absorbed into coping repertoires by the weight of its rationality or demonstrated utility for others and, even if the teaching were successful, the effectiveness of the coping might not be.

There are other organized programs that in crucial respects are very different from those targeted to a particular problem. These programs presumably teach people coping skills for all occasions. They might emphasize meditation, breathing, loyalty to a religious charismatic leader, being upbeat and optimistic, and on and on. Programs of this type, to the extent that they are helpful, probably exercise but one coping function, namely the control of stress of symptoms. If the control or reduction of stress frees people to engage in coping that has other functions, these programs would then indirectly have broader functions. However, programmatic efforts to teach people how to cope in general very likely leave unchanged the particular problems that created the stress in the first place. Moreover, if the teaching convinces people that the origins and persistence of life problems are solely and always the product of their own coping deficiencies, it can be downright misleading and possibly harmful. On top of persisting problems, they are left in a state of blaming themselves for not being clever enough or determined enough to transcend these problems.

Public policy, finally, is a form of intervention distinctly different from others. Like some programmatic efforts, it is geared to special groups having special needs. But on a scope greater than any other form of intervention, it is able to exercise preventive functions. That is, policies may help people to avoid problems, not only to provide amelioration after problems arise. Seatbelt laws are but one of literally hundreds of illustrations that could be provided. If a generalization can be made about public policy, it is that its potential importance is exponentially related to the limitations of individual coping. That, I believe, makes public policy interventions of incalculable importance.

Public policy, of course is forged through a political process, placing it in a world distantly removed from that of individual action. Yet, the two are occasionally treated as though they were intimately related— indeed, interchangeable. Thus, it is often implicitly, if not explicitly, asserted by political leaders that costly policy interventions are not necessary because difficult or harmful circumstances can be changed by the properly motivated and cleverly conceived coping actions of individuals. These kinds of arguments are largely ideologically driven, not empirically. Personal problems are often an extension of social problems, and individual coping will not solve social problems. Public policies and programs are required for this. There are circumstances of individual lives that without doubt are amenable to coping interventions by the individuals. Other circumstances, many of them stemming from the unequal distribution of resources and power in stratified societies, are far beyond the reach of individual influence. Because these kinds of circumstances are likely to affect large collectivities, they are prime targets for public policy interventions. By no means should effective individual coping be confused with or treated as interchangeable with effective public policy.

Although I submit that coping cannot *substitute* for public policy, I would also argue that public policy can enhance coping and coping effectiveness. If there is a policy-based intervention to alleviate onerous circumstances that are beyond the capacities of individuals to change, it might very well be that individuals would then be able to deal more effectively with those circumstances that are within the range of their coping repertoires. For example, if one is lifted from poverty through public intervention, one might then be better able to deal with family problems through one's own coping interventions. In general, it is chimerical to suppose that coping, social support, community programs, and public policy can substitute for each other. Nevertheless, they can support each other in a synergistic fashion.

DISCUSSION

Research provides little justification for an unbridled enthusiasm for the power of coping in the stress process. On the other hand, there is certainly no reason to abandon our interest in its mediating functions. What is necessary, I believe, is to be more aware of its inherent limitations and to build into our research and practices greater sensitivity to the conditions that appear to enhance its efficacy and those that constrain it.

There has been a tendency to attempt to explain outcome variability in terms of coping differences when this variability might better be explained by other factors. Among these factors are differences in the configurations and meanings of stressors. If an appropriate explanatory burden is placed on coping, it might appear to be less an effective mediator than it really is.

Similarly, we have to know where and when in the stress process to look for coping effects. In this regard, it would be useful to search for indirect as well as direct effects, for effects that are slow to develop as well as those whose effects are readily detectable, for both short- and long-run effects, and for negative as well as positive effects.

Finally, the relationship between spontaneous and individual-driven coping interventions and planned, formal interventions deserves more attention. It appears that current attention to these issues involves two assumptions. One is that some formal interventions are useful in teaching people how to cope and the other is that thoughtful and motivated individual coping obviates the need for more formal, external intervention. At best, both assumptions have but limited applicability. It is more reasonable to view naturalistic and formal interventions as very separate and not interchangeable or substitutable. However, they may be mutually enhancing. From the perspective not of individuals but of collectivities sharing difficult life circumstances, each kind of intervention that can be mobilized may make a unique contribution to the relief from or prevention of the circumstances, and, at the same time, each may maximize the usefulness of the other.

My general impression of coping research is that in recent years it has moved forward very slowly, if not actually stagnated. It is not because of the construct of coping itself, and it is certainly not because there is little left to learn. The study of coping can be revitalized, I believe, by expanding our concerns beyond examining how individuals cope to include also the conditions under which coping effectiveness varies. In general, we can predict with confidence that as our study of the larger stress process becomes more refined, so will the study of coping. As this happens, I believe that we shall gain more respect for the mediating power of coping.

REFERENCES

Aneshensel, C. S., & Huba, G. J. (1983). Depression, alcohol use, and smoking over one year. *Journal of Abnormal Psychology, 92*(2), 134–150.

Hyman, H. H. (1953). The value systems of different classes. In R. Bendix & S. M. Lipset (Eds.), *Class, status and power* (pp. 426–442). New York: Free Press.

Lazarus, R. S., & Folkman, S. (1984). *Stress, appraisal and coping* (pp. 77–81). New York: Springer.

Merton, R. K. (1957). The role set: Problems in sociological theory. *British Journal of Sociology, 8*, 106–120.

Pearlin, L. I. (1988). Social structure and social values: The regulation of structural effects. In H. O'Gorman (Ed.), *Surveying social life* (pp. 252–264). Middletown, CT: Weslean University Press.

Pearlin, L. I. (1989). The sociological study of stress. *Journal of Health and Social Behavior,* *30,* 241–256.

Pearlin, L. I., & Aneshensel, C. (1986). Coping and social supports: Their functions and applications. In L. H. Aiken & D. Mechanic (Eds.), *Applications of social science to clinical medicine and health* (pp. 53–74). New Brunswick, NJ: Rutgers University Press.

Pearlin, L. I., & Lieberman, M. A. (1978). Social sources of emotional distress. In R. Simmons (Ed.), *Research in community and mental health.* (Vol. I, pp. 217–248). Greenwich, CT: JAI.

Pearlin, L. I., & McCall, M. (1990). Occupational stress and marital support. In J. Eckenrode & S. Gore (Eds.), *Stress between work and family* (pp. 39–60). New York: Plenum Press.

Pearlin, L. I., & Radabaugh, C. (1976). Economic strains and the coping functions of alcohol. *American Journal of Sociology, 82,* 652–663.

Pearlin, L. I, & Schooler, C. (1978). The structure of coping. *Journal of Health and Social Behavior, 19,* 2–21.

Pearlin, L. I., & Turner, H. A. (1987). The family as a context of the stress process. In S. V. Kasl & C. L. Cooper (Eds.), *Stress and health: Issues in research methodology* (pp. 143–165). New York: Wiley.

Pearlin, L. I., Lieberman, M., Menaghan, E., & Mullan, J. (1981). The stress process. *Journal of Health and Social Behavior, 22,* 337–356.

Pearlin, L. I., Turner, H., & Semple, S. (1989). Coping and the mediation of caregiver stress. In E. Light & B. Lebowitz (Eds.), *Alzheimer's disease treatment and family stress: Directions for research* (pp. 198–217). Washington, DC: National Institute of Mental Health.

Thoits, P. A. (1986a). Multiple identities: Examining gender and marital status differences in distress. *American Sociological Review, 51,* 259–272.

Thoits, P. A. (1986b). Social support as coping assistance. *Journal of Consulting and Clinical Psychology, 54*(4), 416–423.

Turner, R. J. (1983). Direct, indirect, and moderating effects of social support on psychological distress and associated conditions. In H. B. Kaplan (Ed.), *Psychosocial stress* (pp. 105–155). New York: Academic Press.

Wheaton, B. (1990). Where work and family meet: Stress across social roles. In J. Eckenrode & S. Gore (Eds.), *Stress between work and family* (pp. 153–174). New York: Plenum Press.

Williams, R. (1960). *American society.* New York: Knopf.

Index